50 YEARS
lonely planet
OF TRAVEL

BHUTAN

T0273998

Thimphu
p46
★

Western Bhutan
p81

Central
Bhutan
p136

Eastern Bhutan
p167

**Lindsay Fegent-Brown,
Bradley Mayhew, Galey Tenzin**

View from Paro Dzong (p87)

CONTENTS

Plan Your Trip

Bhutan:
The Journey Begins Here 4

Bhutan Map 6

Our Picks 8

Regions & Cities 18

Itineraries 20

When to Go 26

Get Prepared for Bhutan 28

Booking Your
Trip to Bhutan 30

The Food Scene 34

Bhutan's Religious
Festivals 36

Planning Your
Trekking Trip 40

The Guide

Thimphu 46
Find Your Way 48
Plan Your Days 50
Central Thimphu 52
Greater Thimphu 63
The Valley Rim 70
North of Thimphu 73
South of Thimphu 77

Western Bhutan 81
Find Your Way 82
Plan Your Time 84
Paro 86
Beyond Paro 93
Haa Valley 107
Dochu La 113
Punakha 117
Beyond Punakha 123
Phobjikha 128
Phuentsholing 133

Handicrafts Market,
Thimphu (p56)

Central Bhutan 136
Find Your Way 138
Plan Your Time 140
Trongsa 142
Bumthang 147
Zhemgang & Sarpang 162

Eastern Bhutan 167
Find Your Way 168
Plan Your Time 170
Mongar 172
Lhuentse 176
Trashigang 179
Beyond Trashigang 183

Trekking Routes
in Bhutan 189
Find Your Way 190
Plan Your Time 192
Jhomolhari &
the Paro Valley 194
Beyond Jhomolhari
& the Paro Valley 204
Central &
Eastern Treks 210

Toolkit

Arriving 216

Getting Around 217

Money 218

Accommodation 219

Family Travel 220

Health & Safe Travel 221

Food, Drink & Nightlife 222

Responsible Travel 224

Accessible Travel 226

LGBTIQ+ Travellers 226

Nuts & Bolts 227

Language 228

Storybook

A History of Bhutan
in 15 Places 232

Meet the Bhutanese 236

Gross National
Happiness 238

Bhutan:
Beyond Shangri-La 240

Decoding Bhutan's
Temples 195

Monk, Bumthang
(p147)

GERMAN GLOBETROTTER/SHUTTERSTOCK ©

Rinchen Zoe La (p208), Snowman Trek

BHUTAN
THE JOURNEY BEGINS HERE

Bhutan is no ordinary place. It's a land where men wear medieval-looking robes, where Tibetan Buddhism guides official policy, and where the 17th century often feels more relevant than the 21st. I love Bhutan for several reasons: its charming people, its otherworldly monasteries and its beautiful unspoiled forests and stunning mountain scenery.

Bhutan's high-value, low-volume model of tourism has many advantages, at least for those who can afford the eye-wateringly high daily rates. The tourism experience here is almost entirely devoid of the stresses and hassle of other destinations in Asia, and the backpacker scenes of Nepal and India simply don't exist. When you veer off from the country's half-dozen main sights, you'll have exquisite temples, homestays and even entire valleys all to yourself. And maybe that's why I really love it here – it feels like a secret corner, hidden away from the rest of the world.

My favourite experience is to hike downhill from the Dochu La (p113), through gorgeous moss-draped rhododendron forests to the Ser Bhum Brewery for a cold amber ale. It's the perfect mix of the sacred and profane.

Bradley Mayhew

@bradley_mayhew

Bradley is a travel writer specialising in the Himalaya and Central Asia and the author of a dozen guidebooks to the region.

WHO GOES WHERE

Our writers and experts choose the places which, for them, define Bhutan.

LINDSAY FEGENT-BROWN/LONELY PLANET ©

Central and eastern Bhutan (p136, p167) are fascinating parts of Bhutan. Here you'll find a harmony between the long-cultivated valleys and Buddhist heritage of Bumthang on the one hand and the wild topography, traditional cultures and bird-filled jungles of the southern and eastern regions on the other. It's a harmony that is uniquely Bhutanese.

Lindsay Fegent-Brown

@lindsayfegentbrown

Lindsay is a travel writer, focusing in particular on the Subcontinent, Asia and the Pacific.

CAVAN IMAGES/ALAMY STOCK PHOTO ©

Laya (p206) is a place of indigenous culture and tradition, barely influenced by modernisation. This place holds a deep history and a reminder of the old yet rich nomadic life of Bhutanese, a life away from technology, of people living in valleys between the mountains. In recognition of the small number of indigenous highlanders who keep this culture alive, the Royal Highland Festival is celebrated at this place every year to promote the highland culture and highlight the beauty and splendour of Laya.

Galey Tenzin

@gt_tenzin

Galey is an enthusiastic guide who loves travelling and leading tours around his country, Bhutan.

Jhomolhari Trek
Trek to Bhutan's most accessible mountain splendour (p199)

Tiger's Nest (Taktshang Goemba)
Hike up to the iconic cliff-face temple (p96)

Thimphu
Savour the country's best shopping, food and museums (p46)

Paro Valley
Tour temples and soak in a hot-stone bath (p93)

Wagye La

Jejekangphu Gang

Zongophu Gang (Table Mountain)

Masang Gang

Teri Gang

Gangchhenta

○ Laya

Tsenda Kang

Kangphu Gang

Thaga ○

○ Thanza

○ Chozo

Kangri

Gangkhar Puensum

Gieu Gang

GASA

Jichu Drake

Gasa ◉

○ Tsachhu

● Lingzhi

○ Damji

Jhomolhari

○ Tashithang

THIMPHU

PUNAKHA

WANGDUE PHODRANG

Shing Karap

Dodina ○

○ Dawakha

Tseshinang

Pele La

PARO

Punakha ◉

○ Khuruthang

○ Sephu

Dochu La

○ Lobesa

Tashila ○ Nobding ●

THIMPHU ✪

Hongtsho ○

Wangdue Phodrang

Cheli La ◉ **Paro**

Haa ◉

○ Chhuzom

INDIA (SIKKIM)

HAA

○ Genekha

○ Chapcha

Jigme Singye Wangchuck National Park

● Sibsu

SAMTSE

○ Dungna

○ Bunakha

○ Tsimasham

◉ **Chhukha**

Dagana ◉

DAGANA

◉ **Damphu**

● Chengmari

○ Dorokha

CHHUKHA

○ Gedu

○ Jumbja

Lamidrangra

SARPANG

◉ **Samtse**

Rinchending ○

Dagapela ○

TSIRANG

Phuentsholing

○ Sinchula

Phibsoo Wildlife Sanctuary

● Sarpang

INDIA (WEST BENGAL)

○ Kalikhola

Haa Valley
Explore little-visited temples and hiking trails (p107)

Drak Kharpo
Join pilgrims on a sacred *kora* (circumambulation) path (p103)

Punakha
Admire Bhutan's most beautiful building, the dzong (p117)

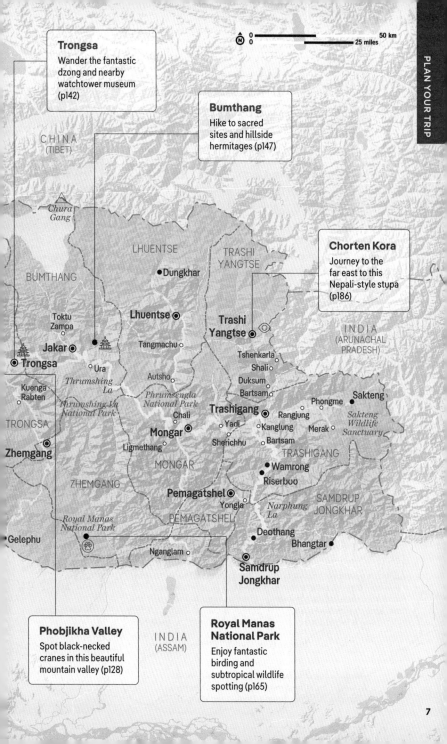

Trongsa
Wander the fantastic dzong and nearby watchtower museum (p142)

Bumthang
Hike to sacred sites and hillside hermitages (p147)

Chorten Kora
Journey to the far east to this Nepali-style stupa (p186)

0   50 km
0   25 miles

CHINA
(TIBET)

Chura Gang

LHUENTSE

●Dungkhar

TRASHI YANGTSE

BUMTHANG

Toktu Zampa

Lhuentse ◉

Trashi Yangtse ◉

Tshenkarla ○
Shali ○

INDIA
(ARUNACHAL PRADESH)

Jakar ◉

Tangmachu ○

Duksum ○
Bartsam ○

◉ Trongsa

○ Ura
Thrumshing La

Autsho ○

Phongme ○

Sakteng ●

Kuenga Rabten

Phrumsengla National Park

Trashigang ◉ ● Rangjung

Sakteng Wildlife Sanctuary

Thrumshing La National Park

Chali ○

○ Yadi ○ Kanglung

Merak ○

TRONGSA

Mongar ◉

Sherichhu ○ ○ Bartsam

◉ Zhemgang

Ligmethang ○

MONGAR

TRASHIGANG

ZHEMGANG

● Wamrong

Riserboo ●

Royal Manas National Park

Pemagatshel ◉

SAMDRUP JONGKHAR

● Gelephu

Yongla ○

Narphung La

PEMAGATSHEL

Deothang ●

Bhangtar ●

Nganglam ○

◉ Samdrup Jongkhar

Phobjikha Valley
Spot black-necked cranes in this beautiful mountain valley (p128)

INDIA
(ASSAM)

Royal Manas National Park
Enjoy fantastic birding and subtropical wildlife spotting (p165)

7

BHUTAN'S INCREDIBLE DZONGS

Bhutan's dramatic dzongs rank as its defining architectural innovation. Built as fortresses, they subsequently took on the roles of administrative and religious centres. Today every district centre, or *dzongkhag,* has a dzong – some dating from the 17th century, others from 30 years ago. They hold the district's most sacred relics and host its most important festivals. Above all, they were designed to impress with their power and wealth, which they still do.

Formal Dress

Bhutan's government has strict rules about dress and etiquette in a dzong. Your guide will have to wear their *kabney* (ceremonial scarf) and come in formal dress.

Dzong Design

Dzongs consist of various *dochey* (courtyards) separated by an *utse* (central tower). Normally only one or two chapels are open to tourists, notably the *kunrey* (assembly hall).

Tsechu Festivals

Bhutan's colourful religious dance festivals, known as tsechu, are all held inside dzongs, notably at Paro, Thimphu, Punakha, Trongsa, Mongar and Wangdue Phodrang.

BEST DZONG EXPERIENCES

Cross the traditional, cantilevered bridge to enter ❶ **Punakha Dzong**, Bhutan's most beautiful dzong, lined with purple jacaranda trees. (p118)

Admire valley views from ❷ **Paro Dzong** and then visit the National Museum in the nearby *ta dzong* (watchtower). (pictured near left; p87)

Make the long drive up to remote ❸ **Gasa Dzong**, with its impressive mountain setting and relics dating from the Zhabdrung's arrival in Bhutan. (p126)

Detour from Thimphu to ❹ **Simtokha Dzong**, the oldest dzong to survive as a complete structure and still boasting some beautiful murals. (p79)

Stop off in ❺ **Trongsa Dzong**, perhaps the most spectacularly sited dzong in Bhutan and long the gateway to central Bhutan. (p144)

ANDREW STRANOVSKY PHOTOGRAPHY/GETTY IMAGES ©

Cheli La (p108)

BHUTAN ON FOOT

Walking is normally the best way to see a country and Bhutan is no different. Take every opportunity you can to get out of the car and hike to a remote hillside meditation centre, monastery or viewpoint. Pause at an ancient stupa in a delightful stretch of old-growth forest and you'll feel the world simply melt away.

Navigation

Bhutan has an excellent network of trails, many of which served as major transport routes until the 1970s. Load the Maps.me app onto your phone for navigation.

Trans-Bhutan Trail

This 403km-long hiking trail traverses Bhutan. We describe several of the best short sections, in case you can't afford the full 30-day through-hike.

BEST HIKING EXPERIENCES

Hike a section of the epic ❶ **Trans-Bhutan Trail**, either in the Haa or Paro valleys, or downhill from the Pele La or Dochu La passes. (p122; p208)

String together a series of day hikes to create a multiday walk in the ❷ **Bumthang valley**, staying at comfortable hotels en route. (p157)

Admire hillsides of red, pink and white blooms on a hike through the towering rhododendron forests of the ❸ **Dochu La**. (p113)

Hear the wind whip through the prayer flags as you hike the roller-coaster ridgeline around the ❹ **Cheli La**. (p108)

Feel the excitement mount as you climb ever closer to the gravity-defying ❺ **Tiger's Nest** at iconic Taktshang Goemba. (p96)

Layap woman, Laya (p206)

ANOTHER BHUTAN

It's not hard to get off the beaten track in Bhutan. Even the popular Paro valley has plenty of charming but little-visited temples, monasteries and hillside pilgrimage sites, where you'll likely be the only foreign visitor that week. Out in the far east, almost everything is away from the tourist trails.

Road Access

New roads now connect almost every monastery and temple in the country, so it's never been easier to get to remote places like Dongkala.

The Deep South

Bhutan's southern *dzongkhags* see almost no foreign visitors, so head to Zhemgang, Tsirang, Pemagatshel or Dagana for real cultural exploration.

BEST OFF-THE-BEATEN-TRACK EXPERIENCES

Hike up to the otherworldly cliff-side hermitage of ❶ **Juneydrak**, for its sacred meditation cave and fine views back to the lovely Haa Valley. (p110)

Spiral up through the inside of the intensely atmospheric, stupa-shaped ❷ **Dumtse Lhakhang**, home to spectacular medieval murals. (p91)

Head out to some of the magical, remoter temples of ❸ **Bumthang**, such as Luege Rowe, the Swan Temple of Ngang Lhakhang or charming Ogyen Chholing Manor. (p147)

Hike for half a day from the road head to get to remote ❹ **Laya**, a fascinating yak-herding community whose women famously wear conical bamboo hats. (p206)

Make the long trip out to the Nepali-style stupa of ❺ **Chorten Kora** in the far east and try to time your visit with the amazing Drukpa Kora festival. (p186)

11

PILGRIMAGE SITES

Bhutanese see their land through the prism of sacred geography. Protector deities and snake spirits lurk behind every pass and body of water, and cliff-side caves mark the site of battles between demons and saints, who have often left their literal imprints in the rock walls. Join pilgrims on a visit to the following sacred sites, partly to gain merit but also to glimpse a world of magic and miracles that has largely disappeared elsewhere.

Pilgrim Etiquette

Always proceed clockwise around a chorten, shrine or sacred site. If you approach a relic or altar, cover your mouth with your hand.

Pilgrim Activities

Pilgrims squeeze through narrow passageways as a form of sin test, rub their backs against sacred rocks and leave donations to gain merit or good luck.

Local Spirits

Most Bhutanese believe in local deities *(nep)*, mermaid-like *tshomen*, snake-bodied *nagas (lu)* and air spirits known as *tsen*.

**BEST PILGRIMAGE
EXPERIENCES**

Follow pilgrims on a *kora*
(circumambulation) of
❶ Drak Kharpo, at one point
descending a ladder into a
sacred cave. (p103)

Test your sin by trying to climb
the sacred rock of **❷ Gom
Kora**, out in the remote far
east. (p185)

Look for visions in the sacred
lake of **❸ Membartsho**, where
Pema Lingpa performed
miracles and discovered
underwater treasures. (p159)

Listen to wild tales of snake
spirits and flying stupas at the
cliff-side temples of
❹ Dzongdrakha. (p101)

Watch new parents make
offerings of milk and alcohol
to the red-faced protector
Tamdrin at Thimphu's
❺ Changangkha Lhakhang.
(p55; pictured far left)

Hot-stone bath

TRADITIONAL CULTURE

Beyond its magnificent temples and mountains, it is Bhutan's unique culture that remains its most intriguing draw. Ask your agent to arrange an overnight in a homestay or visit a temple on a Buddhist holy day, and let your guide help you get under the skin of this fascinating Himalayan culture.

Homestays

Several places are particularly well served by homestays, notably Phobjikha, Haa, Khoma, Nangsiphel and Ngang Lhakhang (the last two in Bumthang).

Khuru

The Bhutanese national sport of archery is difficult to just pick up; try instead *khuru*, a traditional game that uses lawn darts, instead of a bow, to hit a target.

BEST CULTURAL EXPERIENCES

Soak away your worries in a traditional ❶ **hot-stone bath** in the Paro valley, warmed with heated river stones and scented with artemisia and other medicinal herbs. (p101)

Acquire a ❷ *gho* or *kira* (traditional dress for men and women), get a crash course in how to wear it and then wow the locals at a festival. (p61)

Buy a string or two of consecrated **prayer flags** ❸ and hang them at a pass like the Dochu La or Cheli La – your guide will show you how. (p90)

Overnight at a **traditional farmhouse** ❹ and you'll be served *arra* (local homebrew), *zao* (crunchy fried rice) and *sip* (fried beaten corn). (p157)

Attend a weekend **archery march** ❺ to see Bhutan's national sport in action, replete with elaborate victory dances and some incredible skill. (p53)

PRISTINE NATURE

Thanks to its 70% forest cover and a Buddhist-inspired reverence for life, Bhutan has the most pristine natural environment in the Himalaya. The natural diversity is particularly astonishing for such a small country, sheltering everything from Bengal tigers to snow leopards, as well as being a birdwatcher's dream. Oh, and it's the world's only carbon-negative country.

Royal Manas

The 1057-sq-km Royal Manas National Park is home to clouded leopards, rhinos, elephants and golden langurs; visit between November and March.

Red Pandas

Red pandas can be spotted near the Pele La, Thrumshing La and in parts of Gasa district, though they are more commonly seen on beer labels.

Yeti!

The Sakteng Wildlife Sanctuary (p000) in the far east of Bhutan is famous for being the only reserve in the world to officially protect the habitat of the *migoi* (Bhutanese yeti).

BEST NATURE EXPERIENCES

Spot endangered black-necked cranes as they roost and dance in the marshy, high-altitude **❶ Phobjikha valley**, notably between November and February. (p128)

Admire some of the 38 species of rhododendrons that burst into flower each spring in the **❷ Royal Botanical Park** surrounding the Dochu La. (p116)

Catch sight of a takin, Bhutan's endearingly oddball national animal, at the **❸ Motithang Takin Preserve** on the edge of Thimphu. (p72)

Look for one of Bhutan's 100 Bengal tigers – or, more realistically, water buffaloes, langurs, gaurs and hornbills – in steamy **❹ Royal Manas National Park**, bordering Assam. (p165)

Trek into the high mountains of **❺ Jigme Dorji National Park** bordering Tibet to spot iconic species like blue sheep (bharal), wolves, takins, gorals, Himalayan griffons and monal pheasants. (p126)

ARTS & CRAFTS

Bhutan's arts and crafts are an essential part of the country's unique character and the government goes to great efforts to preserve them. You can visit handicraft schools and workshops to see how traditional arts are made, and then shop for everything from Himalayan incense to high-quality Bhutanese *kira* (dresses) at government-sponsored fair-trade shops. Whether it's backstrap weaving or bamboo bow making, you'll find traditional crafts woven into the fabric of Bhutanese society.

Zorig Chusum

The Zorig Chusum are the 13 traditional arts and crafts of Bhutan, as laid down by the fourth Druk *desi* (secular ruler) in the 17th century.

Weaving

Weaving is perhaps the most distinctive and sophisticated of Bhutan's arts, with some elaborate *kushutara* (brocade weaving) pieces taking over a year to complete.

Rigid Rules

Bhutanese traditional painting follows very strict rules of iconography, but a few modern artists have moved beyond them to create a fledgling art scene in Thimphu.

❶❷
❸❺ **❹**

BEST ARTS & CRAFTS EXPERIENCES

Marvel at the skill of students mastering everything from woodcarving to *thangka* painting at Thimphu's **❶ National Institute for Zorig Chusum**. (p66)

Get a sense of the depth and complexity of Bhutan's weaving tradition at Thimphu's excellent **❷ National Textile Museum**. (p55)

Shop for the country's best crafts at the fair-trade shops on Thimphu's **❸ Norzin Lam**, starting at the Craft Gallery. (p58)

Journey out to remote **❹ Khoma** village in Lhuentse, where almost every household has a loom producing incredible brocade-style weavings. (p177)

Breathe in deeply as you tour the manufacturing process at the **❺ Nado Poizokhang Incense Factory**, Thimphu's sweetest-smelling excursion. (p66)

REGIONS & CITIES

Find the places that tick all your boxes.

Thimphu

**WHERE THE 15TH AND 21ST
CENTURIES CONVERGE**

Bhutan's charming capital holds the
bulk of the country's museums and
shops, and its only real nightlife and
dining scenes. There are great hikes
to surrounding hillside monasteries
and several historic temples, but
it's the blending of traditional and
urban life that is perhaps the most
fascinating thing about the city.

p46

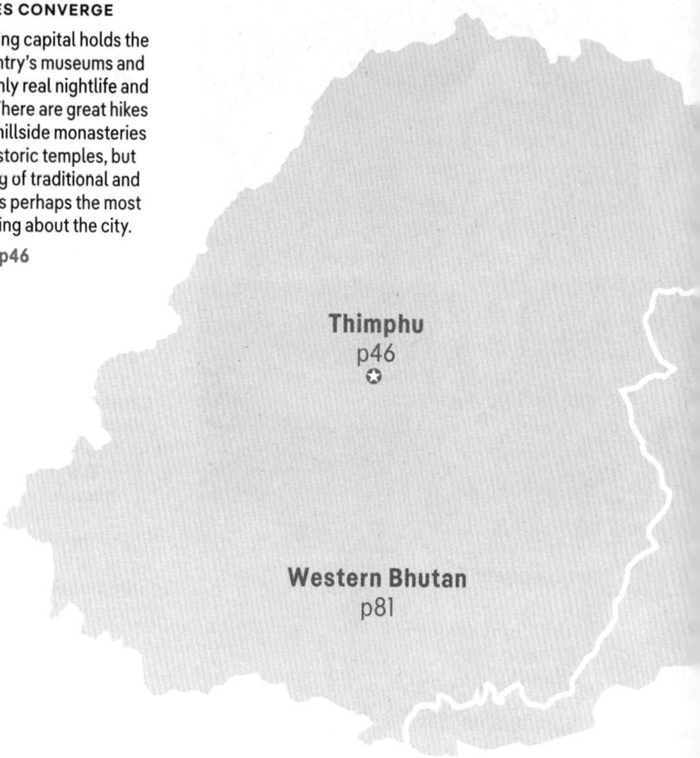

Thimphu
p46

Western Bhutan
p81

Western Bhutan

THE PERFECT INTRODUCTION TO BHUTAN

The west is home to Bhutan's only international
airport, its most dramatic temples and dzongs (fort-
monasteries), some major festivals and the bulk of
its accommodation options, so it's no surprise that
it's the most visited part of the country. Five parallel
valleys each offer their own unique charms.

p81

Eastern Bhutan

**BUDDHIST PILGRIMAGES,
BIRDWATCHING AND TEXTILES**

If you like getting off the beaten track and are
partial to stepping back in time, then head to
Bhutan's wild east. Fascinating ethnic groups, rich
forests perfect for birdwatching and some amazing
festivals are the ample rewards for the few who
invest the time and money to make it all the way
out here.

p167

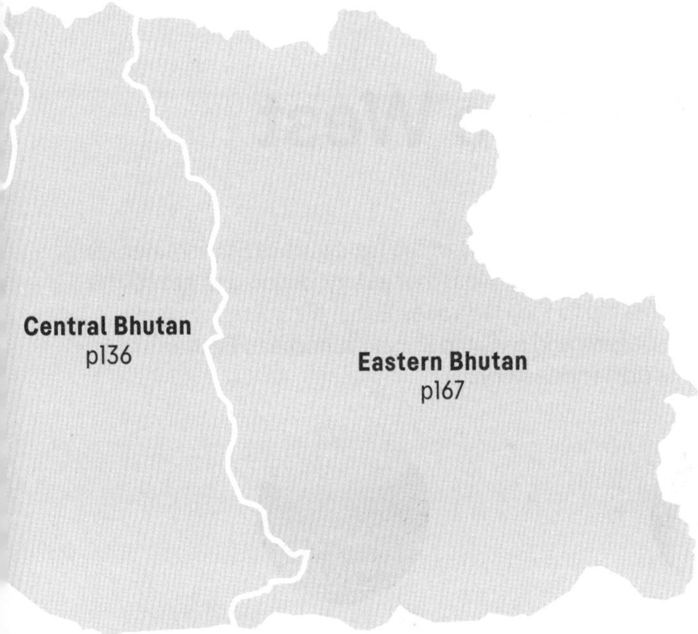

Central Bhutan
p136

Eastern Bhutan
p167

Central Bhutan

**BUDDHIST TRADITION
AND BUCOLIC VALLEYS**

The country's cultural heartland has some
of its oldest and most important temples in a
landscape rich in religious significance. The four
valleys of Bumthang are the big draws, but the
magnificent dzong at Trongsa and subtropical
wildlife in Royal Manas National Park, on the
border with India, are also highlights.

p136

PRITAM, SAHA/SHUTTERSTOCK ©

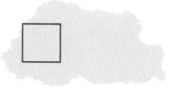

Paro Dzong (p87)

ITINERARIES

Best of the West

Allow: 7 days   **Distance:** 380km

A week allows you to take in many of the highlights of Bhutan, including the iconic cliff-hugging Tiger's Nest monastery, but also to get off the tourist track with a trip to the Haa valley. Other high points include two Himalayan passes and a visit to Punakha, home to Bhutan's most beautiful dzong (fort-monastery).

❶
PARO ⏱ 1 DAY

Fly into **Paro** (p86) and spend the first day visiting dramatic Paro Dzong and the nearby National Museum (pictured), set in a semicircular watchtower and a perfect introduction to the country. Shake off the flight with a 1½-hour walk along the Trans-Bhutan Trail from Girikha Lhakhang to Dop Shari and then celebrate your arrival in Bhutan with a beer at the Outcast Bar.

🚗 3 hrs

❷
HAA VALLEY ⏱ 2 DAYS

For a fine detour off the beaten track, make the drive east over the Cheli La, the highest motorable pass in Bhutan, to overnight in the charming **Haa valley** (p107). Visit either Shelkhar Drak or Juneydrak, two of the country's most atmospheric cliff-side meditation retreats. Haa is a great place for some hiking, either on the Haa Panorama hike or the Trans-Bhutan Trail.

🚗 6 hrs

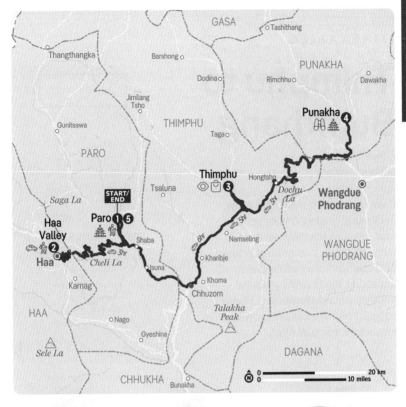

❸ THIMPHU ⏱ 2 DAYS

It's a half-day drive from Haa to **Thimphu** (p46) but there's plenty to see en route, so get an early start and stop off at the magical pilgrimage site of Dzongdrakha and the reconstructed iron-link bridge at Tamchog Lhakhang. In Thimphu visit the National Memorial Chorten and spend some time exploring the shops and restaurants of Norzin Lam.

🚗 3 hrs

❹ PUNAKHA ⏱ 1 DAY

First up is an exciting drive to the Dochu La for potential Himalayan views framed by 108 chortens. The must-see sight in **Punakha** (p117) is the dzong (pictured), probably Bhutan's most beautiful and impressive, but the nearby Chimi Lhakhang is also interesting. Time your visit in March to see the Punakha *dromchoe*, one of the country's most impressive festivals.

🚗 5 hrs

❺ TIGER'S NEST ⏱ 1 DAY

You'll almost certainly fly out of **Paro** (86), so spend your last day there, making the trip up to the dramatic cliff-hugging Tiger's Nest monastery (pictured), and stopping off on the way back at lovely Kyichu Lhakhang, one of the Himalaya's oldest temples. The afternoon is your last chance to pick up a souvenir at Paro's numerous handicraft shops, before flying out the next morning.

ITINERARIES

Thimphu to Bumthang

Allow: 7 days
Distance: 650km

If you can afford a second week in Bhutan, or are on your second visit, be sure to continue east from Thimphu into central Bhutan and spend three or four days exploring the charming alpine valleys around Bumthang, home to great hiking trails and some important spiritual sites.

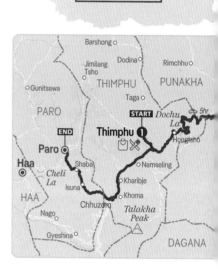

❶ THIMPHU ⏱ 2 DAYS

There's plenty to do in **Thimphu** (p46) – visit the popular Changangkha Lhakhang (pictured) and the huge Trashi Chho Dzong, make the easy hike from the BBS Tower to Wangditse Goemba for its fine views over the Thimphu valley, and then check out the huge neck-craning 51m-tall Dordenma Buddha statue. Be sure to take advantage of the country's best shopping and dining before heading east.

🚗 5 hrs

❷ PHOBJIKHA VALLEY ⏱ 1 DAY

On your second day make the long drive from Thimphu (or Punakha) over the pass of the Lowa La into the **Phobjikha valley** (p128). Between November and February you can spot endangered black-necked cranes here but at any time it's a great spot for hiking, visiting important Gangte Goemba and learning more about monastery life at the nearby *shedra* (Buddhist college).

🚗 3 hrs

❸ TRONGSA ⏱ 1 DAY

From Phobjikha cross the Black Mountains over the Pele La and continue to **Trongsa** (p142), stopping for a short hike on the Trans-Bhutan Trail and a picnic at Nepali-style Chendebji Chorten. Trongsa Dzong (pictured) is well worth a stop for its spectacular location and for the museum house in its nearby watchtower. Overnight here or continue for 1½ hours over the Yotang La pass to Jakar.

🚗 3 hrs

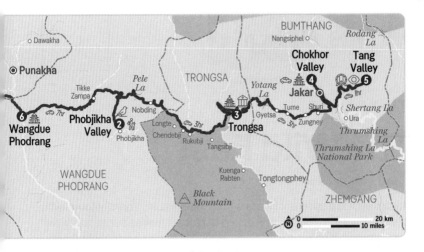

④ CHOKHOR VALLEY ⏱ 1 DAY

Spend a day doing a loop of the **Chokhor valley** (p151), one of Bumthang's four valleys, taking in the historic temples of Jampey Lhakhang and Kurjey Lhakhang (pictured) in the morning and then walking to Tamshing Goemba, one of the most important Nyingma goembas in Bhutan, to try on the cloak of chain mail belonging to Pema Lingpa. Finish the day with a visit to the ancient Konchogsum Lhakhang. 🚗 1 hr

⑤ TANG VALLEY ⏱ 1 DAY

On your second day in Bumthang head up the remoter **Tang valley** (p158) to visit the miraculous pilgrimage site of Membartsho (Burning Lake) and the fascinating museum in the 16th-century Ogyen Chholing Manor. Hikers are spoilt for choice, with excellent trails to Kunzangdrak Goemba or on the Bumthang Cultural Trek. Back in Jakar, visit the Bumthang Brewery for a Red Panda beer and Swiss cheese pairing. 🚗 7 hrs

⑥ WANGDUE PHODRANG ⏱ 1 DAY

The return drive to Paro takes most people two days, so break the trip in **Wangdue Phodrang** (p126), whose dzong (pictured) is once again open to visitors after a decade of reconstruction. The nearby Radak Neykhang is worth a visit for its spooky protector statues. It's also possible to fly back instead from Bumthang to Paro, but add in a buffer day in Paro in case flights are delayed.

Trashigang (p179)

ITINERARIES

The Wild East

Allow: 7 days   **Distance:** 650km

The far east is a different Bhutan; rural, timeless and hardly touched by tourism. There are some long drives here, so it makes sense to throw in a domestic flight one way, to either Bumthang or Yongphula (near Trashigang), or exit the country overland to India via Samdrup Jongkhar, if the border is open.

❶ BUMTHANG ⏱ 2 DAYS

Fly or make the scenic two-day drive from Paro to **Bumthang** (p147). Bumthang is worth a whole trip in itself, so add on a couple of days here if possible, preferably hiking the Bumthang Cultural Trail between the region's two main valleys, or at least doing a couple of day hikes. Accommodation is good here, and there are also several offbeat homestay options.

🚗 6 hrs

❷ MONGAR ⏱ 1 DAY

It's a dramatic day's drive along Bhutan's wildest road, past waterfalls and lush forests and over the Thrumshing La to **Mongar** (p172). Base yourself here for two nights if not overnighting in Khoma. The dzong and Yakgang Lhakhang are worth a visit and there are some interesting hikes. Accommodation and food are limited and simpler in the east.

🚗 2½ hrs

❸ LHUENTSE ⏱ 1 DAY

From Mongar make the day trip up to remote **Lhuentse** (p176), the ancestral home of the royal family, to visit its picturesque dzong and the nearby village of Khoma, which produces some of Bhutan's most exquisite weavings. Also en route is the 45m-high statue of Guru Rinpoche, claimed to be the world's tallest. Return to Mongar or stay in a homestay in Khoma.

🚗 5 hrs

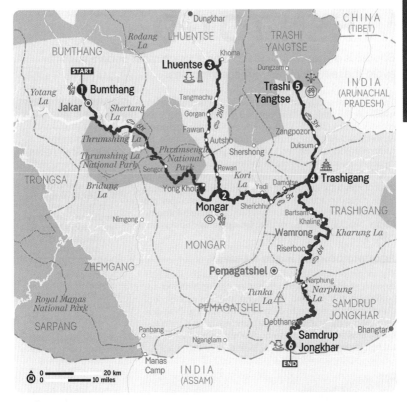

❹ TRASHIGANG ⏱ 1 DAY

From Mongar it's a half-day drive to **Trashigang** (p179), with an optional two-hour detour to Drametse Goemba (pictured), an important Nyingma monastery. Few tourists make it this far, which makes the town and dzong interesting to explore. Hikers use Trashigang as a base to explore the Merak-Sakteng region, home to Brokpa nomads and the odd yeti, in the far east.

🚗 3 hrs

❺ TRASHI YANGTSE ⏱ 1 DAY

Make the day excursion to **Trashi Yangtse** (p186). En route stop at the fascinating pilgrimage site of Gom Kora to test your sin and then visit the large Nepali-style Chorten Kora (pictured). There are spectacular festivals here in February and March. With an overnight in Trashi Yangtse you could continue to the Dechen Phodrang pilgrimage site and Bomdeling Wildlife Sanctuary.

🚗 6 hrs

❻ SAMDRUP JONGKHAR ⏱ 1 DAY

If the border with India has reopened as hoped, take the winding road from Trashigang to the steamy Assam plains at the border town of **Samdrup Jongkhar** (p187), stopping at the National Handloom Development Project. With an Indian visa it's then a three-hour taxi ride to Guwahati. Otherwise, fly from Yongphula airport back to Paro (three flights weekly).

WHEN **TO GO**

Bhutan is a year-round destination, though most people sensibly avoid the rainy summer monsoon months.

There are essentially two main seasons for visiting Bhutan, which are the same whether you are trekking or touring the country. Spring (March, April, early May) brings warm weather, festivals and beautiful rhododendron blooms, while autumn (October, November) is the most popular season, for its clear post-monsoon Himalayan views, stable weather and more festivals. A main consideration is the timing of festivals, most of which are luckily held during the spring and autumn.

The monsoon months from June to mid-September are not popular, due to the rain, clouds and unreliable domestic flights, but this is the prime time for alpine wildflowers, including the famous blue poppy.

Accommodation Highs & Lows

You might get accommodation discounts in the shoulder months of February and December, but only if you are booking hotels yourself. In general, there is an oversupply of accommodation in Bhutan. Hotel rates in Paro and Thimphu spike during their tsechus (religious dance festivals) and you may have to book a minimum number of nights, though your agent will take care of this.

LEFT: JORDISTOCK/SHUTTERSTOCK ©
RIGHT: LINDSAY FEGENT-BROWN/LONELY PLANET ©

Phobjikha (p128) in spring

AUTUMN EXPLORATIONS

PemC, Bhutanese storyteller who makes travel content that delves into Bhutan's culture, people, food and history with a special focus on sustainability.
@yeegetaway

The weather in Bhutan can be unpredictable, especially if you're going hiking in the highlands, but autumn is a special treat. I especially enjoy exploring remote highland trails in eastern Bhutan as it takes you closer to communities in Bhutan's far-flung corners with unique local cultures, folklore and mythologies; October and November are the perfect months to explore here.

SHOULDER SEASON

If you want fewer crowds but still comfortable temperatures, late February to early March, and November are all excellent months, though you'll need to bring an extra fleece for the higher altitudes of Phobjikha and Bumthang.

Weather Through the Year

JANUARY	FEBRUARY	MARCH	APRIL	MAY	JUNE
Avg daytime max: **12°C**	Avg daytime max: **14°C**	Avg daytime max: **16°C**	Avg daytime max: **20°C**	Avg daytime max: **23°C**	Avg daytime max: **24°C**
Days of rainfall (Thimphu): **1**	Days of rainfall (Thimphu): **1**	Days of rainfall (Thimphu): **4**	Days of rainfall (Thimphu): **6**	Days of rainfall (Thimphu): **9**	Days of rainfall (Thimphu): **14**

REGIONAL VARIATIONS

Temperatures vary with altitude in Bhutan. In general, the lower valleys such as Punakha and most of eastern Bhutan are noticeably warmer than Thimphu or Paro. Bumthang and Phobjikha are always a few degrees colder but a warm *bukhari* (wood stove) keep things cosy at night.

The Big Festivals

The **Paro tsechu** (p88) is the single most popular festival in Bhutan, due to its spectacular site, masked dances and the auspicious unveiling of a building-sized *thondrol* (large religious image) at dawn on the last day. 🌸 **March/April**

For sheer spectacle it's hard to beat the **Punakha Dromchoe** (p119), with its dramatic recreation of a 17th-century battle, featuring hundreds of costumed *pazaps* (warriors), followed by a three-day tsechu. ❄️ **February/March**

The **Thimphu tsechu** (p68) is another popular festival with groups, featuring several days of monk dancing in the capital's impressive dzong courtyard. 🌤️ **September/October**

For something a bit unusual try the **Jampey Lhakhang Drup** (p151) in central Bhutan, with its famous midnight naked fire dance, preceded by a four-day tsechu in nearby Jakar Dzong. There are more tsechu dances at the same time at nearby Prakhar Goemba. 🌤️ **October**

Overlooked Festivals

The **Gasa tsechu** (p126) is well worth the three-hour drive from Punakha for its three days of monk dances in a remote and spectacular setting. You won't find many other tourists here. 🌤️ **March**

Way out in the far east, **Chorten Kora** (p186) attracts a fascinating ethnic mix of pilgrims from Bhutan and India's Arunachal Pradesh to its twin fair-like festivals, set two weeks apart. ❄️ **April**

The **Royal Highlander Festival** (p126) in remote Laya includes wrestling, horse races, traditional songs and yak competitions. You need to hike for a day to get here. 🌤️ **October**

The little-visited, three-day **Trashigang tsechu** (p182) in the far east culminates in the unveiling of a *thondrol* and statue of Guru Rinpoche on the last day. Tsechus are also held in Mongar and Pemagatshel on the same dates. 🌤️ **November**

SPRING BLOOMS

The spectacular blooms of the eastern Himalaya are a major draw. March and April bring colour to entire hillsides of rhododendrons (pictured above), with higher altitudes following a bit later, and the beautiful silk cotton trees bloom bright red.

JULY	**AUGUST**	**SEPTEMBER**	**OCTOBER**	**NOVEMBER**	**DECEMBER**
Avg daytime max: **25°C**	Avg daytime max: **25°C**	Avg daytime max: **23°C**	Avg daytime max: **22°C**	Avg daytime max: **18°C**	Avg daytime max: **15°C**
Days of rainfall (Thimphu): **19**	Days of rainfall (Thimphu): **17**	Days of rainfall (Thimphu): **12**	Days of rainfall (Thimphu): **5**	Days of rainfall (Thimphu): **0**	Days of rainfall (Thimphu): **1**

LEFT: ANDREW PEACOCK/GETTY IMAGES © RIGHT: TCD/PROD.DB/ALAMY STOCK PHOTO ©

Traditional Bhutanese clothing

GET PREPARED FOR BHUTAN

Useful things to load in your bag, your ears and your brain

Clothes

Get a *gho* or *kira* Locals love it when foreigners wear a *gho* (robe) or *kira* (dress). Consider getting one made (p61) to attend a festival or a formal occasion.

Shoes Slip-ons for visiting temples, where you must remove shoes before entering every chapel. An extra pair of socks is useful for the dusty floors.

Dress up Locals dress modestly and smartly. Men should wear a shirt with collar and women a long skirt or trousers when visiting a dzong (fort-monastery).

Layers Weather is very changeable, so dress in layers. Bring a fleece or down jacket for the Phobjikha valley, at higher altitudes or in shoulder season.

Hiking gear A rain shell is always useful. See p43 for advice on trekking clothes.

Manners

Remove shoes and hats before entering any lhakhang (temple or chapel), such as in a dzong or goemba (monastery).

Photography is banned inside chapels but permitted in temple courtyards.

Always walk clockwise around stupas, temple buildings and *mani* (carved mantras) walls.

Add the word 'la' to almost any phrase or word to convey respect ('thank you la'), especially to a lama or government minister.

Always refer to the **royal family** in respectful tones.

Reusable carry bag Plastic bags are banned and shouldn't be accepted if offered.

📖 READ

Treasures of the Thunder Dragon (Ashi Dorji Wangmo Wangchuk; 2006) Biography and travelogue from the wife of the fourth king.

The History of Bhutan (Karma Phuntsho; 2014) Comprehensive 650-page history of the country.

The Circle of Karma (Kunzang Choden; 2005) Bhutanese novel about a 15-year-old girl's voyage across Bhutan.

Beyond the Sky and the Earth (Jamie Zeppa; 1999) Memoir of a Canadian teacher's two years teaching in Trashigang.

Words

Kuzu zangbo la Universal greeting, sometimes shortened to 'kuzuu' or 'kuzuu-la'.

La Added onto someone's name or title to convey respect. It also means a mountain pass.

Kadrin chhe la Thank you

Tashi dele Literally good luck, or best wishes, but can also be used for 'welcome' and 'goodbye'.

Chillip Dzongkha name for a foreigner; not disrespectful.

Apa/ama 'Older man/woman', used to respectfully address Bhutanese older than you. **Aum/bum** are similar terms for a lady/girl.

Druk Thunder dragon, the national symbol of Bhutan. Bhutanese call their country Druk Yul, or Land of the Thunder Dragon, and the people and adjective is Drukpa, which also refers to the main school of Buddhism in Bhutan.

Lhakhang Literally 'god house', refers to a chapel or temple. A **goemba** is a monastery, a **goenkhang** is a protector chapel and a **kunrey** is an assembly hall.

Kora Circumambulation; refers to the Buddhist custom of walking clockwise around a lhakhang, shrine, pilgrim site or even an entire mountain.

Mani Literally 'jewel' but refers to prayer wheels and therefore the buildings (*mani lhakhang* or *mani dungkhor*) that house them. A *mani* wall is a wall of stones carved with the Buddhist mantra *'om mani padme hum'*.

Chorten Stupa, a stone Buddhist monument normally built to house relics.

Dzong Dzongkha word for fortress; today refers to the towering complexes that house both government officials and the monastic body.

📺 WATCH

Lunana: A Yak in the Classroom (Pawo Choyning Dorji; 2019) Bhutan's first ever Oscar-nominated movie (pictured), filmed in remote Lunana.

Travellers & Magicians (Khyentse Norbu; 2003) Whimsical fable from the Bhutanese director and reincarnated lama.

Crossing Bhutan (Benjamin Henretig; 2016) Chronicles a 42-day trek across Bhutan, investigating notions of Gross National Happiness.

The Snowman Trek (Ben Clark; 2018) Documentary following marathon runners attempting a speed record along Bhutan's infamously tough Snowman trek.

🎧 LISTEN

Endless Songs from Bhutan (Jigme Drukpa; 1999) An album of (not really endless) traditional folk songs accompanied on flute and lute from the singer and musician.

Music From the Mountains of Bhutan (Sonam Dorji; 2015) Beautiful traditional *drangyen* (Bhutanese lute) music from the Zhemgang native.

Wild Flowers (Misty Terrace; 2020) Third pop album from the popular Bhutanese band led by wild-haired Tandin Wangchuk.

Tibetan Buddhist Rites from the Monasteries of Bhutan Vol 4 (John Levy; 1994) Field recordings of traditional Bhutanese music.

NARONGSAK NAGADHANA/SHUTTERSTOCK ©

Drukair flight arriving in Paro

TRIP PLANNER

BOOKING YOUR TRIP TO BHUTAN

Bhutan's unique model of 'high-value, low-impact' tourism makes a trip to Bhutan more expensive than many other destinations, but not especially difficult to arrange, once you understand its quirks. You can create your own itinerary and travel in any group size – but everything has to be arranged and paid for in advance, including a guide.

The Bhutanese System

The purpose of Bhutan's model of tourism is simple: to maximise the financial benefits of tourism while minimising its environmental and cultural impact. It's an embodiment of the country's guiding policy of Gross National Happiness. Contrary to popular belief, there is no restriction on the number of tourists visiting Bhutan; numbers remain relatively low due to the deliberately high costs.

Up until 2022 Bhutan charged foreign tourists a daily rate of between US$200 and US$290 per person per day to enter the country, and this included almost everything in your tour, from hotels and food to transport and English-speaking guides. In 2022 this all changed.

THE CURRENT RULES

At the time of writing, all visitors to Bhutan have to pre-pay a US$200 per person, per night Sustainable Development Fee (SDF; p33) in order to get visa approval. Travel costs are now in addition to this US$200 per day fee, unlike before, and tour prices now depend on the levels of accommodation, service or activities.

VISAS

- Visas are only granted after you have paid the SDF fee for your entire trip. You can apply yourself online at visit.doi.gov.bt, or get your agent to do it for you.

- You need to show proof of travel insurance as part of the application.

- Visas cost US$40 and are valid for the number of days and exact dates you paid the SDF for.

- Your visa authorisation will be emailed to you. On arrival at Paro International Airport or at the land border with India, you simply present your visa authorisation, and immigration will stamp the visa into your passport.

Tourists have to stay in government-authorised hotels and homestays, which generally means three-star and above, though homestays are possible and a limited number of one- and two-star hotels are being added. Tourists need a guide to visit any temple or dzong (fort-monastery) and to travel beyond Paro and Thimphu, and transportation must be arranged for this.

All this means that most tours cost around US$150 to US$250 per person per day, inclusive of three-star accommodation, transportation, guide and food – on top of the US$200 daily SDF. The actual figure depends on group size, itinerary, standard of accommodation and whether all food and entry fees are included.

There are, of course, plus sides to Bhutan's high costs. Visitor numbers are generally low; tour, guide and accommodation standards are universally high; and the visitor experience is generally excellent.

Moreover, the SDF helps fund free healthcare and education in Bhutan, as well as conservation efforts and improvements in tourist infrastructure and training, so you

BOOK YOUR TRIP: STEP BY STEP

- Start the bureaucratic ball rolling at least a month before your trip; preferably two months or more if visiting in high season or during a popular festival.

- Piece together a personalised itinerary with help from this guidebook and a Bhutanese travel agency, or go with one of their set itineraries.

- Mention your preferred hotels, any hikes or activities you'd like to do, whether you want to try a homestay etc, or any short treks.

- Pay the SDF fee for the number of days of your trip, either directly to the Bhutanese government (credit card or bank transfer) or via your agent.

- Book Drukair or Bhutan Airlines air tickets to Bhutan online (if the tickets are refundable book them as early as possible, especially during high season).

- Fill out the visa form, pay the visa fee and upload copies of your passport, photo and travel insurance (or get your agent to do this). Receive your visa authorisation within five days and print it out to show check-in staff on your Bhutan flight.

- Consider visas for any countries you are transiting through – probably a Nepali visa on arrival in Kathmandu or an Indian e-visa obtained online if travelling via Delhi.

- Pay tour costs to your agent through a bank transfer. If travelling solo, single supplements for car hire and hotel accommodation are at the discretion of the agent, hotel or car-hire company.

know that the bulk of the money you are paying is going to support the country in its admirable environmental and social goals.

INDIAN TOURISTS

The one fact that somewhat undermines the high-value, low-volume mantra is that around 80% of tourists to Bhutan are now Indians, who travel under a different set of rules.

Like other foreigners, Indian travellers must travel with a guide and transportation, but they pay a much-reduced daily SDF of Rs 1200 per person per night. Indian citizens don't need a visa but do require a permit, which can be applied for online or at the border.

Indians also need to show travel insurance but are able to buy a Bhutanese policy on the spot.

Dealing with a Tour Agency

In theory, foreign tourists can now book accommodation and transfers directly with hotels and don't technically need a guide in Paro or Thimphu, so if you are just planning to visit these towns, you could book this through a hotel and arrange the SDF payment and visa yourself.

In reality, for a multiday itinerary that involves visits to dzongs and temples, day hikes, trekking or other activities, you are still better off joining the vast majority of foreign tourists who arrange their trip through an experienced tour agency. Bhutanese tourism infrastructure isn't yet developed enough to offer easily bookable separate transportation and guide services. Guides in Bhutan are almost universally ex-

IPEK MOREL/SHUTTERSTOCK ©

Tour group on trail towards Taktshang Goemba (p96)

Need to Know

	VISA EXTENSIONS	**OFF-SEASON DISCOUNTS**	**CANCELLATIONS**
	Extensions are possible mid-trip, after you've paid the extra SDF for any additional days.	There are no longer discounts on the SDF, only on hotels, so there's little incentive to travel in winter or the monsoon.	If you cancel or shorten your trip you will get a refund on the remaining days of the SDF. For tour cancellation policies, ask your agent.

cellent and they really add to the smooth running and understanding of your trip.

Perhaps the best way to plan your trip is to use an agency's itinerary as a starting point and modify it to your interests. If you have a specific interest in embroidery, hiking or Buddhism, for example, a good agency will adapt the tour to your preferences. This is also the time to mention any extras, such as a traditional hot-stone bath, an overnight in a rural homestay or a day of rafting or mountain biking. You can also specify whether you want a trip that includes all meals in your hotel, or if you want to try restaurants yourself in Thimphu.

CHOOSING A TOUR AGENCY

There are several hundred licensed tour companies in Bhutan, ranging from one-person operations to large organisations with fleets of vehicles and their own hotels.

Large companies, such as Bhutan Tourism Corporation Limited, Druk Asia, Norbu Bhutan Travel and Etho Metho Tours & Treks have more clout to obtain reservations in hotels (some of which they own) and on Drukair, but they are mainly focused on groups.

Companies large enough to handle overseas queries, but still small enough for the owner to pay personal attention to your programme, include: Bhutan Travel Bureau, Bhutan Mountain Holiday, Sakten Tours & Treks, Thunder Dragon Treks and Yu-Druk Tours & Treks. There are dozens more.

A few Bhutanese agencies, such as Blue Poppy Tours & Treks (UK) and Bridge to Bhutan, Windhorse Tours and MyBhutan (USA), have offices abroad, which can be useful when making payments.

Our final piece of advice: you will likely only make one trip to Bhutan in your lifetime, so be sure to invest the time and budget to make the most of it.

THE SUSTAINABLE DEVELOPMENT FEE

The Basic Sustainable Development Fee (SDF) Rules
Foreign tourists (excluding Indian citizens)
A mandatory daily SDF of US$200 per person per night. There is no surcharge for solo travellers.
Children Kids aged six to 12 get a 50% discount; under six are free, over 12s pay the full rate.

Incentives for 2024
In the face of falling tourism numbers, Bhutan announced incentives in June 2023 to encourage longer stays, including treks and trips to the remote east. The following options offer a 50–60% discount on the SDF and are currently only valid for trips made until the end of 2024. The discounts are:

● Pay four days of SDF and get four days free.
● Pay seven days of SDF and get seven days free.
● Pay 12 days of SDF and get 18 days free.

For details visit bhutan.travel. An online calculator at visit.doi.gov.bt will confirm the exact SDF cost for your trip.

Restaurant, Thimphu

MICHAEL GRANT TRAVEL/ALAMY STOCK PHOTO ©

PASSPORT VALIDITY	INDIAN ID	SELF-DRIVE	FLIGHT DELAYS
To enter Bhutan your passport must be valid for six months after your planned departure.	Indian nationals can enter Bhutan with a passport or an Indian voter ID card. Indian under-18s may enter with a birth certificate or passport.	Indians driving their own vehicle must pay a Rs 4500 daily fee. Bring licence, registration, plus insurance, emissions and road-worthiness certificates.	If your flight out of Bhutan is delayed by a day then you won't have to pay an extra day's SDF, but you will be liable for hotel costs.

AS FOODSTUDIO/SHUTTERSTOCK ©

Ema datse (chillies in cheese sauce)

THE FOOD SCENE

Skip the tourist buffets for Bhutan's fiery cuisine, where chillies are a main course, not a condiment.

Like most Himalayan cuisines, food in Bhutan is a blend of Chinese and Indian influences, adapted to local ingredients. Bhutan's national dish is *ema datse,* whole green or red chillies cooked in a soft cheese sauce. The Bhutanese love chillies and mouth-scorching local meals will bring tears of joy to the eyes of chilli lovers.

For visitors the main difficulty with authentic Bhutanese cuisine is finding it. Most tour agencies arrange set lunches in local restaurants and dinner buffets, whose deliberately non-offensive mix of continental, Chinese, Indian and toned-down Bhutanese dishes often ends up a bit bland. For the real firepower, request to eat where, or what, your guide is eating. It will be much tastier, if you can take the heat.

If you do want to explore the dishes available in local restaurants but can't tell your *shakam* (dried beef) from your *sikam* (dried pork) or your *shukam* (dried yellow chillies), then read on.

Staples

Although there is plenty of white rice, the Bhutanese prefer a locally produced red variety, which has a slightly nutty flavour. At high altitudes wheat and buckwheat are the staples. In Bumthang, *khule* (buckwheat pancakes) and *puta* (buckwheat noodles) replace rice as the foundation of many meals, while Haa specialises in *hoentay* (buckwheat dumplings). *Momos* – steamed (sometimes fried) dumplings filled with meat, cheese or vegetables – are a staple throughout Bhutan.

One condiment you'll find everywhere is *ezay,* a salsa of onions, chillies and, if you are lucky, a zingy burst of flower pepper.

Best Bhutanese Dishes	EMA DATSE	KEWA DATSE	SHAMU DATSE	JA SHA MARU
	The national dish: whole chillies *(ema)* smothered in cheese *(datse)*.	Potatoes *(kewa)* in a cheese sauce; rarely spicy.	Mushrooms *(shamu)* with cheese sauce.	Ginger chicken *(ja sha)* in garlic and butter with onion.

Meat & Veg

Some kind of bony chicken is generally available, as are beef and fish, which generally come from India or Thailand. Wind-dried and semi-dried meats are a local staple and include *shakam* (beef jerky), *yaksha* (dried yak) and bacon-like *sikam* (dried fatty pork belly), and all are incorporated into many main dishes.

Beyond potatoes (from Phobjikha) seasonal vegetables to look out for include *nakey* (fiddlehead fern fronds), *olo chato* (literally 'old crow beak'), *khtem* (bitter melon) and wild asparagus. *Lom* (turnip leaves) are dried and preserved for winter, often cooked with *sikam. Shukam* are white-blanched, sun-dried chillies that pack a sour, tangy punch. Bhutan produces some excellent mushrooms *(shamu)* in August and September, including chantarelle, shitake and matsutake, mostly for the Japanese market.

Vegetarians won't have any problems finding a good range of dishes, though things might get repetitive. Vegans have a harder time, as many Bhutanese vegetable dishes come in a cheese sauce. Your guide can make arrangements for most dietary restrictions.

Bhutanese Brews

Traditional Bhutanese tea is known as *sud-ja,* and comes Tibetan style with salt, soda and butter, but you'll also find Indian-style milk tea everywhere. If you visit a homestay you won't get away without trying some *arra,* a sinus-clearing spirit fermented from rice, or *sinchhang,* made from millet, wheat or rice.

Bhutan's best beer is Red Panda, a tangy unfiltered weiss beer brewed in Bumthang but with a short shelf life, so it's found inconsistently elsewhere. Hopheads can also tour and sample local beers at Paro's Namgyal Artisanal Brewery and at Ser Bhum Brewery between Thimphu and the Dochu La. Note that Tuesday is a dry day in Bhutan, so alcohol is not served and bars are closed.

BEST MEALS IN BHUTAN

Bukhari at the Uma (p102) Contemporary and fresh Bhutanese and Western menus at the Uma, one of Bhutan's best hotels. It's best to book ahead.

Babesa Village Restaurant (p69) Popular with tourists but it has a genuine feel and the Bhutanese food is well above average.

Folk Heritage Museum Restaurant (p69) Set meals that go well beyond *ema datse,* best suited to groups.

Jakar Village Lodge (p151) Top-notch Bhutanese food using varied and seasonal local produce and the fluffiest buckwheat pancakes.

Beyond the Ordinary
Dishes Worth Seeking Out

Juma Bhutanese sausage made with minced meat, rice and spices.
Jaju Mild milk and vegetable soup with local greens.
Phak sha laphu Stewed pork with radish.

Dare to Try

Goep Pa Cow tripe with chillies and onions.
Kangchu Maru Pig-trotter curry.
Doma Palm nut (called *paan* in India) mixed with lime ash, rolled up in a betel leaf and chewed slowly. Bittersweet and mildly intoxicating.
Chugo Rock-hard dried squares of cheese, sometimes smoked.

BRADLEY MAYHEW/LONELY PLANET ©

Olo chato

NO SHA HUENT SU	PHAK SHA PHIN TSHOEM	SIKAM PAA	GOEN HOGEY
Braised or stewed beef *(no sha)* with spinach.	Pork *(phak sha)* curry *(tshoem)* with rice glass noodles *(phin* or *fing).*	Wind-dried pork cooked with dried chillies and radish. *Shakam paa* is a beef version.	Salad of cucumber, Sichuanese flower pepper, red chilli, spring onion and tomato.

PEMA GYAMTSHO/SHUTTERSTOCK ©

Dance of the Guru Tshengye, Thimphu tseschu (p68)

TRIP PLANNER

BHUTAN'S RELIGIOUS FESTIVALS

The exotic, arcane and otherworldly side of Bhutanese culture is on glorious display in its religious festivals. With their colourful masked costumes, dances, music and processions, Bhutan's tsechus are a highlight of the social calendar for most Bhutanese, so be sure to build at least one into your itinerary.

Tsechus

Bhutan's most dramatic festivals are its tsechus, a series of ritual religious dances (*cham*) performed by spectacularly masked and elaborately robed monk dancers, who train for months before the event. The dates and duration of the tsechus vary from one district to another, but often take place on or around the 10th day of the Bhutanese calendar, which is dedicated to the saint Guru Rinpoche. Some of the festivals mark specific historic events, others are on auspicious dates and celebrate important moments in Buddhist history.

Usually the tsechus are performed in dzong or goemba courtyards, which can become incredibly crowded as onlookers vie for a position. The tsechu is a grand social event, drawing people far and wide from the surrounding districts. They are not solemn occasions, but rather are marked by a holiday atmosphere as people put on their finest clothing and jewellery, share their picnics and exchange local news, often engaging in a bit of shopping or gambling in the stalls set up just outside the festival grounds.

During the tsechu, *atsara* (masked clowns) mimic the dances and perform comic

Festival dates are determined by the Bhutanese lunar calendar, which in turn is based on the Tibetan calendar, but differs from the latter by one or more days.

There are online Bhutanese calendars to convert dates –

there's even a Bhutanese calendar app! Finding out about smaller festivals can be a challenge, especially as some dates are only confirmed a few weeks beforehand, after the astrologer gives their final seal of approval. Most festivals last

for two or three days, giving you multiple chances to catch them.

The easiest way to determine the main festival dates is on the Department of Tourism (bhutan. travel) website, where over 30 festivals are listed with their upcoming dates.

routines wearing masks with long red phallic noses. While entertaining the onlookers, they also help to keep order.

As much as anything the festival is an opportunity to catch up with far-flung friends and relatives, and to be immersed in Buddhist teachings. The Bhutanese believe that they attain merit simply by attending the tsechus and watching the performances of the highly symbolic dances.

The highlight of many tsechus is the unfurling of a giant *thangka* (painted or embroidered religious picture) from a building overlooking the dance arena before sunrise. Such large *thangka* are called *thondrol* and are usually embroidered rather than painted. The word means 'liberation on sight', and it is believed that one's sins are washed away upon viewing one of these impressive relics.

Cham Dances

The type of dances you see during a tsechu depends on the location and type of festival, though many have become standards.

One of the most common dances is the **Dance of the Stag and Hunter**, which is based on the story of Milarepa's conversion of the hunter Gonpo Dorji to Buddhism. After a comic start, the hunter and his dog are seen in pursuit of a deer when the deer seeks shelter with the yogi Milarepa, identifiable by his white cotton robe, who sings a song that converts all three to Buddhism. The conversion is symbolised by a rope that both the dog and hunter must jump over.

You'll also likely see the dance of the **Guru Tshengye**, the eight manifestations of Guru Rinpoche, who is accompanied by his two consorts, Yeshe Tshogyel and Mandarava. This is both a dance and a drama and starts with the entrance of Dorji Drolo, wearing a

PHOTOGRAPHY ETIQUETTE

During festivals you can photograph from the dzong courtyard where the dances take place but do consider the following etiquette:

● Use a telephoto lens without a flash. Don't let your desire for a close-up get in the way of the dancers or block the view of other spectators.

● Don't intrude on the dance ground or on the space occupied by local people seated at the edge of the dance area, and if you do end up in the front row, remain seated.

● Try not to sit at the entrance to the dance ground or by the main building as it makes it harder for others to avoid having you in their photos.

● Don't photograph a member of the royal family or the Je Khenpo, if they are present.

GNOHZ/SHUTTERSTOCK ©

Jakar tsechu (p151)

terrifying red mask, followed by a long procession with the eight manifestations. Dorji Drolo also takes a central role in the **Dance of the Wrathful Deities**.

The **Black Hat Dance** commemorates the historic killing of the anti-Buddhist Tibetan king Langdarma in 842 by the Buddhist monk Pelkyi Dorji. Like many *cham* dances, it represents the transformation of the dancers into powerful tantric yogis, who exorcise all evil spirits.

The **Dance of the Rashas** is one of the highlights of a tsechu. It represents a spiritual drama as two newly deceased men, one a sinner and the other virtuous, are brought before the Lord of the Underworld, represented by a large mannequin surrounded by an entourage of *raksha* (spirits of the underworld). The sinner, dressed in black, is judged and then dragged to the hell realms by the Black Demon.

Equally chilling is the **Dance of the Lords of the Cremation Grounds**, which occurs on the first day of a tsechu. Four dancers wearing skull masks and long white gloves dance and bend backwards, touching the earth to liberate the spirits of the deceased. The dancers represent Buddhist protectors who live on the edges of the eight cremation grounds on the edges of the symbolic Mt Meru.

Other dances you might see are the **Dance with the Drangyen**, or Lute, which represents the diffusion of the Drukpa lineage in Bhutan, and the **Dance of the Drametse Drummers**, which depicts 100 peaceful and wrathful deities.

LINDSAY FEGENT-BROWN/LONELY PLANET ©

Dance of the Drametse Drummers, Paro tsechu (p88)

Off-the-Beaten-Track Festivals

TRASHI YANGTSE TSECHU
February's three-day tsechu in this remote dzong (p186) ends with the unveiling of a huge Guru Tshengye *thondrol*.

BULI MANI
This three-day festival in February/March at Bumthang's Buli Lhakhang (p112) kicks off with a pre-Buddhist fire blessing.

GOM KORA
A *thondrol* is displayed at this remote site as pilgrims circumambulate the sacred rock (p185) throughout the night. In March/April.

CHARNSITR/SHUTTERSTOCK ©

Thimphu tsechu (p68)

Which Festival?

The Thimphu (p68) and Paro (p88) tsechus are by far the most popular festivals with tourist groups, and increasing numbers of visitors are discovering the theatrical *dromchoe* in beautiful Punakha (p119). These three are the grandest festivals, on the biggest scale and are true spectacles, with hundreds of attendees, but all are popular with tourists.

Some old Bhutan hands prefer the smaller festivals or tsechus held in lesser-known regional dzongs and lhakhangs. They may be lighter on spectacle but they provide a more intimate and traditional experience, and you might be the only foreigners there.

In addition to religious festivals there are other cultural celebrations throughout the Bhutanese year, notably Bumthang's Nomads' Festival (p158) in February and Laya's Royal Highlander Festival (p126) in October.

For a rundown of the most popular festivals see p27.

TSECHU TIPS

What to bring Dances are long and you don't want to lose your hard-fought-for position, so bring a sun hat, water, snacks, camera and spare batteries, and a collapsible seat or cushion.

Dress up Pack a smart set of clothes or even better get a *gho* (traditional Bhutanese men's robe) or *kira* (woman's traditional dress) made up – locals will love it and you'll be accepted with open arms.

Offbeat festivals Try to visit an off-the-beaten-track festival at a smaller temple, lesser-visited dzong or a festival out in the east.

Two-for-one Some auspicious dates are celebrated in multiple locations, meaning you can combine festivals, such as the simultaneous tsechus at Gasa and Talo Goemba, near Punakha.

Book ahead Hotel rooms and flights into Bhutan fill up quickly during the Thimphu and Paro tsechus, and some top-end hotels introduce a tsechu supplement or minimum stay.

Take part You'll get the most out of a tsechu if you come prepared to take part and be part of the crowd, instead of an observer taking photos from the sidelines. Everybody, including visitors, takes part in the final dance (Tashi Lebey), which concludes all festivities.

Clowns Be prepared for clowns to hit tourists up for donations. Take it as a good-natured game. If you contribute, you may even receive a blessing from the wooden phallus they carry.

KURJEY TSECHU	TAMSHING PHALA CHOEPA	JAKAR TSECHU	TRONGSA TSECHU
A one-day festival (p151) in Bumthang coinciding with Guru Rinpoche's birthday in June. The nearby Nimalung tsechu starts two days earlier.	A duet of festivals (p158) in the Bumthang valley, first at Tamshing Goemba and then Thangbi Goemba, in September.	Masked dances occupy the dzong for three days in October/November (p151), a week before the famous Jampey Lhakhang Drup.	One of the least-visited festivals in the country, in December/January (p146). Remote Lhuentse and Dungkhar hold tsechus at the same time.

KATIEKK/SHUTTERSTOCK ©

Trekking near Paro

PLANNING YOUR TREKKING TRIP

Trekking in Bhutan takes you into a rarely seen corner of the Himalaya, opening up a remote region of jagged peaks, pristine forests, high passes and hidden valleys. While treks here certainly entail a physical challenge, logistically things are easy, with every detail taken care of by your tour agency. For the best routes for your trip see p192.

The Nature of Trekking in Bhutan

Treks in Bhutan are physically demanding. The terrain is very rugged, the altitude can be a real challenge and, in general, paths are quite rocky and churned up by horse and yak traffic, making trails muddy after rain. That said, treks do vary greatly in their difficulty and also duration. Some days involve just three hours of walking followed by tea in the sun, while others demand a nine-hour slog with a lung-busting 1000m ascent.

On a logistical level the most notable thing about trekking in Bhutan is that it is fully organised and catered. Even a small group will normally have a guide, cook, helper or two, a horseman and up to eight or more horses, carrying a dining tent, toilet tent and a double tent for every two tourists. Camp helpers will set up your tent and mattress in the afternoon and bring you 'bed tea' and a bowl of hot water for washing in the morning. At night you'll drift off to sleep snuggling with a hot-water bottle.

TREKKING RULES & REGULATIONS

All treks in Bhutan must be fully organised and guided camping treks booked through a Bhutanese tour operator. Your agency must arrange camping gas for fuel (fires are not allowed), as well as a first-aid kit and a toilet tent where no toilet facilities exist.

Trekkers pay the same US$200 per day Sustainable Development Fee (SDF; see p33 for more info) as other travellers. Until the end of 2024 (at least) trekkers can get a 50% discount on the SDF for trips of eight or 14 days (for extra days just add on the daily fee). For a longer trek you can get 18 SDF-free days if you pay the full SDF for the first 12 days (a 60% discount).

Your agency will arrange a slew of permits for national parks and border areas. They are checked by Royal Bhutan Army posts along the trek.

Note that even with comprehensive advanced planning, trek plans do sometimes have to be changed en route, due to weather conditions, snowfall, river flows, illness and the like. Even if you can cross a high, snowy pass your horseman might not want to risk his animals on such a challenge. Be flexible, especially in shoulder seasons, and take disappointment in your stride.

One thing to note is that farm roads are spreading rapidly in Bhutan so you might find that the beginning, or especially end, of your trek is now on a scrappy dirt road, which can be an anticlimactic way to end a fantastic trek.

Food

Your trek staff will provide food of such quality and quantity that Bhutan is one place where you might actually gain weight on a trek! You can rely completely on camp meals, though it's always a good idea to have a few granola bars available during the day and pack some chocolate for moral support. Tell your agency in advance if you have any special dietary requirements.

In general, breakfast usually includes cereal, porridge, toast and jam, sometimes eggs, with instant coffee and tea. You'll sometimes be served French fries for breakfast, proof should you need it that Bhutan really is Shangri-La. Midday meals are hot, usually prepared at breakfast time and packed in a thermos-style metal container with a flask of hot tea.

Your arrival in camp will be met with tea and coffee and maybe popcorn or nuts. For dinner you'll likely to be served rice, chapatis, lentil soup, Bhutanese vegetables and even meat dishes for the first couple of nights.

TREKKING TIPS

● You'll enjoy your trek much more if you are in decent physical shape, so spend a month or more beforehand doing some training hikes and breaking in your trek shoes.

● During the day you won't have access to your main bag, so always carry the following items in your daypack: sun hat, rain shell, spare T-shirt, camera, batteries, phone, fleece, water bottle and purification, and snacks.

● For the same reason always have the following emergency items on your person: toilet paper, blister kit, sunscreen, headache tablets, acetazolamide (Diamox), whistle and torch (flashlight).

● You won't find much electricity on longer treks so consider a solar charger. During particularly cold nights keep your batteries and phone in your sleeping bag to stop them from draining.

PASCAL BOEGLI/GETTY IMAGES ©

**Mules and horses,
Snowman Trek**

PASCAL BOEGLI/GETTY IMAGES ©

Trekking to Thampe Tsho (p208), Snowman Trek

Bhutan's Best Treks for...

BRAGGING RIGHTS
The 25-day Snowman trek (p206) is gruelling, expensive and hard to predict; more people have summited Everest than completed it.

HIMALAYAN PEAKS
The Jhomolhari trek (p199) takes you to within an arm's reach of Jhomolhari and Jichu Drake, two of Bhutan's most beautiful peaks.

MOUNTAIN CULTURE
The Laya trek (p205) takes you past Lingzhi Dzong to experience the unique culture and fantastic hats of the Layap people.

What to Pack

Only very simple trekking gear is available in Thimphu, so bring everything you need with you. Agencies provide tents, mats and sleeping bags but it's a good idea to bring your own down sleeping bag and an extra mattress for comfort. A silk sleeping bag liner is a nice luxury and adds warmth. Pack everything in a lockable, durable duffel bag (maximum 15kg) that is suitable for packing on a horse or yak.

CLOTHES

In terms of clothing you'll need a couple of wickable T-shirts (preferably merino wool), a fleece, a down jacket, quick drying trek pants and several pairs of wool socks. Thermal underwear is a good idea, as are gloves, a beanie hat and a sun hat that covers your ears. A waterproof Gore-Tex jacket is a must, as are trousers, though some trekkers prefer a poncho or sturdy umbrella.

Gore-Tex boots with sturdy Vibram soles are more useful than running shoes on Bhutan's rocky and sometimes snowy trails. Make sure they are broken in but still in good condition. A spare pair of camp shoes are useful for the evenings.

EQUIPMENT

You'll need a daypack, with sun cream and lip balm, toilet paper, sunglasses, a blister kit with scissors and tape, trekking poles, a head torch and spare batteries. Bring a camera or smart phone and a spare battery pack, charging cable and, for long treks, a solar charger. Several of the cooking huts on the Jhomolhari trek have electrical outlets for charging phones. A book is useful for the long afternoons.

For water you should bring your own system of purification, either chemical-, filter- or UV light-based. Camp staff can provide boiling water, so a metal bottle that can handle heat is useful. Don't rely on bottled water.

If you think you might be crossing a snowy pass consider bringing a pair of lightweight mini-crampons such as micro-spikes. In bad conditions they can be priceless.

TREKKING HEALTH

Once you are on a trek in Bhutan you can't rely on getting any medical attention, so be sure to minimise your risks beforehand.

● It is essential to get comprehensive travel insurance that covers medical evacuations up to the maximum altitude you will reach.

● Inflamed knees is a common complaint caused by long trekking descents. Anti-inflammatory pills are helpful, as are walking poles and specialised knee supports.

● Get a dental checkup before flying to Bhutan and bring antibiotics and painkillers in case you have a tooth infection on trek.

● When on the trail remember to always give way to yaks and mules and stand on the upper side of a trail when livestock are passing, as they might just push you off.

● Acute mountain sickness (AMS) is a potentially fatal condition that can affect anybody above 3500m. It's important to read up on the symptoms and treatment beforehand, to keep altitude gain to less than 400m per day and follow recommended acclimatisation days.

● If in doubt, always descend to a lower altitude.

● In an emergency your only solution may be a helicopter medivac, which will cost from US$3000 upwards. The Royal Bhutan Helicopter Service based at Paro airport offers emergency evacuations.

A SHORT TREK	GENERAL TREKKING	SOLITUDE	EPIC TREKKING
The overnight Bumdrak trek (p196) offers luxury glamping, sunset views and a visit to the Tiger's Nest – from above.	The Druk Path trek (p195) combines remote lakes and historical Buddhist sites and is easily combined with sights in Paro and Thimphu.	For high-altitude lakes, panoramic views and remote mountain trails, try the Dagala Thousand Lakes trek (p208).	The 403km Trans-Bhutan Trail (p208) doesn't boast high peaks but it's an incredible cultural journey, traversing the country.

THE GUIDE

Thimphu
p46

Western Bhutan
p81

Central Bhutan
p136

Eastern Bhutan
p167

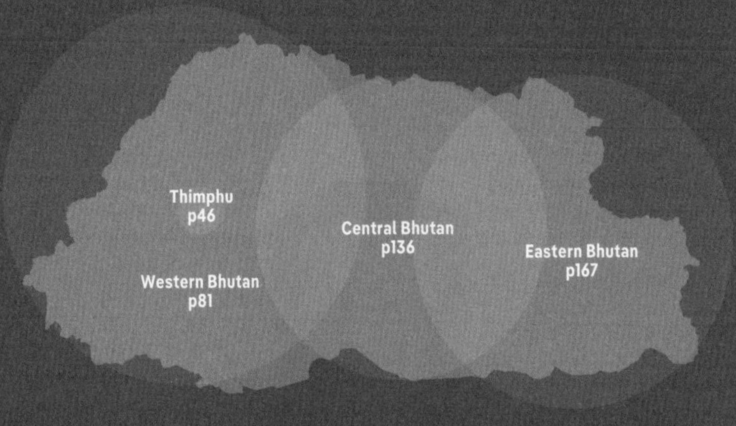

Chapters in this section are organised by hubs.
We see the hub as your base in the destination,
where you'll find unique experiences,
local insights, insider tips and expert
recommendations. It's also your gateway to the
surrounding area, where you'll see what and how
much you can do from there.

View towards Wangdue Phodrang (p126)

THIMPHU

WHERE THE 15TH AND 21ST CENTURIES CONVERGE

Thimphu is Bhutan's only real urban centre, where Gross National Happiness has to coexist with the demands of modern life.

Strung out along the Wang Chhu, Thimphu is Bhutan's own mini-metropolis, an expanding bubble of shopping centres, monasteries and chalet-like apartment buildings that quickly frays at the edges into blue-pine forest.

Travellers expecting a medieval atmosphere may be disappointed – Thimphu's traditional houses have been largely replaced by multistorey concrete towers – but it's this mixture of ancient and modern that makes the city so interesting. Climb up to Changangkha Lhakhang early in the morning and watch parents bring their newborns to receive an auspicious name, or wander the stalls of the Centenary Market in the late afternoon, and you'll see the Bhutan you were expecting: devotees in traditional dress, crimson-robed monks and farmers from the hills coming to trade.

It's the cultural combinations give Thimphu its flavour; you'll see pilgrims paying for amulets and making donations to protector deities using a QR code on their mobile banking apps, or monks taking a break from their tantric studies over an Americano coffee.

For the visitor, central Thimphu offers an opportunity to break away from the rigid tour itinerary and do a bit of solo exploring. The centre has a fascinating array of shops, selling everything from Korean fashion to Buddhist statuary. This is also the only place in the country to boast a dining and nightlife scene. Take the rare opportunity to dine on burgers and craft beer, chat to plugged-in entrepreneurs in the city's surprisingly hip bars or catch some live music in a crowd of tattooed, hoodied (and impeccably polite) youth – most of whom might speak better English than you do.

The Bhutanese capital is changing fast, as more and more rural families migrate here and wealthier city residents plan an escape to Australia (joining the 80,000 who have moved there in recent years). Largely devoid of the stresses and irritations that plague city living, Thimphu in many ways offers the realisation of the Bhutanese dream: a largely contented people embracing the modern world, but doing so on their own terms and while holding on tightly to their traditional culture. Look closely and you'll see that even Thimphu's most modern buildings are adorned with hand-painted Buddhist murals and protector deities.

KHOA NGUYEN/GETTY IMAGES ©

THE MAIN AREAS

CENTRAL THIMPHU	GREATER THIMPHU	THE VALLEY RIM	NORTH OF THIMPHU	SOUTH OF THIMPHU
Downtown shops, cafes and restaurants. p52	Museums and government buildings. p63	Forested trails to monasteries and meditation retreats. p70	Hillside monasteries and temples. p73	Historic buildings and suburban sprawl. p77

Above: Buddha Dordenma (p78). Left: Prayer wheel, Trashi Chho Dzong (p67)

Find Your Way

Thimphu is a miniature capital city, spread along a narrow north–south valley, and getting around is easy, especially as you'll have a car and driver at your disposal. That said, staying in a hotel within walking distance of the centre is useful, to have a bit of independence when visiting restaurants and bars.

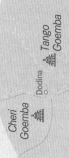

N

0   2 miles
0   4 km

Cheri Goemba

Dodina

Tango Goemba

North of Thimphu p73

Begana

Wang Chhu

Guru Rock Painting

Kabisa

Pangri Zampa

Dechenchoeling

FROM THE AIRPORT

Thimphu is just over an hour (46km) from the Paro international and domestic airport, but there are several interesting sights and potential detours en route, so you could take most of the day. Your guide and driver will meet you and drop you off at the airport.

WALKING

On foot is the best way to get around the centre, at least between the Clocktower Sq and the top of Norzin Lam. The hourlong walks to Wangditse Goemba and the Buddha Dordenma are both lovely, and there are also several full-day hikes up the forested sides of the valley.

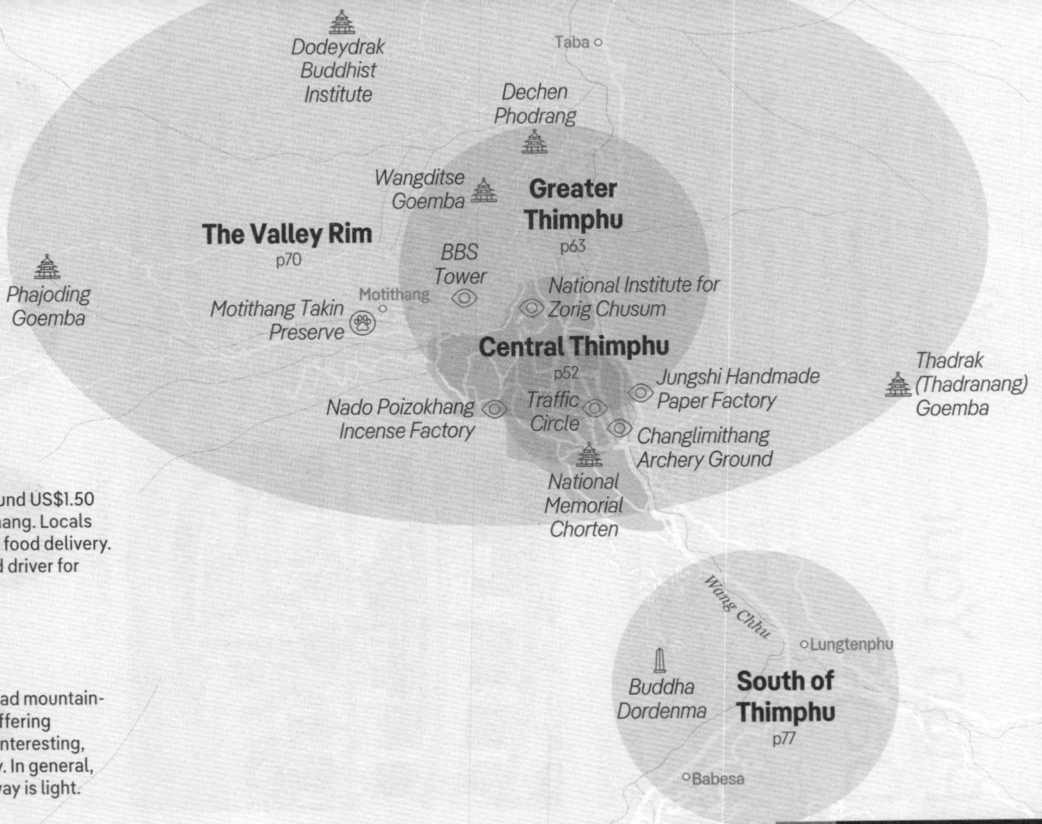

Phajoding
Goemba

Dodeydrak
Buddhist
Institute

Taba

Dechen
Phodrang

Wangditse
Goemba

The Valley Rim
p70

BBS
Tower

Motithang

Motithang Takin
Preserve

**Greater
Thimphu**
p63

National Institute for
Zorig Chusum

Thadrak
(Thadranang)
Goemba

Jungshi Handmade
Paper Factory

Central Thimphu
p52

Traffic
Circle

Changlimithang
Archery Ground

Nado Poizokhang
Incense Factory

National
Memorial
Chorten

Lungtenphu

Wang Chhu

**South of
Thimphu**
p77

Buddha
Dordenma

Babesa

TAXI/CAR

Taxi rides around town are cheap at around US$1.50 for a ride in the centre or to lower Motithang. Locals use the DrukRide app for both rides and food delivery. Most tourists will have their own car and driver for getting around the city.

BIKE

Thimphu has a decent network of off-road mountain-biking trails, as well as several places offering bike hire and guided trips, making it an interesting, alternative way to experience the valley. In general, road traffic off the main southern highway is light.

Plan Your Days

Your guide will help you visit the city's highlights, but budget some time to explore the centre under your own steam; opportunities for such independent exploration are few and far between in Bhutan.

Traffic police (p54)

Day 1

Morning

● Join pilgrims around the **National Memorial Chorten** (p54) and **Changangkha Lhakhang** (p55) and then pop into the **National Textile Museum** (p55) and **National Institute for Zorig Chusum** (p66) for a fine introduction to Bhutan's traditional arts. Take advantage of Thimphu's global food offerings for lunch – **Cloud 9** (p55), **San Maru** (p57) and **Ambient Cafe** (p60) are the standouts.

Afternoon

● Drive south to the epic statue of **Buddha Dordenma** (p78), then north to **Trashi Chho Dzong** (p67), for when it opens to visitors after 5pm (weekdays).

Evening

● Grab a cocktail and a grilled *ema datse* (cheese and chillies) sandwich at the **Drunken Yeti** (p60) and, on weekends, sample the local live-music scene at **Mojo Park** (p57).

You'll Also Want to...

Visit on a weekend for the busiest markets, most active archery contests and pilgrim sights, and the best live music and nightlife (Friday and Saturday).

ATTEND A FESTIVAL
Thimphu is packed to bursting during its colourful *dromchoe* and **tsechu** (p68) festivals in September/ October.

GET A TRADITIONAL MEDICAL TREATMENT
Enjoy an oil massage, **herbal steam bath** or hot oil compression to recharge your humours (p61).

VISIT A CRAFT WORKSHOP
See how Bhutanese incense and traditional paper are made in these two welcoming **workshops** (p66).

Day 2

Morning
● If it's a weekend, check out the action at the **Changlimithang Archery Ground** (p53), before visiting the bustling **weekend market** (p56). Weekends also mean that the dzong is open all day. Budget some time for **handicraft shopping on Norzin Lam** (p58) and then sample Thimphu's best *momos* (dumplings) at **Zombala** (p56) or **Tibetan Uncle** (p60) – if you can find it.

Afternoon
● Enjoy the late afternoon light on the walk from the **BBS Tower** to **Wangditse Goemba** and **Dechen Phodrang** (p65).

Evening
● Check out the Thimphu **bar scene** (p60) at Naughty Pigs and Blackout Bar, except on a Tuesday when all bars are closed.

Day 3

Morning
● Get an early start and pack a lunch for the day trip to **Tango Goemba** (p76) or **Cheri Goemba** (p75), stopping at **Pangri Zampa** (p74) en route. Alternatively, make the full-day hike up to **Pumola**, **Phajoding** and **Chhokhortse Goemba** (p71).

Afternoon
● There's just enough time to visit **Motithang Takin Preserve** (p72) – especially if coming from Phajoding – before some final shopping for festival masks, cordyceps tea or lemongrass fragrance.

Evening
● It's possible to drive to Paro in under 1½ hours if you are catching a flight the next morning, so stop for an early dinner at **Babesa Village Restaurant** (p69) en route.

SPOT A TAKIN
Get a good look at Bhutan's endearingly oddball **national animal** (p72) – part cow, part goat, part moose.

PLAY GOLF
Make your **golf** buddies jealous by playing nine holes within range of Trashi Chho Dzong (p68).

BUY A GHO
Bhutanese love to see a foreigner wearing a traditional *gho* or *kira*, especially at a festival, so get one made or buy one off the peg (p61).

GO CLUBBING
See a different side of Bhutan after midnight on a Friday or Saturday night at **Space 34** (p57) nightclub.

CENTRAL THIMPHU

DOWNTOWN SHOPS, CAFES AND RESTAURANTS

Thimphu's city centre is as urban as Bhutan gets (which isn't a lot). The handful of streets are home to a fascinating collection of shops, selling everything from monks' robes to edgy street fashion, alongside cinemas showing Dzongkha dramas, back-street *momo* joints, glitzy banks and swanky international hotels. Clocktower Sq anchors the south, with the top of Norzin Lam, the main drag, to the north, plus a few blocks on either side.

For visitors, the centre is the place to explore Thimphu's best restaurants, cafes, bars and nightlife, to get a taste of Bhutan's traditional medicine and its modern art scene, or learn more about the nation's twin obsessions – archery and weaving. There are also some fine sights, from the ionic National Memorial Chorten to the medieval Changangkha Lhakhang, and the shopping here is the best in the country.

TOP TIP

Central Thimphu is best explored on foot. You can walk from north to south in 30 minutes. Only the Centenary Market, Changangkha Lhakhang and the National Memorial Chorten are worth driving to. That said, you'll likely combine the sights of central and greater Thimphu into a day's sightseeing.

GFC COLLECTION/ALAMY STOCK PHOTO ©

Clocktower Sq

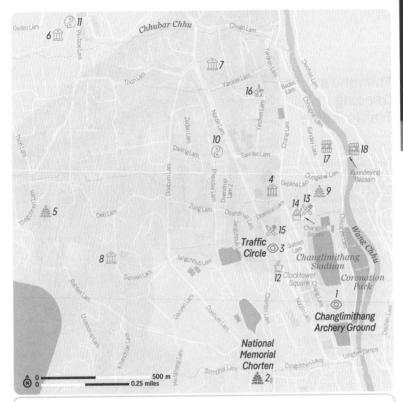

HIGHLIGHTS
1 Changlimithang Archery Ground
2 National Memorial Chorten
3 Traffic Circle

SIGHTS
4 Bhutan Postal Museum

5 Changangkha Lhakhang
6 Faculty of Traditional Medicine
7 National Textile Museum
8 Simply Bhutan
9 Zangto Pelri Lhakhang

ACTIVITIES, COURSES & TOURS
10 33 Soksoom Centre of Wellbeing & Happiness
11 National Institute of Traditional Medicine

EATING
12 Ambient Cafe
13 Chuniding Foods

14 Sonam Tshoey
15 Tibetan Uncle (Achola's)

DRINKING & NIGHTLIFE
16 Drunken Yeti

SHOPPING
17 Centenary (Weekend) Market
18 Handicrafts Market

Changlimithang Archery Ground

BHUTAN'S NATIONAL SPORT

Changlimithang Archery Ground

Head down to the city's premier *bacho* (archery ground) for one of the most enjoyable and quintessentially Bhutanese ways to spend an afternoon. Teams compete to hit targets over a distance of 145m, while their competitors taunt and tease their rivals' poor shots, and sing and dance to big up their own shots on target. Only traditional bamboo bows are used here, and a tournament is quite a spectacle, with lots of good-natured ribbing and camaraderie. The on-site 'Traditional Bow and Arrow Unit' sells traditional bamboo bows, known as *zhug,* and you can see arrows *(dha)* being made on the spot.

53

Thimphu's Dancing Traffic Police

ICONIC SYMBOL OF THE CITY

Thimphu is said to be one of only two capital cities in the world without traffic lights. A set was installed a few years back, but residents complained that it was too impersonal, so Thimphu's beloved white-gloved police returned to direct the traffic with the balletic grace of a 1980s robot dance. As well as being a classic Bhutanese anachronism, this may well be the city's most photographed spectacle. Moonwalk up to the roundabout (known as the **traffic circle**) on Norzin Lam and enjoy the show.

TOP: GNOHZ/SHUTTERSTOCK © BOTTOM: ANANDOART/SHUTTERSTOCK ©

Changangkha Lhakhang

National Memorial Chorten

TRADITIONAL BUDDHIST MONUMENT

National Memorial Chorten

This large stupa, or chorten, is one of the most visible landmarks in Thimphu, and for many Bhutanese it is the focus of their daily worship. The whitewashed Tibetan-style stupa was built in 1974 as a memorial to the third king, Jigme Dorji Wangchuck (1928–72). Early morning is a great time to visit, as elderly people shuffle meditatively around the chorten, families light butter lamps, and kids squeeze in a quick *kora* (ritual circumambulation) on their way to school. The action continues from dawn till long after dark, but tourists are discouraged from visiting during the floodlit night to give devotees some privacy. Clock the dedicated group of old-timers hauling away at room-size giant prayer wheels beside the main entrance.

Consult with a Bhutanese Astrologer at Changangkha Lhakhang

THIMPHU'S MOST INTERESTING TEMPLE

Changangkha Lhakhang is a traditional Bhutanese temple perched like a fortress on a hill above central Thimphu and humming with pilgrim activity. It was established in the 12th century on a site chosen by Lama Phajo Drukgom Shigpo, originally from Ralung in Tibet. The interior murals are particularly fine.

Parents come here to receive auspicious names for their newborns or blessings for their young children from the protector deity Tamdrin (to the left in the grilled inner sanctum). Visitors, especially children, are blessed by a *phurba* (ritual dagger) and given a *sungke* (sacred thread), while their parents make offerings of milk, *arra* (rice spirit) or pear brandy to Tamdrin.

Give the resident astrologer your birth date and he will consult divination charts to decide what kind of protective prayer flags will benefit you. Don't leave without checking out the shrine to the *tshomen* (mermaid-like water spirit) in the central courtyard and then taking in the excellent view from the *kora* path around the compound. Come early in the morning, before groups arrive, to enjoy Changangkha at its most peaceful.

National Textile Museum

THIMPHU'S BEST MUSEUM

Bhutan has one of the most highly developed textile traditions in the Himalaya, so much so that for centuries cloth was used here as currency and a form of tax payment. Anyone who can tell their warp from their weft should visit Thimphu's National Textile Museum to appreciate the incredible skill behind the national arts of *thagzo* (weaving) and *tshemzo* (embroidery). The museum is part of the Royal Textile Academy and features a stunning display of ancient and modern textiles.

The ground floor focuses on royal *gho* and *kira* (traditional dress for men and women, respectively), including the wedding clothes worn by the fourth king and his four wives. The upper floor introduces the major weaving techniques, styles of regional dress and types of textiles made by women and men. No photography is allowed.

Some of the most striking fabrics feature intricate designs called *trima,* an embroidery-like technique where extra

---

BHUTANESE NAMES

You can't tell a lot from a Bhutanese person's name. Although most Bhutanese have two names, the second name is not a family name, and names are generally given by monks or astrologers after consulting a newborn's horoscope. Many names have auspicious or religious meanings, such as Tashi (Good Luck), Sonam (Merit), Kalsang (Good Fortune) or Tshering (Long Life), whereas others refer simply to which day of the week they were born, such as Nyima (Sunday), Dawa (Monday), Migmar (Tuesday) etc. Everyone who gets their name from the Chimi Lhakhang has the name Chimi or Kunley.

Interestingly it's often impossible to tell even the sex of a Bhutanese person from their name. A few names are given only to girls (Choekyi, Drolma and Dekyi) but most names apply to either.

THE GUIDE

THIMPHU

WHERE TO GO FOR INTERNATIONAL FOOD

Cloud 9
The best burgers in Bhutan, plus homemade ice cream, stylish decor and an outdoor terrace; closed Monday. **$$$**

Seasons
Old-school pizza, pasta and salad joint (plus Nepali set meals), with an enclosed outdoor patio. **$$**

Project ZZA
Stylish place on Norzin Lam with the best pizza and calzones in town, plus cocktails; closed Sunday. **$$$**

**BEST LOCAL
BHUTANESE
RESTAURANTS**

Kalden Restaurant
Packed with office
workers at lunch, this
modern space has
authentic local dishes
served with a glass of
buttermilk. $

Yangkhil Restaurant
Recommended
for its *pak* ribs and
bacon-like *sikam,*
dried in house by the
owner 'Uncle' Kado
himself. $

Zombala Restaurant
Excellent choice
for beef *momos* or
bathup, a stew made
from rolled dough
noodle pieces; closed
Tuesday. $

Zombala II
A wider menu than
the original, with more
Bhutanese dishes and
some Continental,
overlooking the traffic
circle. $$

weft threads are coiled around the warp yarns to create distinctive geometric patterns. A *kira* with *trima* designs can take a year to complete and cost over US$1000. Some of the most sought-after styles are *ngosham* on a blue ground and *kushuthara* pieces on a white silk ground.

Shop at Centenary (Weekend) Market

UNIQUE LOCAL PRODUCTS

Thimphu's Centenary Market fills a maze-like pavilion on the west bank of the Wang Chhu, just north of Changlimithang Stadium. The market is open daily but is busiest from Friday until Sunday, when farmers travel here from the surrounding countryside. The incense area is one of the most interesting, full of deliciously aromatic mountain herbs.

Wander around the stalls and you'll find a pungent collection of dried fish, strips of fatty pork and discs of *datse* (soft cheese), as well as dried chillies, local pickles and bottles of wild honey from southern Bhutan. During the winter you can even pick up a leg of yak (with the hoof still attached). Depending on the season, look out for *bacha* (a type of wild cane shoot) and banana flower pods, both used in traditional soups, and the curly fiddlehead fern fronds known as *na-key.* The cereals section has red rice and *kapche,* the ground roasted barley beloved by highland Bhutanese and Tibetans (known as *tsampa* across the Himalaya).

Nearby, across the Kundeyling Baazam traditional cantilevered bridge, is a weekend-only **Handicrafts Market** selling everything from wooden *dhapa* bowls (the best come from Trashi Yangtse) and *mala* (prayer) beads to printing blocks and yak tails. Bargaining is acceptable, but starting prices are generally reasonable. Note that some of the cheaper items sold here are actually imported from Nepal.

Part of the market was under reconstruction at the time of research, so for dairy products and incense head north for a stroll along the riverside **Kaja Throm** market.

Zangto Pelri Lhakhang

TIMELESS CORNER OF OLD BHUTAN

With its endless procession of devotees and the constant chiming of prayer wheel bells, this is one of the most atmospheric corners of traditional Thimphu. The main modern chapel was built in the 1990s as a representation of Guru Rinpoche's celestial abode by Dasho Aku Tongmi, the musician who composed Bhutan's national anthem and features central stat-

WHERE TO GO FOR INTERNATIONAL FOOD

Brusnika Russian Café
Unexpectedly good Russian
breads, *pelmeni* (dumplings),
piroshki (meat pies) and *blini*
(pancakes) with sour cream. $$

The Zone
Old-school cafe-bar-diner with
breakfasts, pizza, burgers and
the like, plus Red Panda on tap;
closed Monday. $$

Shambhala
Stylish restaurant and lounge on
the main Clocktower Sq, serving
up a mix of Bhutanese, Indian
and Continental dishes. $$

Centenary Market

A NIGHT OUT IN THIMPHU

Namgay 'Nala' Phuntsho, co-owner of the Drunken Yeti bar in Thimphu, gives us his favourite spots for a night out in Thimphu.
@drunkenyetibar

The Zone
The Zone is where I grab something to eat before a night out. The owner is a die-hard Manchester United fan, so there's a great atmosphere whenever a game is on TV.

Mojo Park
Easily the best place for live music, with local bands performing every weekend. Plus, it's just down from the Zone.

Space 34
If you're not ready to wrap up your night, then try clubbing Bhutanese style at Space 34. It's popular with a younger crowd, especially after midnight, and has a restaurant that serves food till 2am.

ues of the *Khen Lop Choe Sum* – Guru Rinpoche, his disciple Shantarakshita and Tibetan King Trisong Detsen.

The older **Mani Dungkhor Lhakhang** next door contains some enormous prayer wheels, including some unusual thin corner wheels. Between the two chapels is an elephant skull in a box – reputedly unearthed while digging the foundations.

Art at VAST Bhutan

THE THIMPHU ART SCENE

This studio and art gallery has existed for 25 years with royal support to promote local artists, to provide vocational training for young artists and to act as an artists' creative meeting venue. It's a great place to plug into the Thimphu art scene, check out the latest exhibition and chat with artists.

To view the work of many VAST artists, with an eye to purchasing, visit the **Art Gallery Jatra**, near Clocktower Sq, which shows everything from modern mandala-inspired works to calligraphy and landscapes. Some of the most famous pieces from VAST alumni like Asha Karma are on display in the **international departure lounge** of Paro airport.

 WHERE TO EAT THE BEST EAST ASIAN FOOD

San Maru
Stylish place for excellent *bibambap, bulgogi* and Korean barbecue, plus dried fish soup and *kimbab* rolls. **$$$**

Fu Lu Shou
Set meals, hotpot and whole steamed fish Chinese style, just west of the centre. **$$**

Hayate Ramen
Good-value Japanese diner featuring ramen, sushi, curry and rice, and tofu and seaweed salad, with a kids menu. **$$**

Shopping & Handicrafts Tour of Norzin Lam

This stroll down Norzin Lam is a fascinating tour of some of the most interesting handicrafts in the country. Figure on an hour for the 1.5km stroll, plus shopping time.

Start your wanderings at the **1 Traditional Boot House**, at the northern end of Norzin Lam, which is one of only two shops in the city making traditional Bhutanese formal boots, known as *tshoglham*. Prices range from Nu 3000 up to Nu 15,000 for ornately embroidered leather boots. Tourists can only buy boots with a green band, as the colour denotes rank; orange is for government ministers and yellow is reserved for the king.

At the **2 National Textile Museum** (p55), just to the south, pop into the gift shop for some of the highest-quality *gho*, *kira* and silk scarves around. Just across from the museum on Norzin Lam is the tiny **3 One Gewog One Product store**, part of a royal project to boost local products from each of Bhutan's 205 *gewogs* (districts).

Products include bottled honey with cordyceps from Bumthang and *amla* (gooseberry) fruit candy from Mongar. The next-door **4 Wochu Metal Craft Center** preserves the arts of making traditional swords, knives and daggers (none of which you can put in your check-in luggage).

The centre of Norzin Lam is lined with 80 or so **5 handicraft stalls**, most stocking a fairly repetitive selection of scarves and woven bags. As you walk downhill, at stall 48, cross the gap in the stalls to the west side of the road.

The **6 Craft Gallery** here is a showroom for 13 of the very best Bhutanese brands, including wonderful honeys and oils from Bhutan Natural, body scrubs from Tse organics and beauty products from Mudra.

Traditional Bhutanese boots

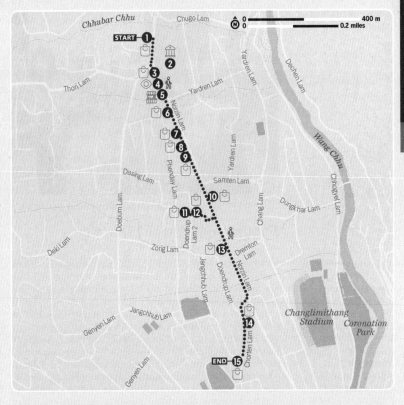

Also worth checking out is the jewellery by Sonam Rabgye (as worn by Kate Middleton), the silk pillows and belts from Kencho Couture and top-end T-shirt company Chhom.

Continue down Norzin Lam to NGO-run **7 Taryana Rural Crafts** to check out its collection of cane boxes, bags and scarves. The impressive building on the left is the five-star Taj Tashi hotel, which houses other Tashi businesses belonging to Bhutan's largest private company, including Tashi Cell and Bhutan Airlines.

A bit further down are **8 KMT Yangkhil** and the smaller **9 Yeshi Dorji Statues**, both fascinating traditional shops, full of holy pills, amulets, spirit traps and ritual implements.

Stop at Project Zza for a pizza lunch, otherwise detour left to the government-run **10 National Handicrafts Emporium**, with its wide range of *kira*, table runners and other weavings at set prices.

If you're in the market for some prayer flags, take the alley off Norzin Lam to the right by Food Express, directly across from the Bank of Bhutan, and then take a right and an immediate left up the steps to the **11 Dhar Tsongkhang** and **12 Lungdhar Tsongkhang** prayer flag shops. All the flags here have been pre-blessed in monastic ceremonies.

Back on Norzin Lam, continue downhill to the **13 Sephub Gyeltsen Tsongkhang** (p62) for the best woven cloth, silks, *gho* and *kira*.

When you reach the traffic circle take a right on Chorten Lam to the traditional **14 Norphel Choechan & Handicraft Shop**, opposite Le Meridien Hotel, which is worth a visit for its prayer wheels, tantric drums and ritual *kangling* trumpets.

Finally, head to the Cafe Himalya Bakery for a break and to visit the upstairs **15 CDK shop**, featuring top-end Bhutanese fashion from designer Chandrika Tamang; it's closed on Mondays.

Bhutanese people wearing *gho* and *kira*

BEST BARS IN THIMPHU

Drunken Yeti
Cosy and cool space on the top floor of Thimphu's narrowest building, with Red Panda on tap.

Blackout Bar
Rooftop bar popular with a younger crowd, with weekend DJs, food specials and great views.

Naughty Pigs
Cool industrial decor, with weekend live music, cocktails and late-night tacos.

Grey Area
Central bar, cafe, restaurant and gallery, featuring the art of owner-actor Kelly Dorji.

High Jinks @ Hotel Druk
A grown-up hotel bar with old-school charm, leather bar stools and Thimphu's most famous barman.

Foodie Highlights of Thimphu

HIDDEN SECRETS AND UNUSUAL FLAVOURS

Thimphu is the only place in Bhutan that has any kind of food scene, so this is the place to break away from the set meals and hotel buffets. Try as many of the city's restaurants as you have time for.

If after days of buffets you are crying out for some fresh, healthy food, head to **Ambient Cafe**. Not only do they roast their own coffee and make their own ice cream but they offer a vegan and gluten-free menu that includes cold-pressed juices, apple cider drinks and build-your-own salads washed in filtered water.

For organic Bhutanese products and packaged snacks, including excellent house-made trekking foods such as granola bars and fruit leathers, **Chuniding Foods** is the place. Fresh Bhutanese dishes are also served for lunch (until 7pm), with *momos* and noodle dishes made from local cassava, banana and buckwheat flours.

The award for best *momos* in town is a hotly contested affair, but many people rate **Tibetan Uncle (Achola's)**, whose delicious beef-filled dumplings are served with soup, fresh tomato *ezay* (salad) and delicious *cha ngamo* (Tibetan milk tea). The unsigned hole-in-the-wall near the cinema off Norzin Lam is ridiculously hard to find; look for the NDG Archery Shop, the 'Seasonal Fashion' sign and the garuda image above the wooden door. Good luck.

For a uniquely Bhutanese beer snack that you won't find anywhere else, order a yeti cocktail (with potent Bhutanese *arra*) at the **Drunken Yeti** bar and try their *ema datse* (cheese and

 PROPER COFFEE NEAR CLOCKTOWER SQUARE

Thijha Cafe
A sunny terrace, warm interior and back balcony, with pizza, sandwiches and Ramyun noodle soup bowls. **$$**

Tower Cafe
A tiny place on Clocktower Sq but everything on the menu is good, including the coffee. **$$**

Ambient Cafe
The best coffee and vibe in town, with excellent, healthy food options. **$$**

chillies) or *no sha* (slow cooked beef) grilled cheese sandwiches, using mozzarella instead of the normal *datse*.

The least expected spot to find a gourmet treat is the **Sonam Tshoey** Swiss watch shop in Changlam Plaza. The owners use real Madagascan vanilla pods for their signature ice cream and also make delicious summer sorbets using passion fruit from Zhemgang and mango from Mongar.

Recharge with a Traditional Bhutanese Medical Treatment

HERBAL TREATMENTS

If you're feeling under the weather and you have an interest in traditional medicine, consider getting a diagnosis and treatments from a Bhutanese traditional doctor. One good place to go is the clinic at the **National Institute of Traditional Medicine**, where a doctor will read your pulse and check your eyes and tongue to tell if your wind, bile and phlegm are in balance and prescribe appropriate herbal medicines or treatments, all free of charge. A total of 23 traditional treatments are on offer, though most foreigners steer clear of the blood-letting and cauterisation.

For a slightly more pampering experience, head to the **33 Soksoom Centre of Wellbeing & Happiness** in the Namseling Boutique Hotel, which also employs graduates of the Faculty of Traditional Medicine but has more of a spa feel. Treatments on offer include *num tshuk* herbal hot oil treatments (for insomnia, tinnitus and migraines), *ching lum* herbal compresses (for backache and poor circulation), *numgi jukpa* oil massage, and *lang lum* herbal steam baths. Book a two-hour general session of relaxing treatments or meet with the doctor for a diagnosis and personalised list of prescribed treatments. The centre has a firm medical basis, unlike most hotel spas.

If you have a particular interest in herbal treatments, visit the museum of the **Faculty of Traditional Medicine**, which has displays on most of the 300 herbs, minerals and animal parts that Bhutanese doctors draw their medicines from. Lasgang root and gentiana are said to do wonders for a sore throat, while *chozen nagsel* helps in curing all diseases caused by evil spirits.

Buying a Gho or Kira

DRESS LIKE A LOCAL

A *gho* or *kira* makes a great, inexpensive souvenir, and locals will be thrilled if you wear one to a festival in Bhutan. Many

BHUTANESE TRADITIONAL MEDICINE

Bhutan's system of traditional medicine, Sowa Rigpa (Science of Healing), is a blending of Tibetan knowledge, Indian Ayurveda and traditional Chinese medicine said to have been handed down by the Medicine Buddha, Sangye Menlha. Based on the concepts of five elements and three humours, with disorders divided into hot and cold conditions, the traditional therapies have been integrated into the national health care system.

For centuries Bhutan was the major exporter of herbs to Tibet, which traditionally refers to Bhutan as Menjong, the 'Land of Medicinal Herbs'. The National Institute of Traditional Medicine still collects medicinal plants from remote corners of the Bhutanese Himalaya, and distributes pills, ointments and medicinal teas to regional health-care units around the country.

WHERE TO STAY IN CENTRAL THIMPHU

Hotel Osel	**Pelyang Boutique**	**Tashi Yoedling**
A great location, a useful cafe-bar and lots of space makes this a popular upper midrange option. **$$**	This modern place has fresh rooms, good service and a lobby cafe near the weekend market. **$$**	Views of the memorial chorten from the rooms and restaurant; executive corner rooms are worth it. **$$**

SOUVENIR SHOPS

Drukpro
One-of-a-kind, limited edition T-shirts and scarves based on original artwork from some of Bhutan's best artists.

DSB Books
Bhutan's best selection of books, with a strong selection on Bhutan and Himalayan titles.

National Institute for Zorig Chusum
Showroom at the national arts school offers a good selection of masks, weavings and traditional boots at fair prices.

Lungta Handicrafts
Good selection of the normal textiles, masks and wooden bowls, with an upper floor of antiques for which staff will arrange customs clearance.

tourist shops sell off-the-rack versions, but specialist robe stores on Norzin Lam offer more choices of styles and colours.

Depending on the fabric, a *gho* can cost from Nu 2300 to over Nu 10,000. To get the best fit, allow a couple of days to have an item tailor-made and expect to pay around Nu 5000. Don't forget you'll also need to invest in a *kera* (narrow woven belt; from Nu 500) and a white *lhagey* (inner liner; Nu 200 to 400). Women can expect to pay Nu 2000 and upwards for a *kira,* and Nu 750 to 1500 for the accompanying *toegu* (jacket) and *wonju* (blouse).

Once you have your *gho* or *kira,* you'll probably need help learning how to wear it. You'll also need some instruction on storing the *gho,* which involves folding the pleats origami-style. Video your guide demonstrating it or you'll never remember how!

Recommended clothing stores include **Sephub Gyeltsen Tsongkhang**, at 30 Norzin Lam, and **Dorji Gyeltshen Tshongkhang**, run by the same family and closer to Clocktower Sq. Both are piled high with ready-made *gho,* as well as silks and woven fabrics from across Bhutan.

Bhutan's Most Unusual Souvenir

POST YOURSELF HOME

The Philatelic Bureau at Thimphu's **main post office** is the place to come for one of Bhutan's most unique gifts. Bring in a favourite digital photo of yourself on a USB stick, and staff will print you a sheet of personalised stamps with your photo on them, superimposed in front of Tiger's Nest. The stamps are fully functional so you can use them to send your postcards home. The process costs Nu 500 for 12 stamps and takes just a couple of minutes.

While you're waiting you can visit the small **museum** dedicated to the history of the Bhutan postal service.

Simply Bhutan

FAMILY FUN

Simply Bhutan is an interactive 'living' museum that gives a quick introduction to various aspects of traditional life in Bhutan. Visitors are greeted with a shot of local *arra* – always a good start to a museum visit – before being encouraged to dress up in traditional clothes, try out archery and hear renditions of the songs sung by Bhutanese women as they build houses out of rammed earth. It's a fun family experience but introverts might find it cringeworthy at times. Closed Tuesdays.

 WHERE TO STAY IN CENTRAL THIMPHU

Hotel Druk
Reassuring option in the main Clocktower Sq, with comfortable rooms, good staff and a fine restaurant. **$$$**

The Willows
Modern and fresh rooms with a pleasant cafe, bar and terrace and a perfect location just off Clocktower Sq. **$$**

Norkhil Boutique Hotel & Spa
An imposing four-star giant with a mix of traditional and modern decor and a fine spa. **$$$**

GREATER THIMPHU

MUSEUMS AND GOVERNMENT BUILDINGS

The area north of central Thimphu is made up of government offices, civil organisations and a scattering of NGOs, mixed in with a few museums that offer some good background on Bhutanese culture. The area further north is dominated by Thimphu's massive dzong and other administrative government offices, such as the striking National Assembly and Supreme Court buildings. The dzong is spectacularly lit up at night.

To the west rise the forested valley sides, offering some fine views of the city and bucolic walks from the BBS Tower at Sangaygang. West Thimphu is largely made up of the suburb of Motithang, a quiet hillside area of hotels, wealthy houses and the occasional royal residence.

Apart from Motithang there aren't many places to stay or eat in these largely suburban areas, so figure on returning to central Thimphu for lunch.

TOP TIP

Combining the sights in Greater Thimphu is the best way to visit them, notably by walking to Wangditse Goemba and Dechen Phodrang and then driving back via Zilukha Nunnery. Remember that the dzong is only open to tourists after 5pm on weekdays (once government offices have closed), but it's open all day on weekends.

TRAVELIB ASIA/ALAMY STOCK PHOTO ©

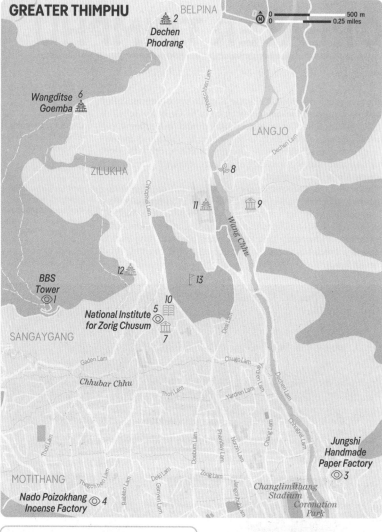

GREATER THIMPHU

BELPINA

2 Dechen Phodrang

0 500 m
0 0.25 miles

Wangditse 6
Goemba

LANGJO

ZILUKHA

8

11 9

BBS Tower
1

12

13

10
National Institute 5
for Zorig Chusum
7

SANGAYGANG

Gaden Lam

Chugo Lam

Chhubar Chhu

Thori Lam

Jungshi Handmade Paper Factory
3

MOTITHANG

Thegchhen Lam

Nado Poizokhang 4
Incense Factory

Changlimithang Stadium

Coronation Park

Wang Chhu

Chhophel Lam

Chubachu Chhen Lam

Dechen Lam

Desi Lam

Yarden Lam

Dechen Lam

Yardren Lam

Chang Lam

Chhogyel Lam

Dechen Lam

Doebum Lam

Phendey Lam

Norzin Lam

Zorig Lam

Rabten Lam

Deki Lam

Gairyen Lam

Jangsa Lam

HIGHLIGHTS
1 BBS Tower
2 Dechen Phodrang
3 Jungshi Handmade
Paper Factory
4 Nado Poizokhang
Incense Factory
5 National Institute for
Zorig Chusum
6 Wangditse Goemba

SIGHTS
7 Folk Heritage Museum

see 10 Lhakhang Sarp
8 Ludrong Memorial
Garden
9 National Assembly
10 National Library
11 Trashi Chho Dzong
12 Zilukha Nunnery

**ACTIVITIES, COURSES
& TOURS**
13 Royal Thimphu Golf
Course

Supreme Court of Bhutan

Hiking from Sangayang to Wangditse

VALLEY VIEWS AND A RENOVATED MONASTERY

For one of the best views over Trashi Chho Dzong and the Thimphu valley get dropped off on the hillside below the **Bhutan Broadcasting Service (BBS) tower** (2685m) at the top end of Sangaygang. This is a popular place for runners, hikers and mountain bikers seeking a quick escape from the city. Photography is best in the afternoon, but be sure not to photograph the telecommunications installation itself.

For a great two-hour hike, follow the prayer-flag-strewn pathway that meanders north along the blue-pine-scented hillside for 2km to the 18th-century **Wangditse Goemba**. The excellent views extend over the yellow-roofed Supreme Court of Bhutan at the bottom of the spur.

Wangditse Goemba has been painstakingly restored by a team of traditional craftspeople from the National Institute for Zorig Chusum. The interior features an impressive two-storey statue of Sakyamuni Buddha, which was salvaged from the original monastery. Have a look to see if there is a game of *khuru* (darts) going on at the nearby ground and then continue steeply downhill to end the hike at **Dechen Phodrang**. Allow a couple of hours for the walk and stops.

DECHEN PHODRANG

At the north end of Thimphu, Dechen Phodrang stands on the site of Thimphu's original 12th-century dzong (p67). Since 1971 it has housed the state *lobdra* (monastic school), providing an eight-year education for more than 270 novice monks.

The attractively proportioned main chapel contains murals dating back to the original 13th-century monastery, and the upper floor features a large figure of Zhabdrung Ngawang Namgyal. The *goenkhang* (protector chapel) here is one of the few open to tourists.

SPRING IMAGES/ALAMY STOCK PHOTO ©

Trail from Sangaygan to Wangditse Goemba 65

Traditional Crafts: Paper & Incense

TWO TRADITIONAL WORKSHOPS

Thimphu has two interesting craft workshops that are open to visitors. The **Jungshi Handmade Paper Factory** on the east bank produces traditional Bhutanese paper *(deshog)* by hand using pulp made from the bark of the daphne bush. You can see the whole production process here, from the initial soaking and boiling of the bark to sorting, crushing, pulping, layering, pressing and drying. Products for sale include lovely decorated paper, plus cards, notebooks, lampshades and calendars.

Further southwest in Motithang, the **Nado Poizokhang Incense Factory** is easily Thimphu's sweetest-smelling excursion, churning out about 10,000 sticks of handmade incense monthly, with each stick hand-rolled between wooden blocks and then stacked in the shade for air drying. You can watch the whole production process (grinding, extruding, fermenting, rolling and drying) at the workshop, or simply shop for the final product at the nearby showroom. Bhutanese generally light incense in their home altars twice a day, both as an offering and to purify the air, an act that has its origins deep in the pre-Buddhist Bön faith.

NETTA AROBAS/SHUTTERSTOCK ©

Trashi Chho Dzong

National Institute for Zorig Chusum

PHOTOGENIC ARTS SCHOOL

The National Institute for Zorig Chusum, commonly known as 'the painting school', operates four- to six-year courses that provide instruction in Bhutan's 13 traditional arts – painting (of both furniture and *thangkas* – religious icons on canvas), woodcarving (masks, statues, bowls), embroidery (hangings, boots, clothes), sculpture (clay statues) and metalsmithing. Students are well used to having visitors watch them while they work and it's fine to take photos.

It's hard not to be impressed by the skill and discipline of the young students, and their work is sold at fair prices in the school showroom. The school is closed at lunchtime and on Sundays and Saturday afternoons.

Trashi Chho Dzong

THIMPHU'S MOST IMPRESSIVE BUILDING

The splendid Trashi Chho Dzong, north of the city on the west bank of the Wang Chhu, dominates the valley, looking out over a cascade of terraced fields. It's Thimphu's grandest building by far, and served as the official seat of the Druk Desi, the head of the secular government that shared power with the religious authorities from the 18th to the 19th centuries. The dzong was the site of the lavish formal coronation of the fifth king in 2008.

When King Jigme Dorji Wangchuck moved his capital to Thimphu in 1962, he began a five-year project to renovate and enlarge the dzong. The royal architect left the *utse* (central tower) untouched, along with the imposing assembly hall, but the rest of the compound was rebuilt in traditional fashion, without nails or architectural plans. The dzong once housed the National Assembly and now houses the secretariat, the throne room, and offices of the king and the ministries of home affairs and finance.

The dzong's whitewashed perimeter walls are guarded by three-storey towers at the four corners, capped by red-and-gold, triple-tiered roofs. The only way to enter the fort is via one of two gateways on the eastern side of the structure. The southern entrance leads to the administrative section (off-limits to visitors), while the northern entrance leads to the monastic quarter, the summer residence of the *dratshang* (central monk body).

Entering the dzong via the northern entrance after a security check, visitors are greeted by depictions of the four guardian kings, while the steps are flanked by images of Drukpa Kunley, Thangtong Gyalpo and Phajo Drukgom Shigpo (the founder of nearby Phajoding Monastery, also known as Togden Pajo). Beyond is the vast, flagstone *dochey* (courtyard) and the *utse*. It's hard not to be humbled by the dramatic proportions of the architecture, and the enclosed silence broken only by the flight of pigeons, the shuffle of feet and the whir of prayer wheels.

The northern part of the compound ends at the towering *utse,* which houses the 3rd-floor funeral chorten of the 69th Je Khenpo, but only Bhutanese are allowed to enter to receive the blessing of betel nut from his nut container.

Nearby in the courtyard is the **Lhakhang Sarp**, a small chapel with handsome mythical beasts supporting its beams. The main **kunrey** (assembly hall) on the northern edge of the

THE GUIDE

THIMPHU

THIMPHU'S ORIGINAL DZONG

The building you see today is not the original Thimphu dzong. The first fortress – the Dho-Ngen Dzong (Blue Stone Dzong) – was erected in 1216 on the hillside where Dechen Phodrang now stands, and it was adopted as the seat of Lama Phajo Drukgom Shigpo, who brought the Drukpa Kagyu lineage to Bhutan. The fort was renamed Trashi Chho Dzong (Fortress of the Glorious Religion) when it passed to Zhabdrung Ngawang Namgyal in 1641.

The Zhabdrung planned to house both monks and civil officials in the dzong, but it was too small, so he built a new dzong lower down in the valley for the civil officials, and this soon become the focus of attention. The upper dzong was destroyed by fire in 1771.

 WHERE TO STAY IN MOTITHANG

The Pema
This four-star boutique hotel has lots of nice touches, including three restaurants and a rooftop bar. **$$$**

Bhutan Peaceful Residency
Modern, fresh and well run, with well-planned details from double glazing to a sunny breakfast terrace. **$$**

Peaceful Resort
The spacious rooms enjoy a peaceful setting here in upper Motithang. **$$**

square enshrines a huge statue of Sakyamuni (the historical Buddha) and the thrones of the current king, past king and Je Khenpo. Look to the ceiling for fine mandala paintings.

Northeast of the dzong is an excellent example of a traditional cantilever bridge, which you can cross to explore the pleasant new **Ludrong Memorial Garden**. To the southeast is the unassuming residence of the current king, while across the river you can see the impressive, step-roofed **National Assembly**.

Royal Thimphu Golf Course

A MEMORABLE 18 HOLES

Ever met anyone who has played golf in Bhutan? No, we didn't think so, but still here's your chance. This delightful nine-hole course sprawls over the hillside above Trashi Chho Dzong. Brigadier General TV Jaganathan got permission from King Jigme Dorji Wangchuck to construct a few holes in the late 1960s, and the course was formally inaugurated in 1971. At around US$60 for nine holes, plus US$40 for club hire, it's not cheap, but how often do you get to tee off in sight of a Bhutanese dzong and have to dodge chorten hazards?

School-age caddies will accompany you for around US$10. You don't need to make an appointment to play, but you may have to wait to tee off on weekends. The new clubhouse canteen has decent food and fine views of the greens.

National Library

SACRED TEXTS AND HISTORICAL DOCUMENTS

The National Library was established in 1967 to preserve ancient Dzongkha and Tibetan texts. For tourists it's of interest mainly for its dzong-like traditional architecture, but the shelves inside are full of important scriptures, some from the famous Tibetan woodblock printing presses of Derge and Narthang, and all made of unbound pages stacked between wooden plates and wrapped in cloth.

Dotted here and there are some fascinating historical photos and on the top floor is a copy of a letter sent from the Druk Desi (secular ruler) to British army officer and surveyor Samuel Turner in 1783. Look also for the oath of allegiance signed at Punakha on the coronation of the first king in 1907, with all the regional leaders' seals attached.

Also on display is a copy of the world's largest published book – a 2m-tall, 68kg coffee-table tome called *Bhutan: A Visual Odyssey Across the Last Himalayan Kingdom*. Its huge illustrated pages are turned one page per month.

WHERE TO STAY IN MOTITHANG

Hotel Damisa	**Thimphu Deluxe**	**Bhutan Suites**
A decent three-star place with a vegetarian restaurant and an outdoor terrace; ask for a balcony room. **$$**	A well-run option at the top end of tourist class, with huge rooms, some with balcony, and a good restaurant. **$$$**	Kitchenette suites by the night, week or month here, with room balconies and a good bakery cafe. **$$**

Zilukha Nunnery

Folk Heritage Museum

BHUTANESE TRADITIONAL LIFE

Set in a small orchard, the restored rammed-earth and timber building of the Folk Heritage Museum is furnished as it would have been about a century ago, providing a glimpse into rural Bhutanese life. Museum details that jump out include the antique noodle press, leopard skin bags and Brokpa yak-hair 'spider' hats (available for sale). There's a short-range archery ground for visitors and the restaurant here serves excellent Bhutanese meals if booked in advance.

Zilukha Nunnery

FRIENDLY MODERN NUNNERY

An alternative descent on foot from Wangditse Goemba (p65) leads you to this small, friendly nunnery of 50 *anim* (nuns) founded in 1976 by the 16th incarnation of Thangtong Gyalpo, the 15th-century builder of chain bridges across Bhutan and Tibet. There's an interesting enclosed chorten in the main courtyard. Alternatively, come here after a visit to Dechen Phodrang.

BHUTANESE WRITING

The Bhutanese script used to write Dzongkha (the 'language of the dzong') is based on the Tibetan script introduced by Tonmi Sambhota during the reign of the 7th-century Tibetan king, Songtsen Gampo. The distinct development of *jo yig,* the cursive Bhutanese script, is credited to a monk by the name of Lotsawa Denma Tsemang.

Woodblock printing has been used for centuries and is still the most common form of printing in the monasteries. Blocks are carved in mirror image, then the printers working in pairs place strips of handmade paper over the inked blocks and a roller passes over the paper. The printed strip is then set aside to dry. The printed books are placed between two boards and wrapped in cloth.

WHERE TO GET A MEAL OUTSIDE CENTRAL THIMPHU

Babesa Village Restaurant
A popular tourist place for tasty set Bhutanese meals in a historic mansion, south of the city. **$$**

Folk Heritage Museum
Some of the best Bhutanese food in town, with set meals best suited to prebooked groups. **$$**

The Pema
Choose from the main classy Zhego Restaurant or bright, cafe-style bistro near reception. **$$**

THE VALLEY RIM

FORESTED TRAILS TO MONASTERIES AND MEDITATION RETREATS

The steep, forested hillsides of the Wang Chhu valley rise up wherever Thimphu starts to peter out. The city's green lungs are its weekend playground, home to a network of hiking and mountain-biking trails that connect viewpoints, temples and meditation retreat centres. The day hike up to Chhokhortse, Pumola and Phajoding is the most popular with visitors, but there are also others, including excellent hikes to Thadrak (Thari) and Dodeydrak, as well as overnight hikes to remoter destinations, such as the sacred mountain lake of Genyen Latsho. The final day and a half of the Druk Path trek (p195) also takes in the valley rim, as does part of the Trans-Bhutan Trail.

For more valley rim hiking ideas, download a PDF copy of Piet van der Poel and Rogier Gruys' booklet *Mild and Mad Day Hikes Around Thimphu* from bhutan-trails.org or contact the Facebook group of the same name.

TOP TIP

Mountain biking is a great way to experience the Thimphu valley. You can hire bikes from Bikeoholic or Wheels for Hills, both in Thimphu, and many agencies can add a day's biking into your itinerary. For longer stays contact the Thimphu Mountain Biking Club about route ideas and weekend rides.

KATERYNA MASHKEVYCH/SHUTTERSTOCK ©

Phajoding Goemba

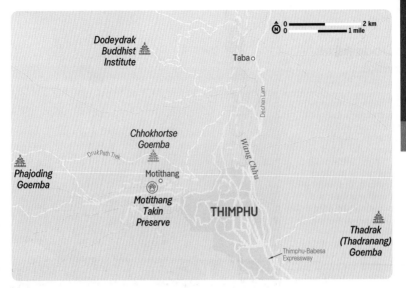

Dodeydrak
Buddhist
Institute

Taba

Chhokhortse
Goemba

Druk Path Trek

Phajoding
Goemba

Motithang

Motithang
Takin
Preserve

THIMPHU

Thadrak
(Thadranang)
Goemba

Thimphu-Babesa
Expressway

Dechen Lam

Wang Chhu

Phajoding Goemba Hike

EXCELLENT FULL DAY HIKE

The tough day hike from Motithang or Sangaygang to **Phajoding Goemba** (3950m) is relentlessly uphill, ascending over 1000m, but very rewarding. The large monastic and retreat complex has several lhakhangs and more than a dozen monastic residences. The hike takes you on the last day of the Druk Path trek in reverse.

Phajo Drukdom Shigpo, a yogi from Tibet, founded the site as far back as the 13th century, but most of the buildings were constructed in 1748 through the efforts of Shakya Rinchen, the ninth Je Khenpo. Don't miss the **Khangza Lhakhang**, with its wonderful ancient statues of the ninth Je Khenpo, and the lower **Jampa Lhakhang**, with its two-storey statue of the Future Buddha.

Most people hike up via **Chhokortse** (2970m), continuing uphill from there through forest for another two or three hours, via a shelter and toilet (3290m). If the ascent didn't knock the curiosity out of you, it's possible to continue to climb another vertical 300m to the cliffside **Thujidrak Goemba**, where Phajo first meditated.

On the way back down you can take the same route back, or descend on a steeper trail to Motithang. Perhaps the best option is to traverse the slopes south from Phajoding for an hour to the temple, pass and chorten of **Pumola** (3640m), where you briefly meet the Trans-Bhutan Trail, before descending 800m to Motithang via a horse pasture and four wooden shelters. You could even take the Trans-Bhutan Trail all the way to the statue of Buddha Dordenma.

CHHOKHORTSE GOEMBA HIKE

From the BBS Tower (2690m; p65) at Sangaygang, a steep trail climbs directly up the ridge, offering stunning views over the valley, framed by ribbons of prayer flags. An hour of hiking gets you to a flat saddle, with a gleaming new chapel and the time-scarred original **Chhokhortse Monastery**, founded in the 14th century and cared for by a long-haired meditator. The ancient-feeling chapel oozes atmosphere and houses an unusual Palace of the Longta (the 'Wind Horse' depicted on most prayer flags).

Dodeydrak Hike

HIKE TO A HERMITAGE

If the hikes to Phajoding or Wangditse Goemba (p65) have whetted your appetite, a two-hour walk up the next valley north will take you to the **Dodeydrak Buddhist Institute**, an atmospheric cluster of chapels and monks' cells founded by the 13th Je Khenpo, Kyabje Yonten Thaye, in 1779. Near the monastery is a 1000-year-old meditation hermitage set into a rocky cleft, where monks meditate for up to 12 years at a time. There are several paths to Dodeydrak – the shortest trail starts near the junction for Samtenling Palace at Jungshina.

View from Phajoding Goemba (p71)

Motithang Takin Preserve

SPOT BHUTAN'S NATIONAL ANIMAL

Off the road leading to the BBS Tower, in Motithang, this preserve for Bhutan's curious national animal was originally established as a zoo, but the fourth king decided this was not in keeping with Bhutan's environmental and religious convictions, and the takin were released into the wild. Unfortunately, the animals were so tame they took to wandering the streets of Thimphu looking for food, so this enclosed area was set aside to keep them safe.

The setting is peaceful and it's worth taking the time to see these unique, slightly oddball mammals, known in Dzongkha as *dong gyem tsey*. The best time to view the takin up close is early morning, when they gather near the fence to feed.

Takin

Thadrak Goemba Hike

HIKE THE EASTERN VALLEY

If you have time for more hiking, a strenuous two-hour uphill walk from the Yangchenphug High School, on the east side of the Thimphu valley, can take you through lovely stands of blue pines to the 17th-century **Thadrak (Thadranang) Goemba** (3270m), said to have been built on a mountain shaped like a *phurba*. The views en route are marvellous and there are several old chapels and monastic cells looking out over the valley.

TOP: KATERYNA MASHKEVYCH/SHUTTERSTOCK © BOTTOM: DE JONGH PHOTOGRAPHY/SHUTTERSTOCK ©

NORTH OF THIMPHU

HILLSIDE MONASTERIES AND TEMPLES

A trip to the forested northern end of the valley to visit Tango and Cheri Goembas makes for an excellent day trip from the capital. As you travel up the east side of the valley you'll get views of Trashi Chho Dzong and the National Assembly, as well as glimpses of Samtenling Palace, the fourth king's residence, and also Dechenchoeling Palace, another royal residence.

Past Pangri Zampa and the photogenic rock painting of Guru Rinpoche, about 12km from Thimphu, the white buildings of Cheri Goemba finally come into view on the sugarloaf-shaped hill at the end of the valley. Shortly afterwards a side road branches right for Tango Goemba; the trailhead for Cheri at Dodina is straight ahead.

North of here lies Jigme Dorji National Park, an important habitat for takins, tigers, snow leopards and Himalayan black bears, and the trailhead for the Laya and Jhomolhari treks.

TOP TIP

There's nowhere to eat near Cheri and Tango Goembas, so ask your guide to arrange a hot packed lunch and bring your water bottle. The only place to stay here is the atmospheric, antique-filled Wangchuk Resort Taba, set in a peaceful pine forest near a small goemba built atop the ruins of a former palace.

KEVIN SCHAFER/GETTY IMAGES ©

Rock painting of Guru Rinpoche (p74)   73

Guru Rock Painting

COLOURFUL SACRED SHRINES

On the west bank of the Wang Chhu near Pangri Zampa, the road passes a huge and very photogenic painted rock painting of Guru Rinpoche and a line of water-powered prayer wheels. Nearby, just before the bridge to the east side of the river at Begana, is a small **Guru Lhakhang**, with some fine murals of protector deities, while on the hillside above is the gleaming white **Jarung Khashor** chorten styled after the great stupa at Bodhnath in Nepal. Just after the bridge, look out for some 'self-arisen' rock images of a fish and mongoose and a collection of chortens.

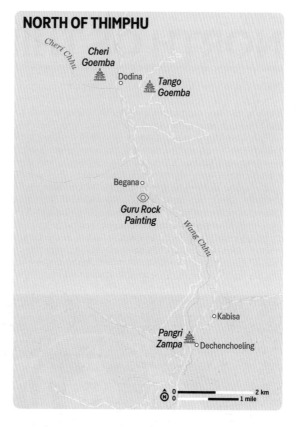

NORTH OF THIMPHU

Cheri Chhu

Cheri Goemba

Dodina

Tango Goemba

Begana

Guru Rock Painting

Wang Chhu

Kabisa

Pangri Zampa

Dechenchoeling

0 —— 2 km
0 —— 1 mile

Pangri Zampa

Pangri Zampa

BEAUTIFUL TRADITIONAL ARCHITECTURE

Founded in the early 16th century, the riverside monastery complex of Pangri Zampa houses Bhutan's most important college for traditional astrology. Zhabdrung Ngawang Namgyal stayed here after he arrived in Bhutan in 1616 because the temple appeared in the vision that directed him from Tibet.

The complex gets its name from the photogenic cantilevered bridge beside the complex. The two huge cypress trees in front of the temple are said to be the biggest in the country; the cypress is Bhutan's national tree. The well-respected head astrologer here was entrusted to divine the auspicious date for the king's coronation in 2008.

The upper floor of the first building on the right has an ancient talking image of the Zhabdrung and you can get a blessing from his 30cm-long walking stick (the rest of the stick has been sliced off over the years for relics and traditional medicine!).

Above Pangri Zampa, the tall **Dechenphu Lhakhang** is home to Gyenyen, the valley's protective deity, and is off-limits to tourists.

Cheri Goemba

BHUTAN'S OLDEST MONASTERY

From Dodina, a handsome covered bridge crosses to a group of Bhutanese-style chortens and carved rock paintings at the confluence of two streams, marking the start of the steep 45-minute climb through forest to Cheri (Chagri) Goemba. Zhabdrung Ngawang Namgyal established the monastery in 1620 as the home for Bhutan's first monk body. A richly decorated silver chorten inside the upper goemba enshrines the ashes of the Zhabdrung's father, whose body was smuggled here from Tibet.

Cheri is currently being restored, so access to chapels is somewhat restricted. Because of the sanctity of the site, labourers have to do manual work in their formal *ghos*. This is an important meditation centre and cells are scattered up the slopes, so be sure not to disturb anyone.

From the main goemba, it's a steep climb (pilgrims aim to do it without pausing) to the **Demon-Subdued Monastery**, built around the cave where the Zhabdrung overcame local demons while meditating here for three years. Look for the unusually wrathful statue of the Zhabrung and ask to see his corner bathroom; possibly the only sacred toilet in Bhutan. Tame brown *goral* (mountain goats) often graze the grounds here.

CHOKI TRADITIONAL ART SCHOOL

This impressive charitable school near Kabisa in the upper Thimphu valley trains around 165 disadvantaged children, aged 14 to 20, in the traditional Bhutanese arts of painting, sculpture, carving, tailoring and embroidery, preparing them for a career while also helping to keep Bhutan's traditional arts alive. Visitors are welcome to tour the school and visit the classrooms, and there is a showroom on-site. Photography is allowed.

The **Choki Handicrafts shop** in Thimphu (near the Folk Heritage Museum) also sells masks, *thangka* and clothes from the school.

S. JAKKARIN/SHUTTERSTOCK ©

Cheri Goemba

WORLDWIDEPHOTOWEB/GETTY IMAGES ©

Tango Goemba

Tango Goemba

HIKE TO A HISTORIC MONASTERY

Tango Monastery was originally founded in the 12th century by Phajo Drukgom Shigpo (the founder of Changangkha Lhakhang and Phajoding), but it was the fourth Druk Desi (secular leader) Tenzin Rabgye (1638–96) who constructed the buildings that you see today. Apart from being the nephew of the Zhabdrung, Rabgye was also the founder of Taktshang Goemba. Tango is today headed by the Gyalse Rinpoche, recognised as the seventh reincarnation of Tenzin Rabgye.

Tango is an important and picturesque monastery and pilgrimage site that has deep connections to the religious history of Bhutan. The main three-storey, 12-sided monastery building is currently under a multiyear reconstruction, so there's not much to see beyond a museum relic room, but it's still an excellent hourlong hike here, taking you past meditation caves, sacred sites and Buddhist quotes to inspire you on the spiritual path.

Notable for its striking curved frontage, Tango is part of the important Dorden Tashi Thang Buddhist University, whose main campus is down by the road junction. Almost all of Bhutan's Je Khenpos (head abbots) completed their religious studies here.

As you climb to the monastery take the left branch to first visit the meditation cave of the Zhabdrung (Tandin Ney) below a rock outcrop. Tango gets its name ('horse head') from the shape of this rocky protrusion and from its associations with the horse-necked protector Tamdrin (Tandin, or Hayagriva). A small chapel here enshrines a crystal that was carried from Tibet and is used in visualisation meditations. The trail also passes a memorial stupa containing the bones and ashes of Tenzin Rabgye.

In 1616 Zhabdrung Ngawang Namgyal visited Tango, carving a famous sandalwood statue of Chenresig, which he installed here. Because of its connections to the Zhabdrung, Tango is a particularly popular place to visit during the memorial of his death in April or May, known as the Zhabdrung Kuchoe.

SOUTH OF THIMPHU

HISTORIC BUILDINGS AND SUBURBAN SPRAWL

There are some interesting things to see south of the capital, including the huge Buddha Dordenma statue and the first dzong built by Zhabdrung Ngawang Namgyal at Simtokha, perched above the road that branches east towards Wangdue Phodrang. Both sights are easily visited as part of a drive between Thimphu and either Paro or Punakha.

Thimphu's southern urban sprawl finally peters out around the suburb of Babesa, where, squeezed between the car showrooms and hardware shops, are a couple of lovely 150-year-old buildings that have been converted into a restaurant and hotel. A couple of five-star resorts here are useful if you want to see the sights of Thimphu but prefer to stay in rural quiet.

Also here is a section of the Trans-Bhutan Trail, dropping down the ridge from Pumola to the Buddha Dordenma, crossing the river near Babesa at Depsi.

TOP TIP

As you leave Thimphu for Paro, the Gagyel Lhendrup Weaving Center in Babesa is worth a stop for its fine weavings, *gho*, belts, women's jackets, scarves, and sashes for women. Five women weave on-site if you want to see how it's done. The owner is a famous weaver and royal dress designer.

IPEK MOREL/SHUTTERSTOCK ©

Buddha Dordenma

GIGANTIC BUDDHA STATUE

One interesting way to reach the Buddha is the hourlong walk through chir pine forest from the Nado Poizokhang Incense Factory (p66) above Changangkha. Hiking in this direction is slightly more strenuous but feels more like a pilgrimage. En route take care passing a cable that transports huge tree trunks down the hillside to a sawmill below. The views of the Thimphu valley are excellent.

The path also makes for a good mountain-biking route, though it's an easier ride heading south to north; in this case take the right (lower) branch at a junction just after the Kuensel Phodrang Park viewpoint.

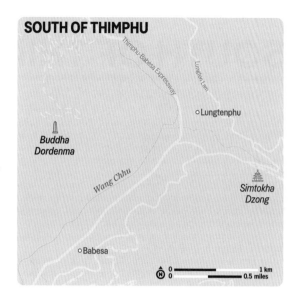

SOUTH OF THIMPHU

Thimphu-Babesa Expressway

Lungten Lam

Lungtenphu

Buddha Dordenma

Wang Chhu

Simtokha Dzong

Babesa

0   1 km
0   0.5 miles

Hiking To/From Buddha Point

THIMPHU VALLEY VIEWS

The huge 51m-tall bronze and steel statue of **Buddha Dordenma** is visible from throughout the Thimphu valley. The massive three-storey base houses a large chapel full of thousands of donated Buddha statuettes, while the body itself is filled with shrines. The chapel roof has some particularly fine mandalas. The Buddha looks amazing when illuminated at night. The area is called Changri Kuensel Phodrang after the former palace of the 13th Druk Desi that once stood here.

The statue was made in China, cut into pieces and then shipped and trucked in from Phuentsholing – we would've loved to have seen the faces of the local farmers as the super-sized features of the Buddha drove by!

The paved road to the site, also known as 'Buddha Point', is a popular biking route, with a further 3.5km mountain-bike route descending from here to Depsi, near Babesa.

Buddha Dordenma

IPEK MOREL/SHUTTERSTOCK ©

Simtokha Dzong

MORE SOUTH OF THIMPHU

Simtokha Dzong

THE ZHABDRUNG'S FIRST DZONG

About 5km south of Thimphu on the old road to Paro, the handsomely proportioned Simtokha Dzong was built to mark the spot where a demon vanished into a rocky outcrop, hence the name Simtokha, from *sinmo* (demoness) and *do* (stone). The site was also a vitally strategic location from which to protect the Thimphu valley and the passage east to the Dochu La and eastern Bhutan. Although expanded many times, it is considered the oldest dzong to have survived as a complete structure.

Officially known as Sangak Zabdhon Phodrang (Palace of the Profound Meaning of Secret Mantras), the squat, whitewashed dzong looks more fortress-like than most, and the only gate is on the south side (though the original gate was on the west wall). The fine murals inside have been restored by experts from Japan.

The central lhakhang in the 12-sided *utse* is of Sakyamuni Buddha, flanked by the eight bodhisattvas and featuring an ancient Indian statue of the Zhabdrung. The dark murals here are some of the oldest and most beautiful in Bhutan.

In the western chapel are statues of Chenresig, green Taras, and an early painting of Zhabdrung Ngawang Namgyal. Check out the tigers' tails and guns hanging from the pillars outside the eastern *goenkhang*, a protector chapel dedicated to the guardians of Bhutan: Yeshe Goenpo (Mahakala) and Pelden Lhamo.

SIMTOKHA HISTORY

Built in 1629 by Zhabdrung Ngawang Namgyal, Simtokha is often called the first dzong built in Bhutan. In fact, there were dzongs in Bhutan as early as 1153, but this was the first dzong built by the Zhabdrung (inspired by a Buddhist institute in Ralung, Tibet) and was the first structure intended to incorporate both monastic and administrative facilities. The main building burned down during a Tibetan attack in 1630 but was restored in the 1670s; descriptions of the original dzong were provided by two Portuguese Jesuit priests who visited in 1629 on their way to Tibet.

 WHERE TO STAY SOUTH OF THIMPHU

Six Senses Thimphu
Sweeping valley views from the suites, meditation room and infinity pond, high above Simtokha. **$$$**

Terma Linca Resort
Impressive riverside stone buildings of huge rooms with a spa and a designated Bhutanese restaurant. **$$$**

Heritage Home Babesa
Two comfortable rooms in a traditional 150-year-old home, with a hot-stone bath, good for a private lunch. **$$**

KEONGDAGREAT/GETTY IMAGES ©

Above: Taktshang Goemba (p96). Right: Carved dragon head, Punakha Dzong (p96)

THE MAIN AREAS

PARO	**HAA VALLEY**	**DOCHU LA**
Temples, hikes and the Tiger's Nest. **p86**	Under-the-radar charm. **p107**	Hikes and mountain views from the pass. **p113**

WESTERN BHUTAN

THE PERFECT INTRODUCTION TO BHUTAN

The west is home to the kingdom's only international airport, its most popular festivals and its most spectacular dzongs (fort-monasteries).

The west is your perfect introduction to otherworldly Bhutan. Straight out of Paro airport, you'll see prayer flags fluttering from rooftops, men and women walking in traditional dress, chortens and stupas marking river and road junctions, and fortress-like monasteries commanding hilltops.

Beyond Paro is Punakha, home to a sublimely beautiful dzong, as well as the nearby newly reconstructed dzong of Wangdue Phodrang. Another hop to the east is the Phobjikha valley and Gangte Goemba, a great place to do some hiking and black-necked crane spotting (November to February).

Beyond the west's big sights, there are lots of little-visited but captivating religious sites – cliff-face temples like Juneydrak in Haa or Dzongkharpo on the road to the Cheli La, as well as active pilgrimage sites like Chumphu Ney and Drak Kharpo, which are peppered with magical rock markings and miraculous caves. Western Bhutan also has some of the most accessible sections of the Trans-Bhutan Trail, offering a taster of the long-distance path in just an hour or two of hiking.

Throw in the country's most popular trekking destination at spectacular Jhomolhari, as well as the country's best roads (and so minimal driving times), and western Bhutan's popularity is obvious. Whether it's the beginning of your trip or the only part of Bhutan that you will see, the west is a spectacular introduction to a magical country.

PUNAKHA
Bhutan's most beautiful dzong. p117

PHOBJIKHA
Black-necked cranes and stirring landscapes. p128

PHUENTSHOLING
Overland gateway to Bhutan. p133

Find Your Way

Western Bhutan is very compact, with short distances and the best roads in the country. You can drive across the entire region in a day. Tourists will have their own transportation prearranged as part of their obligatory tour.

Dochu La, p113
Himalayan views and a photogenic collection of chortens make this pass a natural place to break the drive between Thimphu and Punakha, and it's the trailhead for several excellent hikes.

Paro, p86
The beginning and end of almost everyone's Bhutan trip, featuring an impressive dzong, beautiful temples, the country's best museum and its most popular festival.

Haa Valley, p107
This little-visited area offers great hiking, cliff-side temples, the beginning of the Trans-Bhutan Trail and the sense that you have the entire valley to yourself.

Phuentsholing, p133
Few make it to this subtropical border town, but it's an interesting overland option for entering or exiting Bhutan from India, and the drive from the plains up into the mountains is dramatic.

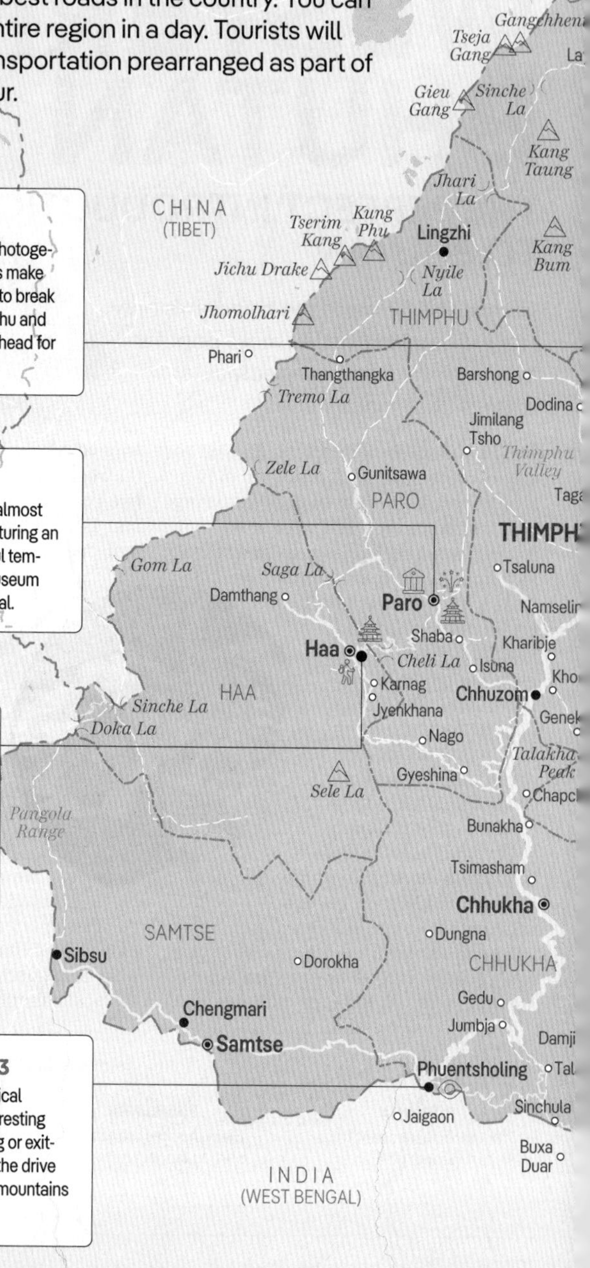

Gangchhen
Tseja
Gang
La

Gieu
Gang
Sinche
La

Kang
Taung

Jhari
La

CHINA
(TIBET)

Tserim
Kang
Kung
Phu
Lingzhi

Jichu Drake

Nyile
La

Kang
Bum

Jhomolhari

THIMPHU

Phari

Thangthangka

Barshong

Tremo La

Dodina

Jimilang
Tsho

Zele La

Gunitsawa

Thimphu
Valley

PARO

Taga

THIMPH

Tsaluna

Gom La
Saga La

Damthang

Paro

Namselir

Shaba

Kharibje

Haa

Cheli La
Isuna

Kho

Karnag

Chhuzom

HAA

Jyenkhana

Genek

Sinche La

Nago

Doka La

Talakha
Peak

Sele La
Gyeshina

Chapc

Pangola
Range

Bunakha

Tsimasham

Chhukha

SAMTSE

Dungna

Sibsu

Dorokha

CHHUKHA

Gedu

Chengmari

Jumbja

Damji

Samtse

Phuentsholing
Tal

Jaigaon

Sinchula

Buxa
Duar

INDIA
(WEST BENGAL)

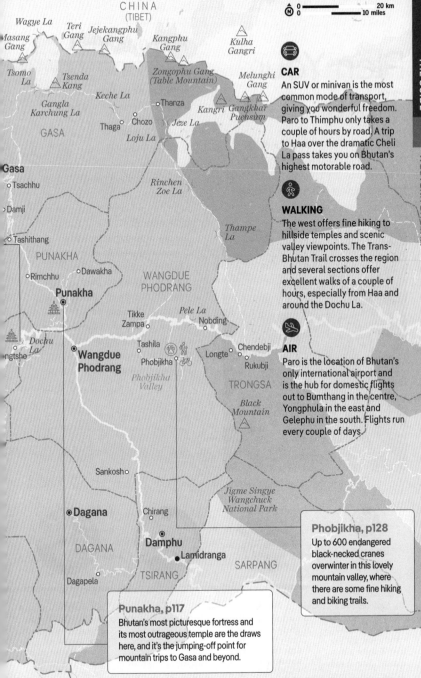

CHINA
(TIBET)

0   20 km
0   10 miles

CAR

An SUV or minivan is the most common mode of transport, giving you wonderful freedom. Paro to Thimphu only takes a couple of hours by road. A trip to Haa over the dramatic Cheli La pass takes you on Bhutan's highest motorable road.

WALKING

The west offers fine hiking to hillside temples and scenic valley viewpoints. The Trans-Bhutan Trail crosses the region and several sections offer excellent walks of a couple of hours, especially from Haa and around the Dochu La.

AIR

Paro is the location of Bhutan's only international airport and is the hub for domestic flights out to Bumthang in the centre, Yongphula in the east and Gelephu in the south. Flights run every couple of days.

Phobjikha, p128
Up to 600 endangered black-necked cranes overwinter in this lovely mountain valley, where there are some fine hiking and biking trails.

Punakha, p117
Bhutan's most picturesque fortress and its most outrageous temple are the draws here, and it's the jumping-off point for mountain trips to Gasa and beyond.

INDIA
(ASSAM)

83

Plan Your Time

Don't miss the popular sights around the Paro and Punakha valleys, but try to also fit in some lesser-visited religious sites, as well as a couple of hikes.

JESSE33/SHUTTERSTOCK ©

Path to Taktshang Goemba (p96)

A Flying Visit

● The one can't-miss activity for every traveller to Bhutan is the two-hour hike up to the gravity-defying cliff-face temples of **Taktshang** (p96) – the Tiger's Nest. The views just before you arrive at the entrance are iconic and an irresistibly photogenic spot for a selfie.

● Combine this with a couple of hours watching spectacularly colourful masked dancing at a festival, preferably the **Paro tsechu** (p88) in April, and you have a perfect two-for-one introduction to Bhutan, for minimum cost. Festival dates change every year in the Gregorian calendar, so be sure to confirm the correct dates when booking your trip.

Seasonal Highlights

Spring (March and April) and autumn (October and November) have the best weather, festivals and trekking in the west, with the summer months (June to early September) bringing monsoon rains.

MARCH
Punakha has two major back-to-back festivals in early March, and the **Gasa tsechu** (dance festival; p126) is also worth catching.

APRIL
The **Paro tsechu** (p88) is a major draw, as is trekking, with spring rhododendron blooms decorating the hillsides.

JULY
The monsoon brings rains but also lush alpine blooms, including blue poppies, plus it's the start of mushroom season.

ANANDOART/SHUTTERSTOCK ©, ARUNLUGOON/SHUTTERSTOCK ©, R R/SHUTTERSTOCK ©

Two Valleys in Four Days

● After arriving at Paro, visit impressive **Paro Dzong** (p87) and then the **National Museum** (p88), which is housed in the nearby *ta dzong* (watchtower) and serves as the perfect introduction to Bhutanese culture.

● On day two drive to Punakha, with a stop at the pilgrimage site of **Drak Kharpo** (p103). After a visit to the sublimely beautiful **Punakha Dzong** (p118) and the temple of the Divine Madman at **Chimi Lhakhang** (p125), head back over the **Dochu La pass** (p114) to Paro.

● The next day visit the Tiger's Nest at **Taktshang** (p96) and then ancient **Kyichu Lhakhang** (p94), one of Bhutan's most charming temples.

A Week to Explore

● With a week up your sleeve you can visit the highlights of Paro and Thimphu and then add a trip over the Dochu La pass to Punakha. You might also have time to visit the low-key but charming **Haa Valley** (p107); if not, at least make the drive up to the **Cheli La** (p108), Bhutan's highest motorable road, stopping to visit the magical cliff-face temples of **Dzongdrakha** (p101) en route.

● Hikers can throw in a section of the **Trans-Bhutan Trail** (p115), most enjoyably from Dochu La west downhill through rhododendron forest, to finish with a Bhutanese amber ale at the **Ser Bhum Brewery** (p114).

SEPTEMBER

Festival season kicks in, with the popular Thimphu tsechu drawing crowds and the Haa (p109) and Wangdue (p127) tsechus two days earlier.

OCTOBER

An ideal month to visit, with clear mountain views, and remote mountain festivals at Jhomolhari and **Laya** (p126).

NOVEMBER

A festival at Gangte celebrates the arrival of **black-necked cranes** (p129) to the Phobjikha valley, with the cranes staying until February.

DECEMBER

Punakha's mild climate guarantees pleasant winter temperatures, and you can catch the **Dochu La Wangyel Festival** (p114).

PARO

Paro ● ✪ THIMPHU

The charming town of Paro lies on the banks of the Paro (or Pa) Chhu, just a short distance northwest of the imposing Paro Dzong. The main street is lined with colourfully painted wooden shopfronts, cafes and handicraft shops, and despite the recent appearance of a few multistorey concrete buildings, Paro remains one of the best Bhutanese towns to explore on foot. It's well worth an hour or two's stroll at the end of a day of sightseeing.

Surrounding the town are a host of interesting temples, the only international airport, one of Bhutan's most impressive dzongs, its best museum, some lovely hiking trails and the densest collection of hotels and restaurants outside of Thimphu. It's also a natural base for exploring the rest of the surrounding Paro valley. No wonder, then, that charming Paro sees more international visitors than anywhere else in the country.

TOP TIP

It's tempting to rush straight out of Paro and visit Taktshang (the Tiger's Nest), but it's better to leave it until the end of your trip. You'll be better rested from your flight and more acclimatised to the altitude. Plus it's always good to end on a high.

GÜNTER FISCHER/EDUCATION IMAGES/UNIVERSAL IMAGES GROUP VIA GETTY IMAGES ©

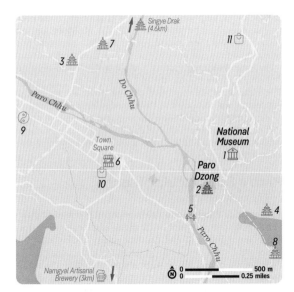

HIGHLIGHTS
1 National Museum
2 Paro Dzong

SIGHTS
3 Dumtse Lhakhang
4 Gönsaka Lhakhang
5 Nyamai Zam
6 Paro Weekend Market
7 Pena Lhakhang
8 Zuri Dzong

ACTIVITIES, COURSES & TOURS
9 Tshetob Yingyum Spa

SHOPPING
10 Lama Tshering Dorji General Shop
11 Tashi Gongphel Bhutanese Paper

The Imposing Architecture of Paro Dzong

PARO'S SEAT OF POWER

Paro Dzong ranks as a high point of Bhutanese architecture. The massive buttressed walls that tower over the town are visible throughout the valley, especially when floodlit at night. It was formerly the meeting hall for the National Assembly and now, like most dzongs, houses both the monastic body and district government offices. Most of the chapels are closed to tourists but it's worth a visit for its stunning architecture and views.

The dzong is built on a steep hillside, and the front courtyard of the administrative section is 6m higher than the courtyard of the monastic portion. The *utse* (central tower) inside the *dochey* (courtyard) is five storeys tall and was built in the time of the first *penlop* (governor) of Paro in 1649.

A stairway leads down to the monastic quarter, which houses about 200 monks. The **kunrey** (assembly hall), which functions as the monks' classroom, is on the southern side (to the left) and centred around an image of Buddha aged 16. Look to the left of the exterior vestibule for the mural of the cosmic

NYAMAI ZAM

Below the dzong, a traditional wooden covered bridge called Nyamai Zam spans the Paro Chhu; it's easily visited via downhill paths. This is a reconstruction of the original bridge, which was washed away in a flood in 1969. Earlier bridges were removed in times of war to protect the dzong.

You can get especially picturesque photos of Paro Dzong from the west bank of the Paro Chhu here, just downstream from the bridge. Nearby is a handsome set of six chortens (stone monuments), as well as the **Ugyen Pelri Palace**, though as a royal residence this is off limits.

 WHERE TO GET A COFFEE IN PARO

Mountain Café	**Brioche Café**	**Book Café**
Spacious seating overlooking the main square, with a full food menu, and they roast their own beans. **$$**	Fantastic pastries, cakes and house-made ice cream, run by a former pastry chef from Amankora. **$$**	Mellow cafe next to Chhencho Handicrafts, also serving homemade *bathup* stew and *kulay* (buckwheat pancakes). **$**

HISTORY OF PARO DZONG

Paro Dzong's formal name, Rinchen Pung Dzong (usually shortened to Rinpung Dzong), means 'Fortress on a Heap of Jewels', referring to the fact that Zhabdrung Ngawang Namgyal ordered the construction of the dzong in 1644 on the foundation of an earlier dzong and an even earlier monastery, said to have been built by Himalayan magician-saint Guru Rinpoche. The dzong survived an 1897 earthquake but was severely damaged by fire in 1907.

The fort was used on numerous occasions to defend the Paro valley from invasions by Tibet. The British political officer John Claude White reported that in 1905 there were old catapults for throwing great stones stored in the rafters of the dzong's veranda.

'mystic spiral', a uniquely Bhutanese variation on the geometric mandala. Another mural here depicts Mt Meru, the legendary centre of the universe, surrounded by seven mountain ranges and four continents.

The large **dukhang** (prayer hall) opposite has lovely exterior murals depicting the life of Tibet's poet-saint Milarepa. The views from the courtyard's far windows are superb. An interesting side note for film buffs: scenes from Bernardo Bertolucci's 1993 film *Little Buddha* were filmed here.

The dzong courtyard is open daily. Foreign visitors should wear long sleeves and long trousers and remove their hats when entering.

Paro's Spectacular Tsechu

A MASKED DANCE FESTIVAL

The four-day **Paro tsechu** in March/April is one of Bhutan's most impressive and colourful festivals and locals travel from across the region to attend. On the first day masked religious dances known as *cham* take place in the lower courtyard of Paro Dzong, which fills to bursting point, before the action moves to the open-air festival ground northeast of the dzong.

The highlight of the festival comes just before dawn on the final day, when a *thondrol* – a huge embroidered image of Guru Rinpoche and his eight manifestations, measuring more than 18 sq metres – is unfurled and the crowd files in front of it to receive blessings and merit. The *thondrol* (the word means 'liberation gained from the sight of it') was commissioned in the 18th century by the eighth *desi* (secular ruler of Bhutan), Chhogyel Sherab Wangchuck. By 9am the *thondrol* is rolled up again and a final day of exuberant *cham* dances finishes off the festival.

The tsechu is probably the most popular festival of the Bhutanese year, so book hotels and flights well in advance.

History & Divinity at the Museum

BHUTAN'S BEST MUSEUM

Perched above Paro Dzong is its *ta dzong* (watchtower), built in 1649 to protect the dzong and renovated in 1968 to house the **National Museum**. The unusual round building is said to be in the shape of a conch shell, boasting immense 2.5m-thick walls, with an underground tunnel thought to lead to a water supply below.

The 4th-floor entrance kicks off with a description of early history that perfectly illustrates how myth and fact are impossible to separate in Bhutan. Information on Stone Age tools

 WHERE TO EAT IN PARO

My Kind of Place	Hotpot Restaurant by Tenzinling	Authentic Pizza
Bhutanese *hoentey* (buckwheat dumplings) and Southeast Asian *laksa* noodles in a serene space. **$$**	Stylish decor and top-end, spicy Chinese hotpot cooked at the table, with a hip bar too. **$$$**	Decent pizza, with delivery to your hotel room if you are tiring of bland buffets. **$$**

Paro Dzong (p87)

sits next to images of 'self-arisen' magical stone mantras. A water clock measures astrological time, which runs 2.5 times slower than actual time; six breaths equals one *chusay,* and 60 *chusay* make one astrological hour. Even time runs differently in Bhutan.

The *thangka* (religious painting) gallery has displays on the four schools of Tibetan Buddhism (Sakya, Nyingma, Gelug and Drukpa). Next is the Namse Phodrang with its collection of bronze statues, notably of the god of wealth Zambala (Kubera), and it's then down to a collection of relics discovered by Bhutan's treasure finders, featuring links from Thangtong Gyalpo's original iron bridge at Tamchog.

More exhibits (festival masks, royal photos and natural history) are on display in an adjacent annex, where you'll discover that living a slothful life greatly increases your chances of seeing a yeti during the transition between death and rebirth. The display on the zombie-like cordyceps fungus is particularly interesting.

PARO'S MUSEUM OF CURIOSITIES

The National Museum is packed with, shall we say, unconventional treasures. The 3rd floor sets the tone with a baking pan crafted by the 15th-century saint Pema Lingpa and a tooth belonging to the pet dog of the Zhabdrung, the 17th-century founder of Bhutan.

Go down two more floors and you'll find the museum's most revered wonders, including a stone egg laid by a mule, a horse horn, a *dorje* (ritual 'thunderbolt') used by Guru Rinpoche, an arrowhead belonging to the army chief of legendary Tibetan warrior Gesar of Ling and even a *wangdril* – a gall-stone-like growth found in the bodies of adept meditators and used as a traditional medicine. After all this surreality, the other displays of tea pots and cane boxes seem a bit tame.

Mountain Cafe
The main street branch of this cafe is particularly popular with Indian tourists for its all-vegetarian food. $$

Momo Corner
Join the locals in the no-frills joint serving up great *momos* and noodle stews. $

Tshongdu Boutique Hotel
Book ahead for a set meal in this bright, modern hotel in the south of town. $$

LAMA TSHERING DORJI GENERAL SHOP

This monk's supply shop in southwest Paro is one of several in town aimed squarely at locals and monks rather than tourists, and it's a fascinating browse. Items for sale include amulets, divination dice and cubes of saffron and camphor used to flavour holy water, plus incense, statuary and butter lamps – everything, in fact, for your own personal altar. There are also some nonreligious items such as *khuru* darts and bamboo arrows.

If you are interested in buying some prayer flags to hang at the Cheli La or another pass, the helpful owner can consult astrological charts and advise on the best types, most auspicious colour and best time to hang them for your birth year.

STEVE ALLEN/SHUTTERSTOCK ©

Market, Paro

Hike to Zuri Dzong

AERIAL VIEWS OF PARO DZONG

A great follow-on to the National Museum is an hourlong hike along the forested hillside high above Paro to Zuri Dzong and then down to the main gate of the Uma Paro hotel, where your vehicle can pick you up. The views over Paro Dzong along this route are unmatched and you'll almost certainly have the trail to yourself.

After just five minutes you'll pass **Gönsaka Lhakhang**, a charming temple that predates Paro Dzong. Ask to visit the meditation cave of Pha Drun Drung, the founder of Paro Dzong.

Zuri Dzong itself was built in 1352 as a fort and the five-storey main building is still well protected by sturdy double walls and a bridge. There are some particularly fine murals in the upper chapels, one of which is dedicated to the protector Zaa (Rahulla). Finding the trail after the dzong can be tricky but it eventually passes a small cave.

On reaching the fence of the Uma Paro hotel, non-guests will have to walk 15 minutes around the perimeter fence to the front gate.

 BEST BARS IN PARO

Outcast Bar
Great views, stylish decor and upstairs meals or a downstairs lounge, with live music on weekends.

Park 76
Paro town's only real bar, with a dark, pub-like atmosphere, beers on tap and comfort food.

Namgyal Artisanal Brewery
House-brewed craft beers, a full food menu and plenty of space, including a sunny terrace.

The Tibetan-Style Murals of Dumtse & Pena Lhakhang

OFFBEAT ANCIENT TEMPLES WITH EXCEPTIONAL MURALS

Just north of Paro town, by the road leading to the National Museum, is the unusual chorten-shaped **Dumtse Lhakhang**, which was built in the early 15th century by the iron-bridge builder Thangtong Gyalpo to subdue a leprosy-spreading demoness. Look for a mural of Thangtong himself on the inner wall by the entrance. As you climb clockwise, spiralling up through the timeless three-storeyed mandala-shaped temple core, you'll pass some of the finest murals in Bhutan. Bring a good torch.

The middle floor is devoted to wrathful protectors and the animal-headed deities that the deceased face on their journey between death and rebirth. The top floor is devoted to the 84 Indian *mahasiddha* (yogic masters) and various tantric deities. Devotees continually circumambulate the outside of the buildings, using white stones to count off sets of 108 circuits. For Nu 50 you can light a butter lamp in the attached hall.

Nearby **Pena Lhakhang** (also called Jangsa Pelnang) is almost completely ignored by visitors to Paro, but it is one of the oldest temples in Bhutan, said to have been founded by Tibetan King Songtsen Gampo in the 7th century. The lovely main inner sanctum has an ancient feel, dominated by a statue of Jowo Nampar Namse that apparently has the power to fulfil wishes. The red-faced protector Pehar lurks in the corner, while to the left is the stone footprint of a former Zhabdrung. The temple is easily missed, just past Dumtse Lhakhang, on the east side of the road.

TSHETOB YINGYUM SPA

If you need a break from a hectic tour schedule, book a massage at this locally owned and professionally run spa in the north of Paro town. Owner Tshewang was a masseuse at the Amankora resort for nine years, so she knows what she is doing. Book a time in advance and choose from a one- or 1½-hour Thai or Bhutanese full body, head and shoulder, foot or signature hot-stone massage, all done in relaxing treatment rooms and excellent value at around Nu 2000 per hour (Nu 3000 for hot-stone massage). It's perfect if you've been trekking or hiking up to the Tiger's Nest.

Paro's Intriguing Weekend Market

TRADITIONAL BHUTANESE FOODS

Paro's weekend market isn't very large but is nevertheless a good introduction to some of Bhutan's unique rural products, from organic Tsirang honey to the dried cow skin known as *khoo* that is boiled up as an ingredient in stews. The market is busiest on Sunday mornings but the vegetable stalls remain open throughout the week.

As you wander the stalls, look for strings of *chugo* (dried yak cheese), either white (boiled in milk and dried in the sun) or brown (smoked). The fruit that looks like an orange egg is actually fresh husky betel nut, or *doma,* imported from India. The jars of pink

THANGTONG GYALPO

Thangtong Gyalpo was a 15th-century bridge-builder, yogi and treasure finder who built 108 iron link bridges across Tibet and Bhutan, including at **Tamchog Lhakhang** (p104) on the road from Paro to Thimphu.

 WHERE TO STAY OUTSIDE BUT NEAR PARO TOWN

Dewachen Resort
Hillside private balcony views of the surrounding rice terraces make this a good choice. **$$**

Gawaling Hotel
A solid riverside hotel with private balconies and helpful staff in the Dop Shari valley. **$$**

Hotel Olathang
Lovely rooms and romantic cottages in pine-scented grounds on a hillside above town. **$$**

TASHI GONGPHEL BHUTANESE PAPER

This small workshop en route to Paro Dzong is worth a visit to see how traditional paper is made from local daphne and edgeworthia bushes. You'll see the steps of soaking, boiling, sorting, pounding and laying out the paper on a bamboo screen and then compressing and drying the sheets, a process that takes three days. You can even make your own scrap of paper here in just five minutes, which is great fun for kids. This showroom has excellent-value notebooks, cards and flower wrapping paper.

If you are headed to Singye Drak you can visit the original factory in the Dop Shari just below the lhakhang car park; turn left at the chorten.

paste contain lime, which is ingested with the betel nut. There is also plenty of powdered incense and patties of *datse,* the cheese used in almost every Bhutanese dish.

The market is currently housed in the **Kaja Throm** market area (which also has a Thai-inspired fast-food dining area), while the main market building to the north is being rebuilt.

The Pilgrimage Site of Singye Drak

A LITTLE-VISITED CLIFF-SIDE TEMPLE

Hidden down the Dop Shari valley, 2km off the road to Paro Dzong, lies the cliff-side temple of Singye Drak, sometimes optimistically called the 'second Tiger's Nest'. The magician-saint Guru Rinpoche meditated here while subduing a demon that had been troubling nearby Jibar village.

A 20-minute uphill walk from the parking area brings you to the main lhakhang, featuring a statue of the guru, as well as local protector Zabu Tsen riding a yak. The cave shrine, or *drubkhang,* has images of blue lion-faced *dakini* (female celestial being) Singye Dongma, who is considered a form of Guru Rinpoche. The cliffs hide lots of self-arisen rock footprints, serpent images and a flat stone said to be shaped like a *dakini*'s tongue. Just above the site is an impossibly narrow 'sin test' rock that only few can squeeze through to prove their lack of karmic baggage. It's a hike into the fantastical.

Sampling Paro's Craft Beer Scene

SIP ON A BHUTANESE PALE ALE

Beer drinkers should make a beeline to the **Namgyal Artisanal Brewery**, Bhutan's biggest microbrewery. The founder caught the beer bug while studying in Switzerland and set up the operation in 2017, using Indian technology and American Cascade hops. The most popular beer is the Red Rice lager, made with local Paro valley red rice, but they also make a wheat beer, a dark ale and a pale ale (both only available on tap), and an oddly refreshing pineapple *gose* (sour beer) made with pink salt and local yogurt. Taste a sampler of all the beers for Nu 180 and add on a brewery tour to the tasting for Nu 450 (the brewery operations close at 5pm and on Sunday).

The huge taproom, restaurant and terrace is a great place to hang out, with live music on Friday and Saturday nights. If you get peckish, try a scoop of local *sikam* (dried spicy pork) or masala peanuts, or there's a full menu offering everything from burgers and nachos to local river trout.

 BEST SOUVENIR SHOPS IN PARO

Collection of Rare Stamps & Souvenir Shop
This tiny shop has some first covers and stamps you can play on a record player.

Chencho Handicrafts
Particularly strong on weavings, antique *kira* (women's dresses) and embroidery, with weavers on-site.

Yuesel Handicrafts
All the normal souvenirs, plus a back room of antiques, for which they provide export certificates.

Beyond Paro

The Paro valley boasts charming rural scenery, scenic hiking trails, excellent accommodation and some of Bhutan's most famous sights.

Taktshang
Drukgyel • Goemba
Dzong
Kyichu •
Lhakhang ● Paro
Dzongdrakha •
Drak ●
Kharpo

The Paro valley is one of the loveliest and most important in Bhutan. For most of the 19th century it was the commercial, cultural and political heart of the country. The upper end of the valley holds the country's most famous sight, the Tiger's Nest monastery at Taktshang, as well as one of its most beautiful temples, Kyichu Lhakhang, and continues towards Bhutan's most popular treks.

Leading off from Paro are several side valleys whose hillsides shelter some magical pilgrimage sites, often perched on cliff-faces or mountaintops, and rich in myth and magic. Though only a few kilometres off the main highways to Thimphu and Haa, a visit here feels like you are connecting with a more ancient Bhutan.

TOP TIP

Don't rush the drive to Thimphu via the lower Paro Chhu valley. Drak Kharpo and Tamchog Lhakhang are both well worth a visit en route.

CRYSTAL IMAGE/SHUTTERSTOCK ©

Kyichu Lhakhang

SUBDUING THE DEMONESS

In 659 the Tibetan king Songtsen Gampo decided to build 108 temples to pin down a demoness that his wife, the Chinese Princess Wencheng, had divined was blocking the introduction of Buddhism to the country. Temples were constructed at the continental-sized demoness' shoulders, hips, knees and elbows inside Tibet, but more had to be built in Bhutan to pin down the troublesome left leg.

The best known of these temples are Kyichu Lhakhang in Paro, which holds the left foot, and Jampey Lhakhang (p151) in Bumthang, which pins the left knee. Among others, Paro's Pena Lhakhang, Konchogsum Lhakhang in Bumthang, Khaine Lhakhang south of Lhuentse, and Lhakhang Kharpo in Haa may also have been part of this ambitious geomantic project.

A Timeless Temple Built to Thwart a Demoness

ANCIENT SONGTSEN GAMPO TEMPLE

Kyichu Lhakhang is one of Bhutan's oldest and most beautiful temples, popularly believed to have been founded in 659 by King Songtsen Gampo of Tibet to pin down the left foot of a giant ogress who was thwarting the establishment of Buddhism in Tibet. Inside the lhakhang look for a framed image of the reclining demoness for whom the temple was allegedly built.

The third king's wife, Ashi Kesang Wangchuck, sponsored the construction of the **Guru Lhakhang** here in 1968. It contains a 5m-high statue of Guru Rinpoche draped in silks and another of Kurukulla (Red Tara) holding a bow and arrow made of flowers. To the right of Guru Rinpoche is a funeral chorten containing the ashes of Dilgo Khyentse Rinpoche, the revered Nyingma Buddhist master. There is a statue of him to the left, as well as some old photos of the fourth king's grandmother and the first king of Bhutan.

The inner hall of the fantastically atmospheric main **Jowo Lhakhang** conceals the valley's greatest treasure, an original 7th-century statue of Jowo Sakyamuni (the historical Buddha)

WHERE TO OVERNIGHT IN NATURE

Tenzinling Luxury Villa Tents
Top-end safari tents high on a forested hillside in the remote upper Paro valley. **$$$**

Himalayan Keys
Four-star tent-cottages in Balakha, with three walls of glass for full forest immersion. **$$$**

Naksel Boutique Hotel & Spa
Big resort hidden 3km up a secluded side valley, right on the Trans-Bhutan Trail. **$$$**

at the age of eight, said to have been cast at the same time as the famous statue in Lhasa, and flanked by eight bodhi-sattvas. In front of the throne you can see the grooves that generations of prostrators have worn into the wooden floor. King Songtsen Gampo himself lurks in the upper left niche of the outer room.

As you leave the lhakhang, join the elderly pilgrims who constantly shuffle around the temple spinning its many prayer wheels and linger for a while; this is one of the most charming spots in the Paro valley.

Hiking the Western Paro Valley: Tengchen & Dranje

EASY STROLL TO TWO HILLSIDE TEMPLES

If you want to shake off Paro's tourist circuit and enjoy a short, easy walk between a couple of off-the-beaten-track small temples with fine valley views, head to Tengchen and Dranje on the western side of the Paro valley, both of which have connections with the group of five mountain protectors known as the Tseringma sisters.

From the road that leads to the Naksel Resort a dirt road branches uphill to **Tengchen (Tenchhen) Chholing Ani Goemba**, re-energised in 2019 by 50 nuns from Kila Nunnery who transformed the run-down former monastery into their *shedra* (Buddhist college). The main lhakhang features Miyo Losangma, one of the Tseringma sisters. The nuns will open the southern gate, from where it's an easy 30-minute stroll through pine forest, in and out of a side valley, to **Dranje Goemba**.

Dranje's monastic school looks deceptively new, but there are some fine ancient darkened murals inside, particularly in the Tseringma Lhakhang, where pilgrims roll dice to test their luck in front of the mask-like statue of Tashi Tseringma, the goddess of wealth, riding a snow lion. A traditional *drangyen* (lute) hangs to the side. Also here is the statue and funeral stupa of the founder Kichu Barawa and puppet-like statues of local protectors Shingkhab (blue) and Gyenyen (red). A second lhakhang houses a metal box containing a building-sized *thangka* of the five Tseringma sisters that is displayed once a year in the ninth lunar month.

From Dranje Goemba you can meet your vehicle and take the tarmac road back to Paro via Olathang. Alternatively, hike the steep footpath downhill to the road to/from Dewachen Resort.

DILGO KHYENTSE

Kyichu Lhakhang has many connections with Dilgo Khyentse (1910–91), the Tibetan Buddhist yogi and reincarnated lama, who was the main spiritual advisor to the Bhutanese royal family. The Kyichu Lhakhang houses his funeral chorten, as well as his former living quarters *(zimchung)*, which still hold his bed and throne. His main residence next door is now a **house museum** and displays his ceremonial hat, slates used for communicating when on silent retreat and even his sinus medication.

Dilgo was a fascinating character, who grew up in Derge in eastern Tibet before the Chinese invasion, and later married and had a daughter. His reincarnation, or *yangsi,* lives in a complex behind the Zhiwa Ling Hotel.

WHERE TO STAY FOR ULTIMATE LUXURY

Amankora Paro
Sleek and stylish rammed-earth buildings hidden in pine forest in Balakha, near Drukgyel Dzong. **$$$**

Uma Paro
Impeccably managed, 15-hectare site with villas, butler service and the famous Como Shambhala spa treatments. **$$$**

Six Senses Paro
Perched high above Paro Dzong, in splendid isolation, with fine views and spa treatments. **$$$**

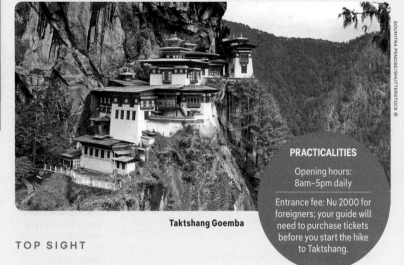

SOUMITRA PENDSE/SHUTTERSTOCK ©

Taktshang Goemba

TOP SIGHT

Taktshang Goemba: The Tiger's Nest

The Tiger's Nest Monastery of Taktshang is one of the Himalaya's most incredible sights, stuck like a limpet on a rock face 900m above the Paro valley. There is a tangible air of magic to the site. Getting here involves a bit of uphill legwork but it's a highlight of any Bhutan itinerary and you'll be joined by many Bhutanese pilgrims.

DON'T MISS

Taktshang
Viewpoint

Views from
Taktsang Cafe

Guru Rinpoche
Cave

Guru Sungjonma
Lhakhang

Langchen Pelgye
Singye Lhakhang

Chapels above
Taktshang

The Hike up to Taktshang

The only way up to the Tiger's Nest is to walk, ride a horse or fly on the back of a magic tiger (the last option generally reserved for tantric magicians). The two-hour uphill hike, gaining 550 vertical metres, is hard work but within the reach of most reasonably fit people, and it's a good warm-up hike if you are going trekking late on your trip.

The trail climbs through blue pines to three water-powered prayer wheels, then switchbacks steeply up the ridge. Once on the ridge there are excellent views across the valley and southwest towards Drukgyel Dzong. After a climb of about one hour and a gain of 300m you will reach a small chorten and some prayer flags on the ridge, which is as far as horses can go. It's then a short walk to the **Taktsang Cafe**, at 2940m, where you can savour the impressive view of the monastery over a well-deserved cup of tea.

The trail continues up for another 30 minutes to a cave and plaque that marks the birthplace of a previous Je Khenpo. A short walk further along the main trail brings you to a spectacular stupa **viewpoint** at 3140m that puts you eyeball to eyeball with the monastery that seems to be growing out of the rocks.

From here Taktshang looks almost close enough to touch, but it's on the far side of a deep valley about 150m away. The trail descends to a waterfall by the **Singye Pel-phu Lhakhang (Snow Lion Cave)**, a meditation retreat associated with Guru Rinpoche's consort Yeshe Tshogyel that's wedged dramatically into a rock crevice. The path then climbs back up to finally reach the monastery entrance.

The Meditation Cave of Guru Rinpoche

As you enter the complex underneath images of the Rigsum Goempo trinity (Jampelyang, Chenresig and Chana Dorje) turn to the right and look for the relic stone; Bhutanese stand on the starting line, close their eyes and try to put their thumb into a small hole in the rock as a form of karmic test.

Pilgrims then visit the **Drubkhang (Pelphu Lhakhang)**, the sacred cave where Guru Rinpoche meditated for three months. The *penlop* of Paro, Gyalse Tenzin Rabgye, built the lhakhang in 1692. Outside the cave is a statue of Dorje Drolo, the manifestation the Guru assumed to fly to Taktshang on a tigress. The inner cave is sealed off behind a spectacularly gilded door, opened only once a year, and is said to hold the *phurba* (ritual dagger) of the Guru.

Murals of the Guru Tshengye, or eight manifestations of Guru Rinpoche, decorate the walls. Behind you, sitting above the inside of the main entrance, is a mural of Thangtong Gyalpo holding his iron chains.

Guru Sungjonma Lhakhang

From the *drubkhang* ascend to this chapel, which has a central image of Pema Jungme, another of the eight manifestations

Hiking trail to Taktshang Goemba

TAKTSHANG FIRE

On 19 April 1998 a fire (rumoured to be arson, to disguise a theft) destroyed the main 17th-century structure of Taktshang and all its contents. It had already suffered a previous fire and had been repaired in 1951. Reconstruction started in April 2000 at a cost of 130 million ngultrum and the rebuilt site was reconsecrated in the presence of the king in 2005.

TOP TIPS

- Bring comfortable walking shoes, a hat and water for the hike. A long skirt or trousers are essential to enter the temples.
- Most people tackle the walk in the morning to avoid strong direct sun, but photographers often opt for the afternoon light.
- It's possible to ride a horse (Nu 1200) halfway up to the temple; your guide can arrange this at the car park, or preferably in advance.
- Bags, phones and cameras have to be checked in to lockers.
- This is a sacred site, so act with respect, removing your shoes and hat before entering chapels.

of Guru Rinpoche. This statue incorporates the ashes of a famous 'talking' *(sungjonma)* image that was lost in the 1998 fire (or is the original statue, saved from the fire, depending on which monk you talk to). Various demonic animal-headed deities and manifestations of the deity Phurba decorate the walls alongside the 25 disciples of Guru Rinpoche.

Langchen Pelgye Singye Lhakhang

Passing a small prayer hall, the Langchen Pelgye Singye Lhakhang on the left has connections to the deity Dorje Phagmo, with a rock image of the goddess's crown hidden in a hole in the floor. The inner chorten belongs to Langchen Pelgye Singye, a 9th-century disciple of Guru Rinpoche, who meditated in the cave. Behind the chorten is a holy spring.

Other Temples

Further on inside the complex to the left is the modern **Dorje Drolo Lhakhang**, while to the right is the **Guru Tshengye Lhakhang**, which features an image of the monastery's 17th-century founder, Gyalse Tenzin Rabgye, to the far right. Look down through the glass into the bowels of a sacred cave.

Further up is a butter-lamp chapel (light one for a donation) and a temple dedicated to Namse, the god of wealth. It's just about possible to climb down into the original Tiger's Nest cave just above the chapel, but take care as it's a dusty path down a hairy series of wooden ladders to descend into a giant slice of the cliff face.

Machig-phu Lhakhang

After visiting the Tiger's Nest and reascending to the previous stupa viewpoint, it is possible to take a signed side trail uphill for 15 minutes to the charming Machig-phu Lhakhang, where Bhutanese pilgrims come to pray for children. Head to the *phu* (cave) behind the chapel and select the image of the Tibetan saint Machig Labdron on the right (for a baby girl),

NOPAWUT KANJANAPINYOWONG/SHUTTERSTOCK ©

Horses on the trail to Taktshang Goemba

DAKINI HAIR

The precariously balanced *ney* (holy place) of Taktshang is said to be anchored to the cliff face by little more than the hairs of *khandroma* (female celestial beings, also known as *dakini*, or 'skywalkers'), who transported the building materials up onto the cliff on their backs.

Singye Pel-phu Lhakhang (Snow Lion Cave; p97)

A LUXURY TAKTSHANG PICNIC

For the most memorable lunch near Taktshang, the MyBhutan agency offers a romantic, high-end picnic of locally sourced dishes, cooked by your personal chef Dekyi and served at a scenic spot at the base of Taktshang. All the food is sourced from the Paro valley and gives you a chance to taste authentic local flavours in a sublime outdoors setting.

or the penis print on the cave wall to the left (for a boy). The chapel is often closed but it's still a lovely spot.

Beyond Taktshang

Several temples dot the hillside above Taktshang and make for fun exploration if you have the energy and time. Very few people make it this far, so you'll have these spots to yourself. The temples can also be visited on the second day of the Bumdrak trek (p196).

To the side of the Machig-phu Lhakhang a trail climbs to a junction where you can head left up to the **Zangto Pelri Lhakhang**, named after Guru Rinpoche's heavenly paradise and perched on a crag with great views from the back down to the Tiger's Nest below.

Back at the junction take the right path for 15 minutes to the **Ugyen Tshemo Lhakhang**, which has an unusual set of four exterior protectors and an interior 3D mandala that you can climb via a series of stairways. Just inside the main entrance are statues of the local protectors Singye Samdrup and red-faced Doley. The only sounds here are the murmurs of wind and water and the creaking of the prayer wheels.

The short 1½-hour hike from Tsendho village offers delightful Paro valley views and will give you a great taste of the epic Trans-Bhutan Trail.

Start off with a visit to Tsendho's 400-year-old **Girikha Lhakhang** and its sacred chorten (if you can find the caretaker). The trail then ascends gently through eroded badlands into pine forest to reveal fine views over the junction of the Paro and Dop Shari valleys, with Paro Dzong and Paro airport in the background. The charming walk ends with a descent to the Dop Shari road, from where you can round things off with a drink at the nearby **Outcast Bar**, itself offering lovely valley views.

A Fortress Reborn

RESTORED HIMALAYAN BORDER FORTRESS

Set high in the upper Paro valley, 16km northeast of Paro town, **Drukgyel Dzong** was built in 1649 by Zhabdrung Ngawang Namgyal to control the trade and military route to Tibet. The building was used as an administrative centre until 1951, when a fire caused by a butter lamp destroyed it. Renovations only finished in late 2023 and the exterior now once again boasts white and ochre paint. On a clear day there are fine views of Jhomolhari's snowy cone from the road leading to the dzong.

The dzong was named 'Druk' (Bhutan) 'gyel' (victory) to commemorate the victory of Bhutan over Tibetan invaders in 1644. One clever feature of the dzong was a false entrance that lured invaders into an enclosed ambush.

As you walk up to the dzong you'll pass a small Drolma Lhakhang on the left, a chorten down a short path on the right, and then the remains of the walled tunnel that was used to obtain water during a long siege. There is another walled tunnel and a *ta dzong* on the other side of the dzong.

After a visit to Drukgyel Dzong, you can take a five-minute stroll from the parking area up to the small **Choedu Goemba**, which houses a statue of the blue-faced local protector, Gyeb Dole. It's just above the village archery ground.

Pilgrim Trails to Chumphu Ney

A REMOTE PILGRIMAGE SITE

For a fabulous trip into the dreamlike world of Bhutan's sacred geography, budget a day for a hike up to one of the country's most famous *ney* (sacred sites). The focal point of the walk is a venerated and miraculous 'floating' statue of tantric goddess Dorje Phagmo (Vajravarahi), who is said to have flown here from Tibet and turned into a statue, but it's the pilgrim trails winding up to the complex that are the real attraction for most visitors.

The three- to four-hour walk to the temple follows a beautiful river and passes dozens of *neydo,* or sacred natural rock carvings, connected to the activities of Guru Rinpoche and his consorts. After two hours or so, a side valley enters from the left and you can spy the lhakhang above you. Shortly afterwards a *kora* (circumambulation) path branches left up the side valley towards a waterfall, before ascending past a remarkable series of sin tests, ladders, ledges, meditation caves and natural stone pools to reach the temple.

 WHERE TO STAY & EAT BY THE TIGER'S NEST ⎯⎯⎯⎯⎯

Paro Dhaba
Trout and other *thali* (set meals) near the Taktshang turnoff by Zhiwa Ling; popular with local monks. **$**

The Taktsang
Vegetarian Western and Southeast Asian food from a Bhutanese chef who trained in Singapore. **$$**

Druk Gatoen Restaurant
Local place serving up delicious authentic Bhutanese cuisine, from dried pork to *datse* dishes. **$**

PETRAKUB/SHUTTERSTOCK ©

Drukgyel Dzong

The main shrine is guarded by police and home to Dorje Phagmo (Vajravarahi), recognisable by the sow's snout behind her right ear. An attendant monk will open a little door under the statue and pass a 10 ngultrum note under her foot to prove that the statue floats unsupported by the ground.

A further 10-minute walk behind the monastery leads to a small prayer-flag-draped waterfall and pool connected to Guru Rinpoche. It's then a two-hour walk back to the car park, which is an hourlong drive from Paro up the Dop Shari valley.

The Cliff-Side Temples of Dzongdrakha

DRAMATICALLY SITED LHAKHANGS ON THE ROAD TO CHELI LA

From the junction at Bondey, south of Paro, the road to Haa climbs for 5km, where a side road branches left for 2km to little-visited **Dzongdrakha Goemba**, a string of chapels perched dramatically on a cliff ledge. The site is one of several where Guru Rinpoche suppressed local demons and it's well worth an hourlong visit.

The first building you come to is the private manor house of **Jongsarbu Lhakhang**, founded in the 18th century by the meditation master Gyanpo Dorje, and fronted by a lovely

HOMESTAYS & HOT-STONE BATHS

Most tour agencies can arrange a visit to a traditional farmhouse, either for an overnight, or just a traditional Bhutanese meal or hot-stone bath. One popular place in Paro's Dop Shari valley is **Tshering's Farmhouse**, which serves authentic home-cooked Bhutanese food, either in the kitchen or a private dining room. Accommodation is also available in the farmhouse on mattresses on the floor. You can play a game of traditional *khuru* (darts) in the garden while waiting for your artemisia-scented wooden hot-stone bath to heat up.

For a higher-end hot-stone bath experience, book a dinner and soak in the myrtle-scented herbal bath of **Nemjo Heritage Lodge**.

Taktsang Cafe
Incredible views and good espresso (but average food) at this revamped cafe halfway up the mountain. **$$**

Taktsang Boutique Hotel
The closest accommodation to the Tiger's Nest, recently renovated with an ornate basement restaurant. **$$**

Bumdrak Camp
Permanent camp with proper beds, high above Tiger's Nest; it's part of the Bumdrak trek (p196). **$$**

BONDEY

At the junction of roads to Paro, Haa and Thimphu, tiny Bondey has a trio of interesting temples worth a quick stop.

Tago Lhakhang
This charming and unusually chorten-shaped temple on the main road near the Bondey bridge was founded by the iron-bridge builder Thangtong Gyalpo. A circular chapel occupies the upper floor; women come here for a blessing when trying to conceive.

Bondey Lhakhang
This 400-year-old temple is on the west side of the river, across the bridge.

Pelri Goemba
A 15-minute uphill hike (or short drive) above Tago is this rare Nyingmapa-school chapel that was reduced in size after an unwise dispute with the dominant Kagyu school.

BRADLEY MAYHEW/LONELY PLANET ©

Drak Kharpo

suntala (mandarin) tree. The main statue is of Sakyamuni Buddha in his princely Jowo form, flanked by local protector Tsethsho Chen and a *tshomen* (mermaid-like water spirit).

As you head along the cliff face, the **Tseringma Lhakhang** is dedicated to the goddess of longevity, depicted riding a snow lion and covered in offerings of necklaces and safety pins. Pilgrims buy amulets here containing a protective pill known as a *rubep*. Climb the log ladder behind the chapel to the cave-like **Doley Lhakhang**, which houses local protectors Doley and Shari Tsen, alongside a couple of papier-mâché heads that were once used during local festivals. Parents who have just given birth to a son are supposed to come to this chapel to receive an auspicious name for their child.

Nearby is the **Guru Lhakhang**, where the caretaker will tell you stories about local demons, flying saints, stone eggs, treasure finders and magical spells, and point out sacred dagger marks in a nearby stone. Behind the main statue is a hidden relic chorten that allegedly has to be enclosed to prevent it flying away; the caretaker can open a little door at the back to reveal part of the chorten.

 MEMORABLE MEALS OUTSIDE PARO

Nemjo Heritage Lodge
Tibetan hotpot on a linen-clad farmhouse table or in a glass-walled private dining room. **$$$**

Bukhari at the Uma
Inventive set meals from chef Tshering make this the best restaurant in the valley (and a royal favourite). **$$$**

MyBhutan Comfort Picnic
Top-end and very romantic mobile catering service with personal chef, making use of the best local ingredients. **$$$**

Detour to a Guru Rinpoche Pilgrimage Site

FANTASTICAL SPOT OF MIRACLES AND SIN TESTS

High above the Paro–Thimphu road, **Drak Kharpo** (White Cliff) is a cliff-side monastery where the Buddhist magician-saint Guru Rinpoche meditated for several months before flying off to Dzongdrakha across the valley. The site is well worth the detour for its delightful 20-minute *kora* walking path, passing numerous sacred stones and a small cave complex, where you can join fellow pilgrims as they squeeze their way through a claustrophobic series of sin-absolving tunnels (bring a torch). The large split stone at the top of the path is where Guru Rinpoche subdued the local demon Draksen and pilgrims rub their backs and joints on the healing stone before squeezing through the crack.

The main lhakhang is built around the meditation cave of Guru Rinpoche and you can see his fingerprints in the rock that he magically displaced when making the cave. Figure on a 2½-hour return detour to visit the complex from the main road or add it on to a visit to Dongkala.

Neyphu to Dongkala Hike

REMOTE RIDGETOP HIKE TO SACRED SITES

If you are looking to really get off the beaten track, drive up to the 16th-century **Neyphu Goemba**, high in the valley above Shaba. The temple will be under reconstruction until 2028 but you can still see the monastery's most sacred relic – a pair of shoes said to belong to 8th-century master Guru Rinpoche.

From Neyphu (actually halfway between Neyphu Goemba and the Menchhu Retreat Centre) a footpath heads uphill up for 1½ hours, gaining 700 vertical metres, to the ridgetop **Benri Lhakhang**, said to have been constructed by *dakini* (female celestial beings). Just below Benri is the sacred pool of Ekajati, whose waters are said to heal any illness. Meditation huts dot the hillside behind, from where 360-degree views take in the Dagala lakes, the Cheli La pass towards Haa, and Jili Dzong back towards Paro.

From here it's a 1½-hour walk along the ridgeline through delightful forest to reach the road just below Dongkala, where you can meet your vehicle for a packed lunch.

VISITING A TEMPLE OR MONASTERY

- It's customary to **remove shoes and hats** upon entering the chapels of a temple. Leave bags outside.
- Always **move clockwise** around a chapel, shrine, chorten or prayer wheel. Don't talk loudly.
- It's customary to leave a **small offering** (Nu 10) on the altar. The monks will likely then pour a small amount of saffron water from a vessel called a *bumpa* into your hand. Make a gesture of **drinking a sip** and then spread the rest on the top of your head.
- Male visitors might be allowed to visit a **protector chapel** *(goenkhang),* but these are off limits to women.
- **Don't take photos** inside any chapel or religious building.

PEMA LINGPA

The miracle-performing 15th-century treasure hunter Pema Lingpa discovered several relics in **Membartsho** (p159) in Bumthang's Tang valley, one time returning from the lake with his lamp still burning and thus giving the lake its name (Burning Lake).

WHERE TO STAY IN THE MIDDLE PARO VALLEY

Tenzinling Resort
Spacious rooms with balconies and helpful staff make this a good semi-rural option. **$$**

Metta Resort
Large, spacious resort with huge rooms makes for a good base, in Shomo village. **$$**

Zhiwa Ling
Astonishingly ornate lobby, decorated in Bhutanese style, with a private chapel and renovated suites. **$$$**

Dongkala Lhakhang has an imposing location, perched on a peak 1500m above the valley floor. Past a shrine to the *tshomen* ask to visit the *goenkhang* (protector chapel), with its 16th-century mummified hand (of a thief) casually hanging from a beam. There are more wonders in the main lhakhang, including a huge butter lamp with powers to 'save souls from seeing the flames of hell' (quote) and a statue of Buddha said to have been pulled from the waters of Membartsho by the saint Pema Lingpa.

After visiting Dongkala drive down the hillside, past Phudue Goemba and Mendrup Goemba, to Drak Kharpo, which is also well worth a stop if you have time.

Heirs to the Iron Bridge Lama
THE CHAPEL OF THANGTONG GYALPO

As you drive from Paro towards Thimphu, near the junction at Chhuzom, you'll see **Tamchog Lhakhang**, a private temple on the far side of the river that is owned by the descendants of the famous Tibetan bridge-builder Thangtong Gyalpo (p106). A traditional iron link **bridge** was reconstructed here in 2005 using some of Thangtong's original chain links and it's well worth a look, though it's since been declared unsafe to walk on. A small cave above the bridge supposedly marks Thangtong's original iron mine.

With time you can make the 10-minute uphill walk to the 600-year-old temple, where you can almost feel time slowing down. A *kora* path circles the inner sanctum whose entry murals include images of Thangtong Gyalpo and his 'heart son', or main disciple, Dewa Tsangpo.

The top floor holds such treasures as Thangtong's original throne, links from one of his iron bridges, the walking stick of the 13th Je Khenpo and a bamboo stick brought back by the monastery's founder from the sacred Tibetan Buddhist peak of Tsari.

Driving from Paro to Thimphu
SCENIC DRIVE TO THE CAPITAL

The 50km drive between Bhutan's two major centres takes about 1½ hours but there are enough sights en route to warrant a half- or full-day trip.

After you pass Paro airport it's worth stopping briefly at Bondey (p102) to admire the charming **Tago Lhakhang**. Just 1km from Bondey is the family-run **Tshenden Incense Factory**, where you can see the deliciously fragrant boiling,

---

SPIRIT SANCTUARY

For the perfect relaxing stay at the start or end of a luxury tour of Bhutan, consider **Bhutan Spirit Sanctuary**, a five-star rural spa resort above Shaba. Rates include a consultation with a Bhutanese traditional doctor and daily Bhutanese herbal treatments, from *numtsug* hot-oil compressions and heat therapy to *kunye* oil massages. Staff also arrange yoga classes, guided meditations and hikes (to Eutok Goemba and Gom Jalo hermitage), and there's even a spring-fed heated pool and a ceramics studio.

The treatments are particularly good for back pain, migraines or digestive and sleep problems, but you need a couple of days to reap the rewards. All-inclusive room rates run around US$900 for double occupancy.

 OVERNIGHT IN TRADITIONAL BHUTANESE ARCHITECTURE

The Village Lodge
Surrounded by rice fields, this charming, converted 13-room farmhouse perfectly balances style, tradition and comfort. $$$

Nemjo Heritage House
Stylish farmhouse with fine food and herbal hot-stone baths; rent an entire floor for privacy. $$$

Paro Village View Homestay
Off-radar option in an apple orchard near Dzongdrakha, with rooms in a traditional farmhouse or modern cottages. $

Bridge at Tamchog Lhakhang

WHY I LOVE THE PARO VALLEY

Bradley Mayhew, Lonely Planet writer

The Paro valley is proof that you don't have to travel far to get off the beaten track. A network of pine-scented walking trails link little-visited but interesting religious sites like Tengchen Nunnery and Dranje Goemba, or you can follow the Trans-Bhutan Trail to traverse the entire valley on foot. Head off up a side valley and you can explore magical pilgrimage sites like Singye Drak or Chumphu Ney that don't see foreign tourists for months at a time. Then when you are done exploring it's just a short drive into Paro for an Americano and blueberry cheesecake or Bhutan's best craft beer. Heaven.

dyeing, extruding and drying processes. Two kilometres further on at Shaba look up to see the **Gom Jalo hermitage** clinging to the hillside.

A little further on, just past the bridge in Shaba, a rough road heads up for 20 minutes to Spirit Sanctuary, with another road passing Eutok (Yutok) Goemba to **Drak Kharpo** and eventually the mountaintop Dongkala Lhakhang.

Just past Shaba you'll pass the new **Chorten Drimed Namnyi**, a large whitewashed stupa built in 2017 by the fourth king. Cross the Paro Chuu at Isuna, 12km from Bondey, and then 3km later you will see the Tamchog Lhakhang on the left.

Chhuzom marks the juncture of the Paro Chhu and the Wang Chhu (*chhu* means 'river', *zom* means 'to join'). Because

 WHERE TO STAY NEAR PARO AIRPORT

Tashi Namgay Resort	**Paro Grand**	**Hotel Aari Sangdrup**
Sprawling resort with riverside rooms and cottages, plus draught beer from the nearby craft brewery. **$$**	Modern and spacious riverside hotel with a cafe, 3km from the airport, south of Bondey. **$$**	Modern, roadside hotel with excellent staff, good food and 12 pleasant rooms. **$$**

THE IRON BRIDGE BUILDER

Thangtong Gyalpo (1385–1464) was a wonder-working Tibetan saint and engineer who built 108 chain link bridges throughout Tibet and Bhutan, earning himself the nickname Lama Chakzampa (Iron Bridge Lama).

He first came to Bhutan in 1433 in search of iron ore and ended up building eight bridges here, from Paro to Trashigang. Sadly, the only surviving Thangtong Gyalpo bridge, at Duksum on the road to Trashi Yangtse in eastern Bhutan, was washed away in 2004.

Among this Himalayan Renaissance man's other achievements was the invention of Tibetan *lhamo* opera. In Paro he built the marvellous chorten-shaped Dumtse Lhakhang (p91). Images of Thangtong depict him as a stocky shirtless figure with a beard, curly hair and topknot, holding a link of chains.

Three chortens, Chhuzom

Bhutanese tradition regards such a joining of rivers as in-auspicious, there are **three chortens** here to ward away the evil spells of the area. Each chorten is in a different style – Bhutanese, Tibetan and Nepali.

Chhuzom is a major road junction, with roads leading southwest to Haa (79km), south to the border town of Phuent-sholing (121km) and northeast to Thimphu (31km). Road-side stalls here offer a good selection of local products, from apples and chillies to dried cheese and jars of *ezey* (chilli, Sichuan pepper, garlic and ginger).

About 6km from Chhuzom is the **Sisichhum Heritage Home**, a charming centuries-old farmhouse set up to re-ceive visitors. You can see the wooden grain storage bins, old leather bags and a fine altar room. The 19th Druk Desi was born here in 1788 and the family has lived here for 11 gener-ations (the owner's baby grandchild is the 13th generation).

The Thimphu expressway drops towards the valley floor and enters Thimphu from the south. A second, older road travels via Babesa and Simtokha, enabling you to visit the Simtokha Dzong or bypass Thimphu completely on the way to Punakha.

WHERE TO STAY & EAT BETWEEN PARO & THIMPHU

Your Café
Bright, stylish cafe-bar in Shaba with a full vegetarian menu, owned by nearby Neyphu Goemba. **$$**

Sisichum Heritage Home
Book a lunch or overnight at this authentic, atmospheric and historic manor house. **$$**

Postcard By Dewa
Five-star Indian-run resort with a pool that is open to the public; popular on the weekends. **$$$**

✪ THIMPHU

Haa Valley

HAA VALLEY

The isolated Haa valley lies southwest of the Paro valley, hidden behind the high ridge of the Cheli La. Despite easy access to Tibet, the remote valley has always been off the major trade routes and continues to be on the fringes of tourism, which is one reason why we like it. The valley is the ancestral home of the Dorji family, to which the Queen Grandmother, Ashi Kesang Wangchuck, belongs. It is the only one of Bhutan's main north–south valleys that is too high for growing rice.

Less than 10% of visitors to Bhutan make it to Haa, but it's a picturesque valley that is ideal for hiking, and there is real scope for getting off the beaten track. There are at least a dozen monasteries in the valley and some great hiking trails. It's worth budgeting a full day here, especially if you like a bit of exploring.

TOP TIP

The town of Haa sprawls along the Haa Chhu. The southern town is dominated by the Indian Military Training Team (IMTRAT) and a Bhutanese army camp. Near here is the small dzong and Lhakhang Kharpo monastery. The central bazaar, a couple of kilometres to the north, has the main shops and restaurants.

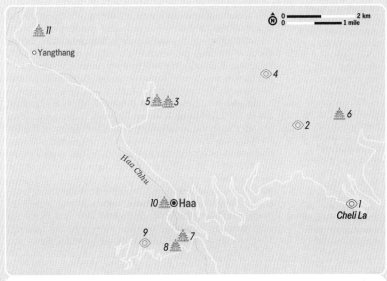

HIGHLIGHTS
1 Cheli La

SIGHTS
2 Gung Kharpo Sky

Burial Site
3 Juneydrak Hermitage
4 Kaley La
5 Katsho Goemba

6 Kila Dechen Yangshi
Nunnery
7 Lhakhang Kharpo
8 Lhakhang Nagpo

9 Shelkar Drak
10 Wangchuck Lo Dzong
11 Yangthang Goemba

Established as a meditation site as early as the 9th century and reputedly the oldest nunnery in Bhutan, **Kila Dechen Yangshi Nunnery** is reached via a dirt road and short walk from the road between Paro and Haa. In 2019 most of the younger student nuns moved to Tengchen in the more clement Paro valley but around 20 meditators remain at Kila in a series of houses pressed dramatically against the cliffs. One excellent way to visit Kila is on a scenic hourlong downhill hike from just below the Cheli La, passing chortens, prayer flags and a delightful stretch of forest en route.

Nuns have traditionally been discriminated against in Bhutan, neither receiving the government financial support available to monasteries nor enjoying the level of religious education and status open to monks. There are around 1300 nuns in official nunneries in Bhutan, with likely the same number again practising privately.

Bhutan's Highest Motorable Pass

PRAYER FLAGS AND RIDGE HIKES

At 3810m the **Cheli (or Chele) La** is Bhutan's highest motorable pass and an interesting destination in its own right. Several ridgetop hikes start or end near the pass, which is festooned in thousands of multicoloured prayer flags, and on a clear day (most likely in October and November) there are views of Jhomolhari. A drive from Paro to the pass can include worthwhile visits en route to Dzongdrakha (p101) and Kila Nunnery.

As you drive up to the pass, look for the roadside *drub chhu* (spring) with rock paintings of Guru Rinpoche and his two consorts. About 20km from the turnoff to Dzongdrakha Goemba a dirt road leads to remote Kila Nunnery.

When you finally crest the Cheli La, join the Bhutanese in a hearty cry of *'lha-gey lu!'* ('May the gods be victorious!'). A sign says the elevation of the pass is 3998m; it's really more like 3810m. If it's raining in Paro, it's likely to be snowing here, even as late as the end of April. A van offers a welcome hot cup of tea.

From the pass it's a steep, switchbacking 26km drive down to Haa.

Exploring Haa Town

HAA'S MOST IMPORTANT TEMPLES

Haa town's commercial centre is limited to a few streets of shopfronts but the traditional settlement spreads further south.

Haa's small dzong, known formally as **Wangchuck Lo Dzong**, is one of Bhutan's newest, built in 1915 to replace a smaller structure. It is inside the Indian army compound (an impressive two-legged chorten marks the camp entrance) and so houses several Indian army offices. There's not a great deal to see.

Haa's 50-strong monk body is housed not in Haa's dzong but in the **Lhakhang Kharpo** commplex, just south of the dzong. The atmospheric central chapel has statues of the Tse-La-Nam Sum trinity (central Tsepame, Namgyelma and Drolma) and of local protector App Chhundu, and there are also a couple of bamboo-framed mannequins once used during *cham* (dances).

A 10-minute walk or short drive behind the Lhakhang Kharpo is the grey-walled **Lhakhang Nagpo** (Black Chapel), one of the oldest temples in the Haa valley. It is said that when searching out auspicious locations for two new temples the Tibetan king Songtsen Gampo released one black pigeon and

 WHERE TO STAY NEAR HAA TOWN

Lhayul Hotel
Modern, comfortable hotel rooms and a good restaurant in the centre of the sleepy town. **$$**

Risum Resort
Spacious, heated, duplex suites and a cosy lodge-like dining room make this a popular choice. **$$**

Urgyen Homestay
Charming family hospitality and atmosphere in simple rooms with modern bathrooms. **$**

ZAKIRI346/SHUTTERSTOCK ©

Cheli La

one white pigeon; the black pigeon landed here, the white one at Lhakhang Kharpo (White Chapel).

The inner shrine has an ancient statue of Jowo Sakyamuni wearing an elaborate crown. The outer chapel houses a shrine to red-faced protector Drakdu Tsen beside a trapdoor that leads to the underground pool of a *tshomen*. In the grounds outside look for the clay representations of the valley's three sacred mountains.

A Winding Drive to the Crystal Cliff

CLIFF-SIDE MEDITATION RETREAT

A short excursion up the valley behind the Lhakhang Kharpo is **Shelkar Drak** (the 'Crystal Cliff'), a tiny, charming retreat centre perched on the limestone cliff face. Take the unpaved side road past the Lhakhang Nagpo, by Domcho village, and drive up switchbacks towards the ridgetop **Takchu Goemba** (8km). From the small private lhakhang and white chorten of Lungsukha village, a 15-minute walk along a new road leads to the small chapel attended by one lama and one monk.

Inside the main lhakhang look for statues of local protector Dorji Zebar and the site's founder, Choling Jigme Tenzin. Those with a spiritual bent can follow the monks on a

WHERE TO STAY IN THE HAA VALLEY

Lechuna Heritage Lodge
A luxury traditional farmhouse renovation with just seven rooms, in Hatey, 9km north of Haa town. **$$$**

Soednam Zingkha Heritage Home
A 150-year-old manor house in Hatey village, with a room that the King himself stayed in. **$$$**

MyBhutan Comfort Camp
Luxury wilderness tented camp featuring bonfire masked *cham*, herbal massages and astrology readings. **$$$**

MERI PHUENSUM TRAIL

The three hills to the south of Haa town are named after the Rigsum Goempo, the trinity of Jampelyang (left), Chenresig and Chana Dorje (right); they also represent the valley's three protector deities. You can see them from almost everywhere in the valley.

Hardcore hikers up for a long eight-hour day hike can follow the pilgrim path around the three sacred hills from south to north, starting in Baysa village south of Lhakhang Kharpo and finishing in Haa town by the suspension bridge. You'll need a full day, so bring water and a packed lunch; there are several wooden shelters en route. The initial ascent takes three to four hours but from then on it's mostly flat or downhill.

Hiking trail to Juneydrak Hermitage

10-minute scramble to the meditation cave of the 11th-century female tantric practitioner Machig Labdron. It's possible to hike downhill from the lhakhang via the prayer-flag-draped **Chimey Dingkha** pool to rejoin the main dirt road further down, for a charming two-hour excursion.

A Pilgrimage to Miraculous Remains

ATMOSPHERIC CLIFF-SIDE TEMPLE

About 1km north of Haa, just before the main bridge, a paved road branches east past the ancient Bali Lhakhang towards Katsho village, from where you can take a lovely 20-minute hike to the cliff-side **Juneydrak Hermitage** (also known as Juneydrag). The retreat contains a footprint of Machig Labdron (1055–1132), the female Tibetan tantric practitioner who perfected the *chöd* ritual, whereby one visualises one's own dismemberment in an act of 'ego annihilation'.

En route to the parking area you'll pass the **Chorten Dangrim** *mani* (carved mantra) wall, to start walking by a two-legged archway chorten, known as a *khonying*. Cross the stream and at a red sign in Dzongkha script, take the trail to the left and climb up to a chorten that marks the entry to the hermitage. Entry to the chapel involves squeezing between a stone entryway guarded by the faded rock painting of a green-faced demon.

 MORE HAA TEMPLES TO TRACK DOWN

Chhundu Lhakhang	**Tengchu Goemba**	**Jamtey Goemba**
The main shrine to the valley's blue-faced protector deity, 11km north of Haa in Chenpa (Lechuna) village.	Chhundu's summer residence, visible across the valley from Chhundu Lhakhang and a 40-minute walk away.	A historic hillside *lobra* (monastic school) 2km north of Talung village, not far from Yangthang Goemba.

The lhakhang has been restored with new wall murals. The photo on the altar of the young boy is the grandson of the fourth king, who was recently recognised as the reincarnation of the 8th-century translator-scholar Vairotsana; his newly built residence sits just below Juneydrak. The cave was visited by Guru Rinpoche and numerous red signs point out a string of miraculous sites, including one rock where the great guru urinated! Meditation huts dot the hillside above.

Valley Views on the Haa Panorama Hike

TEMPLES AND VALLEY SCENERY

The excellent three-hour hike from Yangthang Goemba to Katsho and Juneydrak links three of the valley's most interesting Buddhist sites via fine views of the scenic valley, making it our favourite hike in the valley.

Start with a visit to **Yangthang Goemba** to see the pool just outside the walls said to be inhabited by *tshomen*. The fenced plant in the courtyard is an *udumbara* ('Auspicious Flower from Heaven'), which produces a small, white, tulip-like bloom for one day a year.

The start of the 11km walk is clearly marked but the first junction isn't, so keep to the left, high above the valley instead of descending to Yangthang village. The trail passes two farmhouses and then climbs steeply, switchbacking up to 3100m by the end of the first hour. You can just make out the Jana Dingkha temple on the hilltop across the hazy valley. After cresting a ridge you'll reach a wooden shelter that offers views of the Rigsum Gompo hills.

The path then swings downhill through a burnt side valley to pastures around the **Katsho Eco Camp**, before ascending towards some white prayer flags on the high footpath to Katsho. When you hit the road, follow it uphill and then veer right downhill past a house to drop down to **Katsho Goemba**. It's then up and over a ridge to descend down past meditation huts to Juneydrak, where your vehicle can pick you up.

Trans-Bhutan Trail Hike: Haa to the Cheli La

REMOTE DAY HIKE ADVENTURE

You can get a taste of the Trans-Bhutan Trail by following its first half-day route from Haa and then veering off on an unmarked ridge, past a remote sky burial site, for a great six-hour day hike.

APP CHHUNDU

Like most valleys in Bhutan, Haa has its own protector deity, known as App Chhundu. Troublesome Chhundu is said to have been banished to Haa by the Zhabdrung after an altercation with Gyenyen, Thimphu's protector. He also had a quarrel with Jichu Drakye of Paro, resulting in Paro's guardian stealing all of Haa's water – and that's why no rice grows in Haa.

Ceremonies dedicated to Chhundu are still carried out in the open **ceremonial ground** *(pang)* below nearby Yangthang Goemba, about 5km from Haa on the east side of the river. Until 2016 these included yak sacrifices, highlighting just how intertwined Bhutan's roots are with its pre-Buddhist animist past.

 SHORT HIKES FROM THE CHELI LA ROAD

Haa Valley View Trail	**Kila Nunnery Hike**	**Cheli La**
Easy 30-minute walk from a bend in the road above Haa to charming Wangtsa village.	Hourlong downhill hike from just below the Cheli La through forest to the nunnery.	A short walk to the prayer flags north of the pass is windy but worthwhile.

POPPY HUNTING IN HAA

If you wish to photograph the famous Himalayan blue poppy (*Meconopsis gakyidiana*, Bhutan's national flower), Haa is a good place to start your expeditions. From mid-June to late July, several varieties of *Meconopsis* open their showy blooms on the high passes surrounding Haa, including the Cheli La, though amateur plant hunters will need to be prepared for rain and the odd leech. The blue poppy is notoriously hard to grow, taking several years before it flowers once, produces seeds and dies.

There are five species of Himalayan blue poppy found in Bhutan, as well as red, yellow and white poppies. Aficionados seek the large cream-white *M. superba*, which is endemic to Haa.

Yak

Pop into the small but ancient **Buli Lhakhang** for a blessing near the official start of the Trans-Bhutan Trail then pick up the trail at the Juneydrak car park, heading straight up the valley, away from the Haa Panorama trail, through beautiful pine forest and meadows of mauve primulas. It's a 2½-hour hike, gaining 900m, to the **Kaley La** pass at 3800m.

From here you can follow the Trans-Bhutan Trail as it descends into the Paro valley to the **Naksel Resort**. Alternatively, strike south along the ridge past yak pastures until you reach a small pass and rhododendron forest. A hard-to-find trail leads through the western side of the forest to climb above the tree line up to a series of chortens and a lunch spot. (If you lose the trail you face a tough bushwhack through the rhododendrons.) Lammergeyers soar thermals along the ridgeline here.

Climb past chortens to reach the windy hilltop **Gung Kharpo sky burial site** at a high point of 4140m. The Tibetan custom of sky burial involves taking a dead body to a high, remote site, performing rituals and prayers, then chopping it up and feeding it to vultures, though it's rarely practised in Bhutan these days.

Descend to the left of some hilltop telecom towers and continue to descend the ridge past chortens and hillsides of prayer flags to reach the **Cheli La** (3810m), where you can meet your car.

 BEST LOCAL DISHES TO EAT IN HAA

Hoentey
Buckwheat dumplings stuffed with spinach or turnip leaves and cheese and served with spicy *ezay* sauce.

Khurley
Spongey buckwheat pancake served at breakfast and best eaten alongside savoury Bhutanese dishes.

Yak Meat
Availability depends on the season but Haa's yak meat is renowned as the best quality in Bhutan.

DOCHU LA

THIMPHU ✪● Dochu La

Just 23km east of Thimphu, the east–west highway to Punakha climbs to the Dochu La (3140m), an important pass separating Thimphu from Punakha and marked by an impressive collection of 108 chortens. The chortens were built in 2005 as a Buddhist atonement for the loss of life caused by the flushing out of Assamese militants in southern Bhutan.

On a clear day (most likely October to February), the pass offers a panoramic view of the Bhutan Himalaya – some groups make special predawn trips up here to catch the views. A panorama painting labels the peaks on the horizon, including Gangkhar Puensum (7570m), which is the highest peak inside Bhutan and is considered the world's highest unclimbed peak.

Beware, though: the area near the pass is believed to be inhabited by numerous spirits, including a cannibal demoness. The Chimi Lhakhang in Punakha commemorates Lama Drukpa Kunley's subjugation of these spirits and demons in the 15th century.

TOP TIP

The best time to hike around the Dochu La is in spring, between April and June, when you'll be surrounded by red and pink rhododendron blooms. The hills around the pass are home to 36 of Bhutan's 46 species of rhododendron, as well as 220 species of birds.

KATERYNA MASHKEVYCH/SHUTTERSTOCK ©

HIGHLIGHTS
1 Dochu La

SIGHTS
2 Chandana Lhakhang
3 Druk Wangyal Lhakhang
4 Lungchutse Goemba
5 Royal Botanical Park
6 Thinleygang Lhakhang
7 Trashigang Goemba

DRINKING & NIGHTLIFE
8 Ser Bhum Brewery

SER BHUM BREWERY

Just south of the main Thimphu–Punakha road near Hongtsho, at the end of a bumpy 4WD track, is the Ser Bhum Brewery, where visitors can tour the tiny craft brewery and enjoy a malty Bhutan Glory amber ale (named after a Bhutanese butterfly) or pitch-black Dragon Stout in the small taproom or on the sunny deck (closed Sundays). It's the perfect end to a hike along the Trans-Bhutan Trail from the Dochu La, or just as a pit stop between Punakha and Thimphu. The oddly remote location is down to the purity of the local spring water. A *ser bum* (golden vase) is one of the eight auspicious symbols of Tibetan Buddhism.

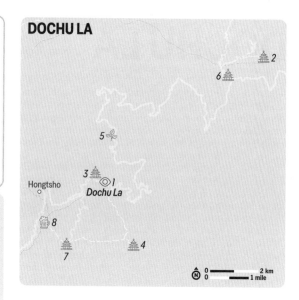

DOCHU LA

Epic Himalayan Views

A MOUNTAIN PASS, MEMORABLE SCENERY AND CHORTENS

Everyone en route to Punakha stops at the **Dochu La** for a look around the photogenic collection of chortens, the (possible) panorama of Himalayan peaks, and for a warming cup of tea at the cafe here.

The adjacent **Druk Wangyal Lhakhang** is also worth a visit to view its unique cartoon-style modern murals on the upper floor. Images include the fourth king battling Indian rebels in the jungle, a Druk Air plane and monks using a laptop or reading the *Kuensel* newspaper, alongside a modern history of the kingdom. It's a quintessentially Bhutanese fusion of the 21st and 15th centuries. The giant central butter lamp was offered by the Queen Mother on the occasion of the fourth king's 60th birthday and features images of the first three kings.

On 13 December the royal-supported **Dochu La Wangyal Festival** holds cham dances here against the dramatic background of peaks.

 WHERE TO EAT BETWEEN THIMPHU & PUNAKHA

Druk Wangyal Café
Espresso coffee, biscuits and a warming *bukhari* (wood stove) atop the Dochu La pass. **$$**

Menchuna Restaurant
A popular group lunch spot run by a master *thangka* and *thondrol* creator. **$$**

My Kitchen Restaurant
A simple local place offering a perfect lunch spot for Trans-Bhutan Trail hikers. **$**

Forest Trails to Lungchutse & Trashigang Monasteries

HIKE TO REMOTE MONASTERIES

There are several good hiking trails around the Dochu La. Perhaps the best walk in the area is the 7km, three-hour round trip from the Dochu La to the hilltop **Lungchutse Goemba**, which offers excellent views of the Bhutan Himalaya. From a signed trailhead just below the 108 chortens the trail climbs gradually through rhododendron forest, with some steep sections, for 80 minutes, before branching left to the goemba (right to Trashigang). The 18th-century goemba was founded by the treasure hunter Drakda Doji and is dedicated to local protector Tashi Barwa.

Trashigang Goemba (3200m) is easily combined with Lungchutse Goemba for a fine half-day walk. It's an easy one-hour downhill stroll from Lungchutse; just follow the electricity pylons. Built in 1782 by the 12th Je Khenpo, Trashigang is an important meditation centre for around 60 monks and a few *anims* (Buddhist nuns). In the main chapel ask to see the small chorten that encases a tiny statue made from a tooth of the 22nd Je Khenpo. The various chapels hold statues of 10 or more Je Khenpos who have meditated here over the years. The inner sanctum of the ground-floor *goenkhang* is said to conceal the preserved flesh of the goddess Palden Lhamo.

Watch out for the aggressive dogs here; carry a stick and make sure they are tied up before approaching. A paved road now leads to Trashigang, so you can meet your vehicle here.

Trans-Bhutan Trail: Hiking West From the Dochu La

HIKE DOWNHILL TO A BREWERY

The Trans-Bhutan Trail crests the Dochu La, following footpaths traditionally used by the monk body on its biannual migrations between Punakha and Thimphu. Several day hikes are possible around here.

If you are headed west, a lovely section of trail leads downhill for 1½ hours from the Dochu La to Hongtsho and the Ser Bhum Brewery. The forest of rhododendrons and Spanish moss has some steep sections but it's generally an easy stroll, with the second half following a stream after crossing the road to Trashigang Goemba. Note that the first half follows a different route than that marked on Maps.me. For the perfect end to the hike, finish with a cold amber ale from Ser Bhum Brewery, a 400m detour from the trail.

HANG SOME PRAYER FLAGS

One way to bridge the cultural distance between visitor and local is to hang some prayer flags at a high pass. Your guide can help buy the flags in Thimphu or Punakha and then show you how to correctly hang them. There are plenty of potential locations on either side of the Dochu La or at other passes like the Cheli La (p108). It's quite a bonding cultural experience.

Specialised *lungdhar* (prayer flag) shops sell preconsecrated prayer flags printed with the *lungta* (windhorse) design and can advise on the different quality, appropriate size and most auspicious colours (most come in strings of five colours). Vertical white *manidhar* are generally only erected in memory of a deceased person.

 MOUNTAINS VISIBLE FROM THE DOCHU LA

Masang Gang (7194m)	Zongophu Gang (7094m)	Gangkhar Puensum (7570m)
First climbed in 1985, the trident-shaped peak's base camp is accessible on foot from Laya.	Known as Table Mountain for its flat top, it's visible from up close on the Snowman trek (p206).	The world's highest unclimbed peak, off limits to climbers since 1993, like all mountains in Bhutan.

CHANDANA LHAKHANG

When the 15th-century saint Drukpa Kunley fired an arrow from Tibet to determine his future path it is said that it landed in Chandana ('Where the Arrow Landed'), causing the saint to detour into Bhutan. The outrageous Kunley promptly seduced his host's wife (after tying his hosts' sword into a knot in the face of his understandable objections), thus creating a bloodline that continues to this day.

The log-cut wooden ladder that the arrow struck is still preserved in the next-door farmhouse, whose family have cared for the shrine for 15 generations. The arrow and miraculously knotted sword are enshrined in the relic room of Tango Goemba outside Thimphu.

FORBITIOUS/SHUTTERSTOCK ©

Lungchutse Goemba (p115)

Trans-Bhutan Trail: Hiking East From the Dochu La

WALK ANCIENT TRAILS

Headed east from the Dochu La, the Trans-Bhutan Trail follows two pre-existing trails. The **Dochu La Nature Trail** (1.3km, 45 minutes) starts near the 108 chortens and ends just past some picnic tables by the road at the Public Works Department, offering a short but sweet downhill walk.

The **Lumitsawa Ancient Trail** (4km, two hours) then continues downhill from here through rhododendron forest to Chamzena village and its lhakhang, once again meeting the main road at Lumitsawa by the My Kitchen Restaurant.

The Trans-Bhutan Trail continues down for 40 minutes to **Thinleygang Lhakhang** via a side gully and a wooden bridge. The handsome lhakhang is the overnight spot for the *dratshang* (central monk body) every November as they move from their summer residence in Thimphu to their winter base in Punakha.

Continue downhill in the shadow of the lhakhang steeply into the main valley and cross a side stream 30 minutes from Thinleygang. The Trans-Bhutan Trail crosses the main river on a suspension bridge and then cuts right under the bridge to follow the curving river, past rice terraces to two Bhutanese-style chortens just before **Chandana Lhakhang** (one hour from Thinleygang). The Thinleygang to Chandana section also makes for a nice hourlong taster if you are tight on time.

You can meet your car at Chandana, or continue all the way along the hillside and then down to Punakha, for a long day's walk from the Dochu La.

 POSSIBLE STOPS BETWEEN DOCHU LA & METSHINA

Royal Botanical Park
Keen gardeners should visit this 97-sq-km park, especially during April's rhododendron festival.

Chorten
The white chorten below the pass was built to reduce the high number of accidents here. Gulp.

Drubchhu
East of Thinleygang is this roadside spring whose holy water is said to come from a lake far above.

PUNAKHA

THIMPHU ⚙ ● Punakha

Punakha sits in a sultry, fertile and beautiful valley at the junction of the Mo Chhu (Mother River) and Pho Chhu (Father River). Commanding the river junction is the gorgeous Punakha Dzong, perhaps Bhutan's most impressive building.

Punakha served as Bhutan's capital for over 300 years. The first king was crowned here in 1907 and the third king convened the Bhutan National Assembly for the first time in 1952. In 2008 the fifth and current king underwent a secret ceremony in the Punakha Dzong, receiving the royal raven crown, before proceeding to a formal coronation in Thimphu.

Most people spend one night in Punakha, visiting the dzong and nearby Chimi Lhakhang before heading on to Phobjikha, but you'll need two nights here if visiting remote Gasa. With plenty of excellent accommodation, good hiking and mountain-biking routes, it's easier to spend a bit more time.

TOP TIP

At 160m long, the suspension bridge northeast of Punakha Dzong is one of Bhutan's longest and has become Punakha's most popular Instagrammable selfie spot. It's fun to cross the swaying, prayer-flag-draped walkway over the Pho Chhu. The drive here from the dzong takes you past a royal palace and a cremation ground.

SABINE HORTEBUSCH/SHUTTERSTOCK ©

Punakha Dzong (p118)   117

HISTORY OF PUNAKHA DZONG

Construction on the current dzong finished in 1638, when the building was christened Pungthang Dechen Phodrang (Palace of Great Happiness). Later embellishments included the construction of a chapel to commemorate the victory over the Tibetans in 1639 and the dzong's brass roof, a gift from the seventh Dalai Lama, Kelzang Gyatso, a century later. Many of the dzong's other features were added between 1744 and 1763 during the reign of the 13th *desi*, Sherab Wangchuk.

Frequent fires (the latest in 1986) have damaged the dzong over the centuries, as did the severe 1897 earthquake and the bursting of a glacial lake on the Pho Chhu in 1994.

PUNAKHA

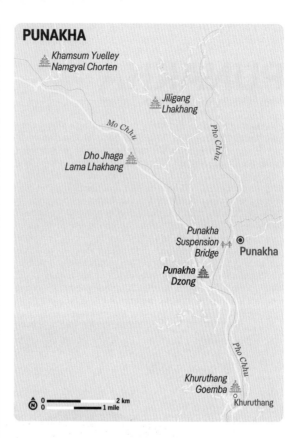

The Dzong's Sublime Architecture

BHUTAN'S MOST BEAUTIFUL BUILDING

Punakha Dzong is arguably the most beautiful building in the country, especially in spring when the lilac-coloured jacaranda trees bring a lush sensuality to the dzong's towering whitewashed walls. This dzong was the second to be built in Bhutan and it served as the capital and seat of government until the mid-1950s. All of Bhutan's kings have been crowned here.

Guru Rinpoche foretold the construction of Punakha Dzong, predicting that a person named Namgyal would arrive at a hill that looked like an elephant. When the Zhabdrung visited Punakha he chose the tip of the trunk of the sleeping

 WHERE TO STAY IN PUNAKHA

Dhumra Farm Resort
Fine views of the dzong, excellent organic food and a friendly owner make this a great choice. **$$**

Happiness Field Homestay
The excellent rural homestay of master dyer Aum Karma, accessed via its own suspension bridge. **$**

Spirit Village Lodge
Eight-roomed place with restaurant views of the dzong, from across the river in Dzomisa. **$$**

elephant at the confluence of the Mo Chhu and Pho Chhu as the place to build a dzong. He later established a monk body here with 600 monks from Cheri Goemba; the dzong is still the winter residence of the *dratshang*.

Access to the dzong is across the **Bazam** (suspension bridge), which was rebuilt in 2008 after the original 17th-century bridge was washed away in floods in 1958. In addition to its strategic position at the river confluence, the dzong has several other features to protect it against invasion. The steep wooden entry stairs are designed to be pulled up, and there is a heavy wooden door that is still closed at night.

The dzong is unusual in that it has three *dochey* instead of two. The first (northern) courtyard is for administrative functions and houses a huge white Victory Chorten and bodhi tree. In the far left corner is a collection of stones and a shrine to the Tsochen, queen of the *naga* (snake spirits), whose image is to the side.

The second courtyard houses the monastic quarters and is separated from the first by the *utse*. In this courtyard there are two halls, one of which was used when Ugyen Wangchuck, later the first king, was presented with the Order of Knight Commander of the Indian empire by John Claude White in 1905.

At the south end is the *kunrey* or 'hundred-pillar' **assembly hall** (which actually has only 54 pillars). The exceptional murals, which were commissioned by the second Druk Desi, depict the life of Buddha. The massive gold statues of the Buddha, Guru Rinpoche and the Zhabdrung date back to the mid-18th century, and there are some fine gold panels on the pillars. The elaborately painted gold, red and black carved woods here add to the artistic lightness of touch, despite the massive scale of the dzong. This is the only chapel that is reliably open to visitors.

After you exit the dzong from the north you can visit the **Dzong Chung** (Small Dzong) and get a blessing from a wish-fulfilling statue of Sakyamuni Buddha. The building marks the site of the original dzong, built in 1326.

Attend the Spectacular Punakha Dromchoe

WEEKLONG SPRINGTIME FESTIVAL

The three-day **Punakha Dromchoe** (or *drubchen*) festival in February/March is a dramatic celebration of a 17th-century battle scene and is one of Bhutan's most interesting festivals. It's the type of event that you should design your entire itinerary around.

PUNAKHA DZONG'S HIDDEN TREASURES

Bhutan's most treasured possession is the **Rangjung Kharsapani**, an image of Chenresig naturally formed from the vertebrae of the Drukpa Kagyud founder Tsanpa Gyare, which is kept in the off-limits Tse Lhakhang in the *utse*. It was brought to Bhutan from Tibet by the Zhabdrung and features heavily in Punakha's famous *dromchoe* festival.

In the southernmost courtyard is the Machey Lhakhang where the remains of the Pema Lingpa and Zhabdrung Ngawang Namgyal are preserved. The Zhabdrung died in Punakha Dzong, and his body is still preserved (*machey* means 'sacred embalmed body'). The casket is sealed and may not be opened. Other than two guardian lamas, only the king and Je Khenpo may enter this room. Both come to take blessings before they take up their offices.

Zhingkham Resort	Khuru Resort	Meri Phuensum Resort
Large, impressive resort offering fabulous views of the dzong from private balconies and an inviting terrace. **$$**	Spacious rooms with balconies at this sprawling place near Khuruthang that is popular with large groups. **$$**	Popular old-school resort with a garden gazebo and cottages cascading down the hillside above Wolakha. **$$**

JORDISTOCK/SHUTTERSTOCK ©

Rafting, Mo Chhu

HOTEL LOCATIONS IN PUNAKHA

Hotels in Punakha are widely spread out throughout the valley in distinct areas. Know in advance where you want to be based.

Wolakha
A group of mostly midrange hotels occupy the hillside above the main road, halfway between Punakha and the Chimi Lhakhang.

Upper Valley
This is where almost all the five-star resorts are concentrated; it's good if you intend to luxuriate in your resort, less useful if you plan on a lot of sightseeing.

Khuruthang
A group of modern hotels line the east bank of Pho Chhu near the modern town.

Metsina/Lobesa
Closest to the Dochu La or Wangdue Phodrang, if you plan an early start to Thimphu or Phobjikha.

In 1639 a Tibetan army invaded Bhutan to seize its most precious relic, the Rangjung Kharsapani. The Zhabdrung concocted an elaborate ceremony in which he pretended to throw the relic into the Mo Chhu, after which the disappointed Tibetans withdrew.

On the final day of the *dromchoe* festival (the ninth day of the first Bhutanese lunar month), a group of 136 lay people dressed as *pazaps* (warriors) perform a dance in the main courtyard, then shout and whistle as they descend the front stairs of the Punakha Dzong.

Next, a procession of monks led by the Je Khenpo proceeds to the river to the accompaniment of cymbals, drums and trumpets. At the river the Je Khenpo throws a handful of oranges symbolising the Rangjung Kharsapani into the river. This is both a recreation of the Zhabdrung's trick and also an offering to the *naga* (*lu* in Dzongkha), the spirits in the river. The singing and cheering warriors then carry their generals back into the dzong as firecrackers explode around them, and mask dances celebrate the Zhabdrung's construction of the dzong.

The three-day **Punakha tsechu** follows on the next day, featuring masked *cham* dances in honour of Guru Rinpoche, and on its final day a *thondrol,* which features an image of the Zhabdrung, is displayed. It's a week of amazing colour and drama and is not to be missed.

 WHERE TO GET LUNCH IN PUNAKHA

Hotel River Valley
Reliable food and riverside views at a hotel run by Bhutan's most famous bodybuilders, near Khuruthang bridge. **$$**

Phuenzhi Diner
Tasty Bhutanese meals at the 'Four Friends' restaurant in Khuruthang; you can arrange a hot picnic here too. **$$**

Kuzuu Café
Thai-inspired dishes at Zomlingthang, north of Punakha, run by the De-suung (Guardians of Peace) civil organisation. **$**

Rafting the Mo & Pho Rivers

RIVER FUN

Sitting at the junction of two pristine rivers, sultry Punakha is the site of Bhutan's most popular rafting trips.

The Khamsum Yuelley Namgyal Chorten bridge, 6km above Punakha Dzong, is the put-in spot for relaxing, two-hour scenic float trips down the **Mo Chhu**. As the river meanders through the wide valley, you float past one of the queen's winter residences, the king's weekend retreat, several luxury resorts and some beautiful farmland before taking out just above Punakha Dzong. It's perfect for families.

Trips on the more exciting **Pho Chhu** start with a hike up the side of the river through forest and farmland to the put-in at Samdingkha. The rafting has a couple of Class III rapids and ends with a bang in the 'Wrathful Buddha' rapid next to Punakha Dzong. It's hard to find a more scenic rafting destination or a more unusual way to view Punakha Dzong.

Valley Views on the Jiligang Ridge Hike

HIKE TO A LITTLE-VISITED TEMPLE

An interesting hike from Punakha's road bridge takes you up the ridge behind Punakha Dzong for 1½ hours to the 300-year-old temple and monastic school of **Jiligang Lhakhang**, offering fine views over the rice terraces of the Pho Chhu valley. The main chapel is connected to Drukpa Kunley (you'll get blessed by a stone phallus) and is home to some appropriately adorable kittens (*jili gang* means 'Cat Hill').

From the lower trail behind the temple it's 1½ hours downhill (don't take the upper trail to Sewla Goemba) past valley viewpoints above the Amankora resort to arrive at Yambesa village near the Khamsum Yuelley Namgyal Chorten. From here you can meet your vehicle, hike up to the chorten or follow a charming riverside trail downstream to the Amankora footbridge.

Temples of the Upper Punakha Valley

TRAPPED SPIRITS AND PROTECTIVE CHORTENS

Drive north up the Punakha valley and after 4.5km you'll reach the **Dho Jhaga Lama Lhakhang**, whose pretty gardens surround a huge boulder split in two. It is said that the Indian guru-magician Nagi Rinchen sent lightning and hail to split the rock to liberate his mother's spirit, which was trapped inside. The chapel houses a statue of the guru (to the far right), who is recognisable by the scriptures in his topknot. Rinchen

KHURUTHANG NEW TOWN

Bhutan has built several new towns in recent years, including Bajo, outside Wangdue Phodrang, and Khuruthang, 4km south of Punakha, to where all of Punakha's shops and offices were relocated in 1999. Punakha's restaurants, local hotels and Saturday vegetable market are all located here.

To the side of the road is the new **Khuruthang Goemba**, built by the Royal Grandmother and consecrated in 2005. The main Zangto Pelri Lhakhang has excellent ceiling mandalas. The entry murals in the side building depict the Zhabdrung and the various dzongs he established.

The large **Nepali-style chorten** here was built by the Indian guru Nagi Rinchen and is said to enshrine a speaking image of Guru Rinpoche known as Guru Sungzheme.

 WHERE TO OVERNIGHT IN LUXURY

Amankora Punakha
Eight beyond-luxury rooms at this intimate resort centred around the former residence of the Queen Mother. **$$$**

Uma Punakha
An intimate property of faultless rooms and villas in a peaceful rural location with lovely views. **$$$**

Six Senses Punakha
Spa treatments, a heated pool and a dramatic cantilevered lounge make this a relaxing choice. **$$$**

WHERE TO HIKE THE TRANS-BHUTAN TRAIL

Rabsel Dorji, advisor to the Trans-Bhutan Trail, shares his favourite sections of the epic new 403km-long hiking route.

Day Hikes
The section of trail around the Dochu La to Chandana is fantastic as a day hike because of its combination of natural beauty and religious significance. I also love the sections around Paro and Thimphu for their easy access, yet still retaining the feeling of remoteness, plus fabulous views.

Pele La
My personal favourite, though, is from the Pele La to Rukubji village, which is a great downhill day hike through an amazing range of landscapes.

Camping
For a three-day section, camping en route, I recommend Punakha to Samtengang, which takes you to remote villages and isn't too demanding.

FRAMALICIOUS/SHUTTERSTOCK ©

Khamsum Yuelley Namgyal Chorten

meditated in a cave across the river (behind Sona Gasa, the former palace of the third king), and so is depicted here as a long-haired *drubthob* (hermit-magician). To the far left is a statue of the local female protector, Chobdra, riding a snow lion.

In Yambesa, 7km north of Punakha, is the eye-catching **Khamsum Yuelley Namgyal Chorten**, perched high on a hill on the opposite bank of the river. The 30m-tall chorten (also known as the Nyzergang Lhakhang) took eight years to build and was consecrated in 1999. The chorten is dedicated to the fifth king and serves to protect the country, so it is stuffed with a veritable 'who's who' of Bhutanese demonography; some with raven or elephant heads, others riding snow lions, and most covered in flames. Look in the ground-floor stairwell for one protector riding a brown, hairy *migoi* (yeti). Go to the roof for fine views of the valley.

A bridge provides access to a sweaty 45-minute hike uphill to the chorten. Head off in the morning to avoid the subtropical heat. Ask your guide to point out the wonderfully fragrant *tingye* (flower pepper) plants that grow along the trail.

 WHERE TO OVERNIGHT IN LUXURY

AndBeyond
A new arrival from the Africa-focused safari company, with luxury tents in a charming riverside location. **$$$**

Pemako
Luxury hillside tents with private pools and a spacious riverside location from this new Bhutanese brand. **$$$**

Dhensa
Calming Singaporean resort in Wolakha, mixing sleek style with Bhutanese architecture; try the wooden hot tub. **$$$**

Beyond Punakha

Timeless temples, hiking trails, mountain-biking routes and adventurous mountain roads are the attractions around Punakha.

The valleys and hillsides around Punakha hide some intriguing lesser-visited sites. Head up the hillside southwest of the dzong and you can track down a sprinkling of important monasteries and temples, many of which have royal connections. Drive north towards the mountains and you'll eventually get to remote Gasa with its mountain dzong and famous hot springs. Even further north, a half-day walk north of the road head takes you to the exotic region of Laya, once the exclusive preserve of trekkers and now accessible to adventurous travellers.

South of Punakha is the Chimi Lhakhang, with its associations with the colourful lama Drukpa Kunley, while beyond is the highway to Wangdue Phodrang, with its recently reconstructed dzong.

TOP TIP

Visit in March and you can combine the Talo and the Gasa tsechus, as the three-day festivals share the same dates.

Wangdue Phodrang Dzong (p126)

LAMA DRUKPA KUNLEY

The 15th-century Tibetan magician-saint Lama Drukpa Kunley (1455–1529) is one of Bhutan's most beloved saints. He travelled throughout Bhutan and Tibet as a *neljorpa* (yogi) using songs, humour and outrageous behaviour to dramatise his teachings to the common people, earning him the nickname 'Divine Madman'.

He felt that the stiffness of the clergy and social conventions were keeping people from learning the true teachings of Buddha and his often obscene actions and sexual antics drew on the Tibetan tradition of 'crazy wisdom' to shake people out of their preconceptions. Nothing, it seems, was off limits; Tango Goemba is the proud owner of a *thangka* that Kunley urinated on, turning it (literally) golden.

IPEK MOREL/SHUTTERSTOCK ©

Chimi Lhakhang

Monasteries & Nunneries En Route to Nobgang

TRADITIONAL TEMPLES AND VILLAGES

By the village of Wolakha, 6km south of Punakha, a road peels off to the west and climbs the hillside to the **Sangchen Dorji Lhendrub Choling Nunnery**, a Buddhist college for 120 resident *anim* which was financed by the fourth king's father-in-law. The attached ridgetop Nepali-style chorten is visible from as far away as the Dochu La–Metshina road. Help out the nuns by buying one of the attractive woven bracelets they make on-site.

High up on the hillside, the side road continues uphill for 8km to **Talo Goemba**, which comes alive in March during its four-day tsechu, held at the same time as the Gasa tsechu (p126).

Around 5km before Talo, a 1km side road branches left to **Drolay (Dalay) Goemba**, a *shedra* that is home to 150 monks. The monastery was founded by the ninth Je Khenpo and is commonly known as Nalanda, after the famous Indian Buddhist

  WHERE TO EAT NEAR CHIMI LHAKHANG

Lobesa Organic Café
Fine window seat views and interesting Bhutanese dishes, such as *juma* (beef sausage). **$$**

Rinchenling Café
Bright and spacious place that is popular with guides, with some Indian dishes on the menu. **$$**

Drubchhu Café
A place for an espresso recharge, with pleasant terrace seating and home-cooked Bhutanese dishes. **$**

university in Patna. Local protectors here include Pelzom Gyelmo, the female consort of Drukpa Kunley.

Back down at the junction just above the nunnery, it's worth branching right to reach the lovely village of **Nobgang**, or Norbugang (Jewel Hill). A community of meditators formed here after the ninth Je Khenpo saw a miraculous light at a spot now marked by a chorten in the Laptshaka Lhakhang monastic school. A tourism project has converted one of these meditators' houses into a **traditional restaurant**, serving up the local specialty *gegyu* (beef, pork and noodle soup with *shukam* chillies), and a four-room homestay-style guesthouse allows for peaceful overnights in the traditional village, with cooking classes and village walks available.

Visit the Temple of the Divine Madman

PHALLUSES AND CRAZY WISDOM

On a hillock in the centre of the valley below Metshina, 11km south of Punakha, is the yellow-roofed **Chimi Lhakhang**, built in 1499 in honour of the 'Divine Madman' Lama Drukpa Kunley.

Inside the lhakhang you'll see the central statue of the lama and his dog Sachi, as well as statues of the Zhabdrung, Sakyamuni and a 1001-armed Chenresig. To the right is a statue of Kunley's cousin, Lama Ngawang Choegyal, the founder of the temple. Make a small offering and you'll be rewarded with a blessing from the lama's wooden and bone phalluses and his iron archery set.

Childless women come to receive a *wang* (blessing or empowerment) from the saint, while mothers-to-be select their future baby's name from a collection of bamboo slips, leaving with either Chimi or Kunley as one of their child's two names. Other women carry a large wooden phallus three times around the building perimeter in order to boost their chances of conception.

Murals to the right of the chapel depict events from Kunley's colourful life. Local protectors depicted in the chapel include Dochu La Dom, the demon who Drukpa Kunley subdued at a spot just outside the lhakhang, marked by a black, white and red chorten. The nearby bodhi tree is believed to have been brought from Bodhgaya in India (where Buddha achieved enlightenment under a bodhi tree).

Budget some time for shopping after your visit. The collection of shops by the car park are mostly run by graduates of Thimphu's National Institute for Zorig Chusum (p66), and they sell a good range of woodcarvings, *thangka* and weavings.

BHUTAN'S PHALLUS OBSESSION

Drukpa Kunley's sexual exploits are legendary across Bhutan, and the flying phalluses that you see painted on houses and hanging from rooftops recall the ribald lama. The eyebrow-raising and often comical penises work on many levels – to protect fertility, as a symbol of Drukpa Kunley's unorthodox 'crazy wisdom' or, as one noticeboard says, to 'symbolise the discomfort that society expresses when facing the truth'.

Perhaps inevitably, the handicraft shops around Chimi Lhakhang offer visitors an unrivalled choice of souvenir wooden phalluses, from discreet keyring-sized options to ostentatious tiger-striped varieties. It's the quintessential Bhutanese souvenir. Let's just hope you don't get stopped at customs.

 WHERE TO STAY IN METSINA/LOBESA ——————————

Hotel Lobesa	**Drupchhu Resort**	**Hotel Vara**
Well-run roadside hotel with spacious rooms and an airy restaurant overlooking a red silk cotton *(Bombax ceiba)* tree. **$$**	Spacious resort in Metsina with fine terrace views, built next to a holy spring *(drub chhu)*. **$$**	Spacious rooms with balconies make up for the somewhat unreliable hot water and electrical plugs. **$$**

A Day Trip to Gasa

INTO THE MOUNTAINS

The road up the Mo Chhu valley north from Punakha eventually enters **Gasa Dzongkhag** and **Jigme Dorji National Park**. Recent road improvements mean that you can now visit Gasa comfortably as a long (148km) day trip from Punakha. The rewards are wonderful birdwatching, dramatic Gasa dzong and the potential for an adventurous trip to remote Laya.

Gasa's remote 17th-century **Trashi Thongmoen Dzong** was built to protect against Tibetan invasions and is surrounded by a dramatic mountain setting. The dzong's *utse* sits atop the meditation cave of Drubthob Terkhungpa, the 13th-century Tibetan master who subdued the local protector Gomo and banished him to the pond just behind the dzong. The dzong's eclectic treasures include the skeleton of the sheep that followed the Zhabdrung on his journey from Tibet's Ralung Monastery (in the Chanzoe Lhakhang), and the remarkably preserved saddles of the Zhabdrung and his companions that sit in the *kunrey*.

The wonderful three-day **Gasa tsechu** in March is particularly worth making the trip for. Beyond the spectacular masked dances, it includes the performance of a 300-year-old folk song called *goenzhey*, believed to have been composed by Zhabdrung Ngawang Namgyal when he first came to Bhutan via Laya in 1616. The newly built festival ground lies just to the north of the dzong.

The famous riverside **Gasa tsachhu** (hot springs) are far below the dzong and reachable by road. The communal baths are primarily a destination for sick or elderly locals who shoehorn themselves into the pools seeking relief from joint pain and other ailments. Homestays around Gasa offer simple accommodation if you need to overnight.

LAYA'S ROYAL HIGHLANDER FESTIVAL

Gasa is the jumping-off point for a visit to fascinating Laya, once impossibly remote but now just a half-day walk from the road head near Koina. Laya is famous for the unusual bamboo hats, known as *zham,* worn by Layap women and for the harvesting of cordyceps, which has made many Layap families very rich. Laya has long been a major trekking destination but there are also good day hikes and the village boasts many homestays.

Perhaps the best time to visit Laya is during late October's two-day Royal Highlander Festival, which features yak and horse races, wrestling, strength competitions, traditional songs and dances, yak hair tents and even a royal visit. It's a true mountain gathering.

Wangdue Phodrang's Rebuilt Dzong

PHOENIX-LIKE FORTRESS

Wangdi's dzong was founded by the Zhabdrung in 1638 as the country's third dzong, 17km south of Punakha, atop a strategic ridge between the Punak Tsang Chhu and the Dang Chhu valleys. Legend relates that as people searched for a site for the dzong, four ravens were seen flying away in four directions. This was considered an auspicious sign, representing the spreading of religion to the four points of the compass.

After Trongsa Dzong was established in 1644, the *penlop* of Wangdue Phodrang became the third-most powerful ruler,

---

 WHERE TO STAY IN WANGDUE PHODRANG

Wangdue Ecolodge	**Kichu Resort**	**Hotel Pema Kharpo**
A recommended sustainable rural resort of eight spacious rooms with balconies; look for the wind turbines. **$$**	Charming riverside location, 9km east of Wangdi, with a bar and rooms on the river. Vegetarian food only. **$$**	Echoing hallways but large rooms and helpful staff, on the quiet north bank of the river, west of Bajo. **$$**

Gasa tsechu

WANGDI

The scenic *dzongkhag* (district) of Wangdue Phodrang stretches all the way from Punakha to the Pele La and Phobjikha valley. As you drive the half-hour from Punakha to Wangdue Phodrang the newly restored dzong comes into view as you pass a series of eight chortens.

Legend says that the Zhabdrung Ngawang Namgyal met a small boy named Wangdi playing in the sand on the banks of the Punak Tsang Chhu and was moved to name his new dzong Wangdi – later Wangdue – Phodrang (Wangdi's Palace). The town is still known colloquially as Wangdi.

The highlight of Wangdue's year is the third and final day of September/October's tsechu, when the Guru Tshengye Thondrol, depicting the eight manifestations of Guru Rinpoche, is unfurled at dawn in the dzong.

after Paro and Trongsa. The dzong's strategic position gave the *penlop* control of the routes to Trongsa, Punakha, Dagana and Thimphu.

The dzong burned to the ground on 24 June 2012 (as it had done in 1837) and rebuilding only finished in 2022. The dzong is made up of three courtyards, each smaller than the last. Several chapels are open, including the Zhabdrung Tongku Lhakhang with its golden statue of the Zhabdrung in Buddha-like pose, and the final *kunrey*.

The Warrior Temple of Radak Neykhang

SPOOKY PROTECTOR SHRINE

By the tall cypress trees of the Wangdue district court is this timeless 17th-century temple dedicated to an ancient warrior king. The anteroom has a collection of helmets, knives and shields, some with battle marks on them. Inside are five versions of the local protector deity Radrap, one of whom protects the local police, army and royal bodyguards. To the far left is a statue of a local *tshomen*. Roll the chapel dice and the resident monk will predict your future.

 LUNCH OPTIONS NEAR WANGDUE PHODRANG

Hotel Dekyiling
A good local restaurant in Bajo new town, serving up *no shapa* (fried beef) and chicken *momos*. **$**

Hotel Kuenphen
Popular group lunch spot at Nobding, 40km east of Wangdue Phodrang, en route to Trongsa or Phobjikha. **$$**

Wangdue Ecolodge
A 3km detour from Wangdue but a fine location and great organic food; book ahead. **$$**

PHOBJIKHA

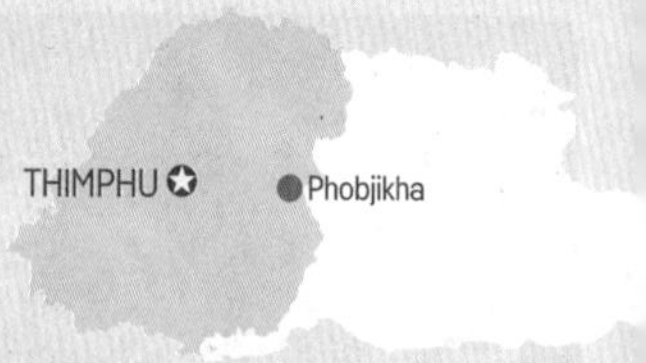

THIMPHU ✪   ● Phobjikha

Phobjikha is a dramatic, bowl-shaped glacial valley on the western slopes of the Black Mountains, bordering the Jigme Singye Wangchuck National Park. It's most famous for the large flock of endangered black-necked cranes that winters here every year, but it's also a great place for exploring on foot or mountain bike. Some people refer to this entire region as Gangte (or Gangtey), after the goemba that sits on a ridge above the valley. The 4500 local residents are known as Gangteps and speak a dialect called Henke.

The road to Phobjikha diverges from the main Trongsa road 3km before the Pele La, to climb through forest to the Janchab Chorten marking the Lowa La (3360m). From here the scenery switches dramatically to low-lying dwarf bamboo and yak pastures until yielding to extensive russet-coloured fields of potatoes. Gangte potatoes are the region's primary cash crop and one of Bhutan's important exports to India.

TOP TIP

Phobjikha is often snowbound in winter and many of the valley's 4700 inhabitants, including the monks, shift to winter residences in Wangdue Phodrang in December and January, just as the cranes move in to take their place. Even outside winter, temperatures can plummet in the afternoon, so be sure to pack warm clothes.

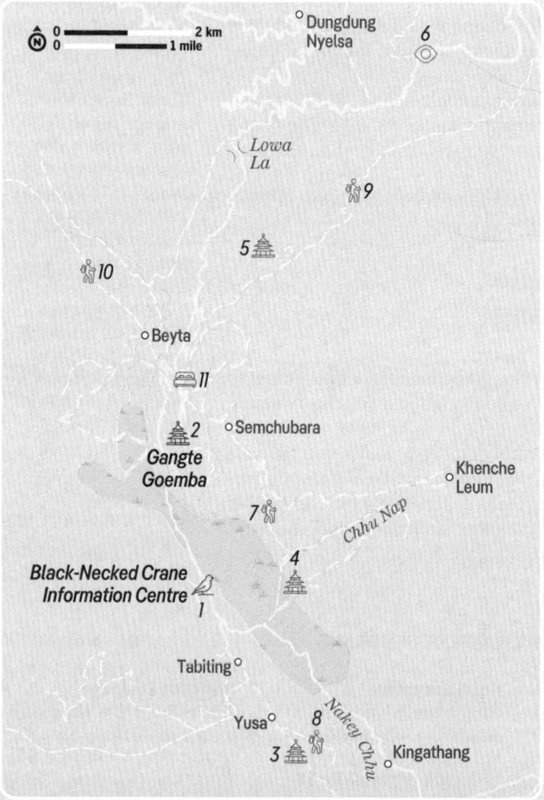

HIGHLIGHTS
1 Black-Necked Crane Information Centre
2 Gangte Goemba

SIGHTS
3 Damcho Lhakhang
4 Khewang Lhakhang
5 Kumbhu Lhakhang
6 Pele La

ACTIVITIES, COURSES & TOURS
7 Gangte Nature Trail
8 Kilkhorthang Trail
9 Longte Trail
10 Shashi La Nature Trail

SLEEPING
11 Gangtey Lodge

FRAMALICIOUS/SHUTTERSTOCK ©

Black-necked crane

Phobjikha's Black-Necked Cranes

ENDANGERED SEASONAL VISITORS

The marshy centre of the Phobjikha valley means it's best avoided on foot, but it's a perfect winter residence for the flock of around 600 rare and endangered black-necked cranes (triple the number of 15 years ago) that migrate from the Qinghai-Tibet Plateau to Bhutan in late autumn, typically in the last week of October. Between mid-February and mid-March the cranes circle Gangte Goemba and fly back across the Himalaya to their summer breeding grounds in Tibet. The Bhutanese have great respect for these 'heavenly birds' (known locally as *thrung thrung kam*), and one of the most popular Phobjikha folk songs laments the time when the cranes leave the valley.

Your first stop in Phobjikha should be the **Black-Necked Crane Information Centre** of the Royal Society for Protection of Nature (RSPN), which has informative displays about the cranes and the valley's environment. If the weather's iffy, you can browse the library and watch a 15-minute video.

SPOTTING BLACK-NECKED CRANES

Jigme Tshering, Black-Necked Crane Conservation Programme Coordinator at RSPN.

November is a good time to spot cranes, as the weather is not too cold and you can attend the Black-Necked Crane Festival. To witness a large flock it's best to come in January, when up to 600 cranes gather in one spot, but be prepared for the cold. In late February/early March the courtship dance starts.

Early morning and evening are the best times for spotting, as up to 300 cranes roost together in shallow, clear ponds and their calls echo around the valley.

Definitely visit the Black-Necked Crane Information Centre, as your visit there supports conservation and you can use the spotting scopes in relative warmth without disturbing the cranes.

 BEST FESTIVALS IN PHOBJIKHA

Black-Necked Crane Festival
This RSPN-sponsored, conservation-focused festival on 11 November sees folk dances staged by local schoolchildren.

Gangte Tsechu
Three-day tsechu in the eighth lunar month (September/October), ending with the hanging of a *thondrol*.

Khewang Lhakhang Tsechu
The small temple celebrates an ancient victory over local demons on the third day of the ninth month (October).

OTHER TEMPLES IN THE PHOBJIKHA VALLEY

Kumbhu Lhakhang
A dirt road leads from the *shedra* up to this protector chapel and meditation-retreat centre dedicated to the ancient Bon deity Sipey Gyalmo.

Khewang Lhakhang
On the east side of the Phobjikha valley, opposite Tabiting, is this 15th-century chapel, featuring three impressive two-storey statues of the past, present and future Buddhas *(dusum sangay).*

Damcho Lhakhang
South of Tabiting, the unpaved road winds past Yusa village to this small but charming chapel, said to be the oldest in the valley, dating to the 14th century.

CHARLES O. CECIL/ALAMY STOCK PHOTO ©

Gangte Goemba

The stars of the centre are Karma and Pema, two injured black-necked cranes who now live in a newly expanded enclosure. It's a rare chance to see the magnificent birds up close.

A Hilltop Monastery over the Valley

THE SPIRITUAL HEART OF THE VALLEY

Gangte Goemba enjoys prime real estate, on a forested hill overlooking the entire Phobjikha valley. The extensive complex consists of the central goemba, monks' quarters, a small guesthouse and outlying meditation centres. Much of the interior woodwork of the 450-year-old goemba was replaced between 2001 and 2008 due to a beetle-larvae infestation.

During a visit to the Phobjikha valley, the 15th-century treasure-finder Pema Lingpa prophesied that a goemba named *gang-teng* (hilltop) would be built on this site and that his

 WHERE TO STAY IN PHOBJIKHA

Dewachen Hotel
A stylish stone lodge and cosy restaurant that offers fine valley views; a good first option. **$$**

ABC Resort
A quiet location and spacious rooms in stone and wood cottages, plus a cosy restaurant with open kitchen. **$$**

Hotel Gakiling
Wood-panelled rooms and valley views from the shared balcony, behind the crane centre. **$$**

teachings would spread from here. Pema Thinley, the grandson and reincarnation of Pema Lingpa, built a Nyingma temple here in 1613, and the larger goemba was built by the second reincarnation, Tenzing Legpey Dhendup. The current Gangte *trulku,* Kunzang Pema Namgyal, is the ninth reincarnation of the 'body' of Pema Lingpa.

The *tshokhang* (prayer hall) is built in the Tibetan style with 18 great pillars around an unusual three-storey inner atrium, one of the tallest in Bhutan. The inner sanctum houses the funeral chorten of Tenzing Legpey Dhendup and a steel box that stores the *thondrol* displayed once a year during the monastery tsechu.

Upstairs is the Machey Lhakhang, holding the central funeral chorten of the sixth Gangte *trulku.* Monks will tell you that when the lama died, his body shrank down to the size of a baby and then the size of a peanut.

Style & Luxury at Gangtey Lodge

THE BEST HOTEL IN BHUTAN

In a country full of uber-luxury hotels, Gangtey Lodge manages to stand out. The architecture is certainly charming, with a main open-plan lodge built in a farmhouse style, and the rooms are close to perfect, with underfloor heating, warming fireplaces and dreamy in-room bathtubs with valley views. The service is also impeccable. But it's the range of activities and community cultural interactions offered by the lodge that really propels Gangtey Lodge into a league of its own.

Included in room rates are guided hikes and mountain biking, archery lessons and a prayer-flag hanging ceremony. Staff can also provide you with traditional Bhutanese dress for a memorable dinner or visit to Gangte Goemba. Extra activities on offer include guided meditation classes, evening prayers or a special butter lamp ceremony at the local *shedra* (prices include a donation to the monastery), or a lunchtime picnic at a scenic ridge viewpoint above the valley. There is also a full range of spa treatments. To boost your karma the lodge can arrange for you to make a donation to the *shedra,* providing a robe to a local monk or feeding all 300 monks in the *shedra* for a day.

This is one five-star property that aims to connect you to the community, not shelter you from it, which is why it ranks as our favourite accommodation in Bhutan. The only downside? All-inclusive high-season rates are US$1000 per night for two.

KUENZANG CHHOLING SHEDRA

The Nyingma-school *shedra* (Buddhist college) of 300 student monks in upper Gangte village has a unique fledgling tourist outreach program. Ask your guide to contact the office (via email: gangteyshedra@ gmail.com) at least a day before to arrange either a late-afternoon meditation class (not Sundays), to attend an early-morning or early-evening prayer meeting, or to just chat and learn more about the life of a monk. They also plan to offer purification rituals, overnight accommodation, dinners and even astrology consultations, as part of an effort to become financially self-supporting. It's a rare chance to gain a deeper understanding of this essential part of Bhutanese life, and all fees go to the upkeep of the *shedra.*

 PLACES TO OVERNIGHT IN A HOMESTAY

Homestays	**Phuntsho Choling Farm House**	**Tokha Menchu Homestay**
At least 20 simple homestays are dotted around the valley. Ask your agent or visitcommunitytourism.bt. **$**	Traditional creaking farmhouse rooms (shared bathrooms) or a modern block, both sharing a warm dining room. **$**	A welcoming, traditional homestay known for its medicinal hot-stone bath; past the Amankora. **$**

Hiking the Phobjikha Valley

EXPLORING THE VALLEY ON FOOT

The beautiful drive from Wangdue Phodrang towards Trongsa over the 3420m Pele La takes you over the rugged Black Mountains, the physical boundary between western and central Bhutan. The pass also marks the western border of the Jigme Singye Wangchuck National Park.

The pass is marked by a new chorten and an array of prayer flags but no real mountain views. For views on a clear day (admittedly rare in these parts) of Jhomolhari (7314m), Jichu Drake (6989m) and Kang Bum (6526m), you'll have to head back to a viewpoint 500m down the old road west of the pass. The Trans-Bhutan Trail crosses the pass, offering some good hiking opportunities.

Phobjikha is an excellent place to explore on foot or even a mountain bike (though you'll have to bring your own). The most popular short walk is the delightful **Gangte Nature Trail** (1½ hours), which leads downhill from the *mani* stone wall just north of Gangte Goemba to the Khewang Lhakhang (p130). The trail descends to Semchubara village and drops down right at the chorten into the edge of the forest, before descending to a valley viewpoint, a crane-watching hide and finally the interesting lhakhang.

The tougher three- to four-hour **Shashi La Nature Trail** leads up the valley from the track behind the Amankora resort. This was the traditional route taken by the Gangte monks and local farmers when they left the valley for the winter. The path branches off the dirt road by an electrical transformer and climbs gently to a *mani* wall, then swings into a side valley of yak pastures to ascend gently to a white chorten and prayer flags at the Shashi La. The stone throne here was once used by the Gangte *trulku* when resting at the pass. From here it's a long, steep descent through old-growth forest to Kalekha on the main Wangdue Phodrang road, where you can meet your car (by the T Wangmo Village Restaurant). This descent is great for birders, who can expect to spot pheasants along the trail, including the beautiful western tragopan.

A lesser-used short route is the **Kilkhorthang Trail**, connecting two religious sites, from the large modern nunnery at Kilkhorthang Lhakhang across the valley to the Damcho Lhakhang (p130), south of Tabiting. A couple of wooden bridges cross the river, one below the lhakhang, another just north of the nearby village of Kingathang.

Finally, the **Longte Trail** is an excellent half-day option that connects Phobjikha's Kumbu Lhakhang with Longtey village on the Trongsa side, via the 3640m Jiche La pass. Most people start from Longtey, but hiking from Phobjikha makes more sense if you are headed on to Trongsa. The hike is of similar difficulty in either direction, gaining and then losing 400m of altitude over the three-hour walk. Expect yak pastures, a mix of dwarf bamboo and rhododendron forest, and fine views over the Phobjikha valley.

A delightful section of the **Trans-Bhutan Trail** also passes through Longtey, so you could add on a downhill section from the Pele La to Longtey (3km), or from Longtey on to Rukubji (7km), depending on your direction of travel.

 PHOBJIKHA'S LUXURY ACCOMMODATION ────────

Gangtey Lodge
Huge, classy rooms, spa treatments and valley views at this faultless farmhouse-style lodge. **$$$**

Amankora Gangtey
The smallest and most intimate of Bhutan's five Amankora properties, with eight sleek and stylish rooms. **$$$**

Six Senses
All the spa treatments you could hope for, with fine valley views and just nine rooms. **$$$**

PHUENTSHOLING

The sweltering Bhutanese border town of Phuentsholing sits opposite the Indian bazaar town of Jaigaon, separated by a border fence and the much more colourful Bhutan Gate. Coming from elsewhere in Bhutan, low-lying Phuentsholing feels like a congested, noisy settlement bustling with Indian migrant workers. Come from India, however, and you will notice an instantaneous improvement in municipal cleanliness and organisation. The mix of cultures is fascinating.

You are only likely to visit Phuentsholing if crossing overland from India. The region gets uncomfortably hot and humid in summer, when monsoon road blockages are common.

The road from Phuentsholing up into Bhutan is a dramatic drive past silver-threaded waterfalls and dripping ferns, from the sweltering Indian plains to cool pine-clad Himalayan heights, and offers a satisfying sense of geographical continuity that flying into Paro can't match. The journey to Thimphu that once took up to 10 days before the highway now takes around five hours.

✪ THIMPHU

● Phuentsholing

TOP TIP

Current tourism rules mean that foreign travellers should get the US$200 per day sustainable development fee waived for a night in Phuentsholing. Phuentsholing is a much nicer place to overnight than Jaigon, so, given this, it makes sense to stay on the Bhutanese side for your first or last night.

BHAVEN JANI/SHUTTERSTOCK ©

Bhutan Gate 133

CROSSING THE INDIA BORDER

Bhutanese Immigration
Meet your guide and clear immigration at the pedestrian gate, just northwest of the Bhutan Gate vehicle crossing.

Indian Immigration
Remember to detour to the Indian immigration office down a side street in Jaigon to get an Indian entry or exit stamp. Indian time is 30 minutes earlier than Bhutan time. Note that you currently can't enter India overland on an e-visa.

Transport
Indian taxis run between Jaigon and Bagdogra airport, Siliguri or New Jalpaiguri train station in West Bengal for Nu 3500 (four hours). There is a prepaid taxi stand at Bagdogra airport. Bhutanese vehicles can travel freely in India, so your Bhutanese tour company can drop you in Siliguri for a fee.

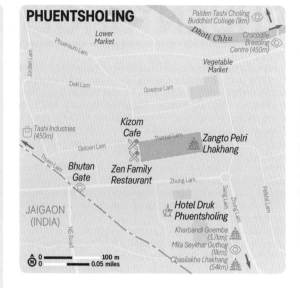

PHUENTSHOLING

Palden Tashi Choling Buddhist College (1km)
Lower Market
Dhoti Chhu
Crocodile Breeding Centre (450m)
Phuensum Lam
Jordan Lam
Deki Lam
Goedoe Lam
Vegetable Market
Kizom Cafe
Tashi Industries (450m)
Tharpei Lam
Zangto Pelri Lhakhang
Gatoen Lam
Thuen Lam
Bhutan Gate
Zen Family Restaurant
Zhung Lam
JAIGON (INDIA)
Sang Lam
Zhung Lam
Pekhril Lam
NS Road
Hotel Druk Phuentsholing
Kharbandi Goemba (3.7km)
Mila Seykhar Guthog (1km)
Chasilakha Lhakhang (54km)
0 — 100 m
0 — 0.05 miles

A Half-Day in Phuentsholing

INDO-BHUTANESE FLAVOURS

If you are entering or leaving Bhutan at Phuentsholing you'll likely have an evening here before or after crossing the border. If you have time to kill head first to the main plaza to join pilgrims walking around the modern **Zangto Pelri Lhakhang**, a replica of Guru Rinpoche's celestial abode (though we're guessing the original paradise wasn't made of concrete!). It's a pleasant place on a balmy evening.

With more time you can visit sleepy marsh muggers and gharials at the **Crocodile Breeding Centre**, just to the west, or drive five minutes to the **Palden Tashi Choling Buddhist College**, which is home to around 70 students aged between six and 25 and has some fine murals in its central *tshuglhakhang*.

If you've had your fill of goembas, get the map out and track down the **Tashi Industries** handmade-carpet factory hidden in the north of town. The factory specialises in bulk orders for many of Bhutan's monasteries. At 49 knots per square inch, woven from Indian wool and coloured with synthetic

WHERE TO STAY IN PHUENTSHOLING

Hotel Druk Phuentsholing
The best place in town, with comfortable rooms, a secluded lawn and good Indian food. **$$**

Orchid Hotel
A modern three-star place with spacious rooms, some with French-window balconies. **$$**

Hotel Bhutan Ga Me Ga
Central four-star option with indoor pool, cafe shop and roof bar-restaurant. **$$**

dyes, the carpets are not top-notch, but the prices are right, with a 1m-by-2m carpet selling for Nu 11,000, so you might just find a last-minute souvenir.

For dinner try the Thai and Chinese dishes at **Zen Family Restaurant** or pizza at **Kizom Cafe**, both on the Zangto Pelri square, or head to the food stalls at the **Kaja Throm** on the rooftop of the multistorey car park north of Zangto Pelri. Finally, toast your trip with a bottle of cold beer in the garden of the **Hotel Druk Phuentsholing**.

Road Trip from Phuentsholing to Thimphu

DRAMATIC MOUNTAIN JOURNEY

The drive from Phuentsholing to Thimphu is a dramatic, twisting drive along Bhutan's first highway. The road starts to switchback uphill almost immediately from Phuentsholing, offering spectacular views back down to the Torsa Chhu valley as it spills on to the plains. Just above Phuentsholing is the small **Kharbandi Goemba**.

From the immigration check at Rinchending, it's 2km further to the newly built **Mila Seykhar Guthog**. Passing the yellow-roofed Kuenga Chholing Lhakhang in the village of Kamji, the road turns a corner and begins to climb steeply towards the huge **Jumja slide** that often wipes away the road during the monsoon.

A descent leads to **Gedu**, a biggish highway town with a large royal-sponsored business college, several small restaurants, a line of eight chortens and the Laptshakha Lhakhang at the south end of town.

Chasilakha (*la kha* means 'grazing field') has an atmospheric **lhakhang** worth visiting; nearby is the village of Asinabari (Field of Hailstones). From here you climb over the ridge that separates the Wang Chhu valley from the Torsa Chhu drainage. Look out for the spectacular high waterfall visible to the east across the valley.

Past the lunch spot of **Wangkha** the road climbs to a lookout over the 1020MW Tala hydroelectric project, from where you can see the yellow-roofed Zangto Pelri Lhakhang and the site of the old Chhukha Dzong.

Past the Thegchen Zam (Strong High Bridge), the new highway passes beneath **Dobji Dzong**, which sits high above the river on the road to Haa, and soon arrives in Chhuzum junction; go left to Paro (24km) or right to Thimphu (31km).

BEST STOPS ON THE PHUENTSHOLING–CHHUZOM ROAD

Kharbandi Goemba
A small monastery below Rinchengang built in 1967 by the late Royal Grandmother Ashi Phuentso Choedron, who had a winter residence here. Eight different styles of chortens decorate the lush grounds.

Mila Seykhar Guthog (Milarepa Tower)
This modern (2022) replica of a famous nine-storey tower built in southern Tibet by the 11th-century Tibetan sage Milarepa is 500m off the road. Climb to the top for fine views.

Chasilakha Lhakhang
A Nyingma-school temple and monastic school featuring the throne of Gangte *trulku*, who supervises the lhakhang. Look for statues of the local deities Tsanglhep and Am Khangchima.

WHERE TO EAT BETWEEN PHUENTSHOLING & CHHUZOM

Doejung Paksam Hotel
Good range of Bhutanese dishes, just south of Gedu, 43km from Phuentsholing. **$**

Dantak Canteen
Worth a stop for cheap and tasty Indian dishes such as *masala dosa* and milky chai. **$**

Wangkha
D2K Hotel and Dam View Restaurant both offer good lunches overlooking the Tala hydro project. **$**

CENTRAL BHUTAN

BUDDHIST TRADITION AND BUCOLIC VALLEYS

Bhutan's cultural heartland dwells in the idyllic valleys of Bumthang; its royal heritage was born in Trongsa and its natural heritage flourishes in national parks.

Central Bhutan's wide, fertile and neatly cultivated valleys, fringed by evergreen-clad mountains, paint a picture of rural nirvana. Crystal-clear brooks gurgle past grazing cattle, frolicking ponies and lush fields of buckwheat, millet and potatoes. This postcard landscape is also Bhutan's cultural heartland, accented by several of the country's oldest and most significant temples and monasteries. In these venerable places of worship tradition is preserved and passed on to new generations of monks. They also set the stage for ancient and spectacular festivals celebrating Bhutan's singular Buddhist tradition.

Guarding the valleys in all directions are imposing mountains and formidable gorges, penetrated only by a few high passes, daunting roads and well-designed bridges. Across the 3420m-high Pele La and the conifer-clad Black Mountains is the magnificent Trongsa Dzong, the western gateway to central Bhutan. From Trongsa, a short drive over the Yotong La (3425m) leads to the four valleys of Bumthang, a magical region rich with relics, hermitages and sacred sites from the visits and activities of Guru Rinpoche and Pema Lingpa.

Central Bhutan sees fewer tourists than western Bhutan, yet in many ways this is Bhutan 'unplugged': authentic and intact. Nature lovers will relish the opportunities for day hikes and multiday treks along uncrowded trails. To really get off the beaten track, you can head south to the wildlife-filled jungles of Royal Manas National Park.

RICHARD I'ANSON/GETTY IMAGES ©

THE MAIN AREAS

TRONGSA
Strategic dzong and royal heritage museum. **p142**

BUMTHANG
Valleys rich in Bhutan's Buddhist tradition. **p147**

ZHEMGANG & SARPANG
Wildlife and Royal Manas National Park. **p162**

Above: Trongsa Dzong (p144). Left: Prayer wall, Chendebji Chorten (p144)   137

Find Your Way

Central Bhutan is believed to be the first part of Bhutan to have been inhabited, and the first region to be converted to Buddhism. Numerous impressive monasteries, royal residences and country estates adorn the region.

Bumthang, p147
Bhutan's historic and religious heartland boasts ancient Buddhist temples and monasteries, bucolic and luxurious accommodation, and some excellent hiking.

Trongsa, p142
Stunning, strategic and central, Trongsa Dzong, and the modest town that supports it, is a natural halt on any journey across Bhutan.

Zhemgang & Sarpang, p162
Wildlife and bird enthusiasts flock to the fabulous southern forests. Meanwhile, sleepy Gelephu is being touted as the site for a major new metropolis.

Kangri

Melung Gang

Gangkhar Puensum

GASA

Gokthon L

Thampe La

WANGDUE PHODRANG

Pele La

Nobding

Sephu

Trongs

Longte

Rukubji

Tangsibji

TRONGSA

Kue Rab

Black Mountain

Korp

Jigme Singye Wangchuck National Park

Dagana

TSIRANG

DAGANA

Damphu

Gongchuandgaon

S

Lamidranga

SARPANG

Dagapela

Sarpang

Gele

Dadgari

Phibsoo Wildlife Sanctuary

Kalikhola

MERTEN SNIJDERS/GETTY IMAGES ©

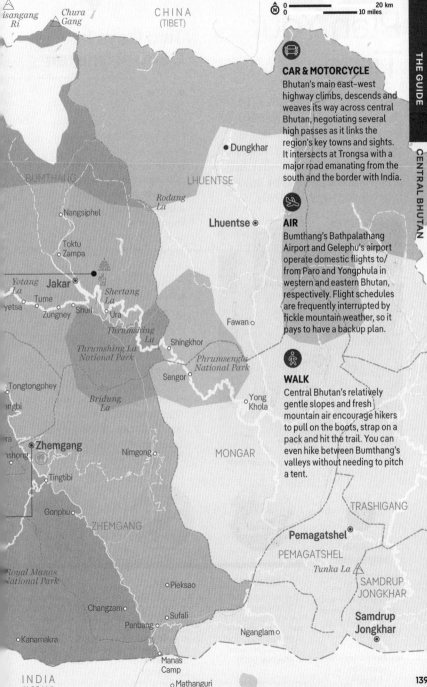

CAR & MOTORCYCLE

Bhutan's main east-west highway climbs, descends and weaves its way across central Bhutan, negotiating several high passes as it links the region's key towns and sights. It intersects at Trongsa with a major road emanating from the south and the border with India.

AIR

Bumthang's Bathpalathang Airport and Gelephu's airport operate domestic flights to/from Paro and Yongphula in western and eastern Bhutan, respectively. Flight schedules are frequently interrupted by fickle mountain weather, so it pays to have a backup plan.

WALK

Central Bhutan's relatively gentle slopes and fresh mountain air encourage hikers to pull on the boots, strap on a pack and hit the trail. You can even hike between Bumthang's valleys without needing to pitch a tent.

CHINA
(TIBET)

isangang
Ri

Chura
Gang

Dungkhar

LHUENTSE

BUMTHANG

Rodang
La

Nangsiphel

Lhuentse

Toktu
Zampa

Yotang
La

Jakar

Shertang
La

Tume

yetsa

Zungney

Shuri

Ura

Fawan

Thrumshing
La

Shingkhor

Thrumshing La
National Park

Phrumsengla
National Park

Tongtongphey

Sengor

Bridung
La

Yong
Khola

ngbi

ra

MONGAR

Zhemgang

Nimgong

shong

Tingtibi

TRASHIGANG

Gonphu

ZHEMGANG

Pemagatshel

PEMAGATSHEL

Royal Manas
National Park

Tunka La

SAMDRUP
JONGKHAR

Pieksao

Changzam

Sufali

Panbang

Samdrup
Jongkhar

Kanamakra

Nganglam

Manas
Camp

INDIA
(ASSAM)

Mathanguri
(Assam)

0   20 km
0   10 miles

Plan Your Time

Don't miss Trongsa's powerful dzong and museum. Stretch your legs on one of several hikes to take in the scenery and history of Bumthang. Or, head south into a green world inhabited by golden langurs and regal hornbills.

Trongsa Dzong (p144)

Two Days in Central Bhutan

● You've scrambled up to Taktshang and explored Thimphu and now you only have a couple of days in central Bhutan. Start by discovering the courtyards and ancient lhakhangs (temples) of **Trongsa Dzong** (p144). Next is the **Tower of Trongsa** (p146), the erstwhile *ta dzong* (watchtower), housing an excellent museum dedicated to Bhutan's monarchy, as well as a cafe and souvenir shop.

● From Trongsa head to **Jakar** (p151), the administrative centre of Bumthang, where you should visit the impressive **Jakar Dzong** (p151) and **Wangdichholing Palace** (p150), and a select few of the region's many temples and monasteries. Additionally, take it easy in one of the luxurious resorts, learn archery and sample rustic Bumthang cuisine.

Seasonal Highlights

Autumn (September to November) hosts the best weather and most festivals. Spring (March to May) is best for bird- and wildlife-watching in the southern *dzongkhags* (administrative districts).

FEBRUARY

Bhutanese celebrate the new year, Losar, between mid-January and March. Nangsiphel, Upper Bumthang, hosts the annual **Nomads' Festival** (p158).

APRIL

Warming weather stirs the magnificent rhododendrons into flowering, while down south **golden langurs** (p163) and hornbills nurture their next generation.

MAY

Warmth, more rain and peak rhododendron flowering. Mountain views are fleeting, tourists are scarce. Ura hosts its **Yachoe Festival** (p161).

CAVAN IMAGES/ALAMY STOCK PHOTO ©, WATHANYUSOWONG/SHUTTERSTOCK ©, SOUMITRA PENDSE/SHUTTERSTOCK ©

Four Days to Travel Around

● Make **Jakar** (p151) your base to further explore the Chokhor valley with its rich history and Buddhist tradition. If you time it right, experience a mysterious and colourful masked dance at an annual tsechu (dance festival). Consider hiring a bike to tackle the roads and farm tracks and pack lunch as there are many riverside locations perfect for a picnic.

● Spend a day hiking from the **Chokhor valley** (p151) to the **Tang valley** (p158), where you can stay overnight in a grand country manor at **Ogyen Chholing** (p159). Further hikes are possible to remote monasteries, beneath whispering blue pines and alongside mountain streams.

If You Have More Time

● From **Trongsa** (p142), head south via the atmospheric **Kuenga Rabten** (p163) and ancient **Yundrung Chholing** (p163) to **Zhemgang** (p164), where you can wander through a little-changed medieval village and a 12th-century dzong. From here roads lead south to the warm climes and bird-filled jungles of **Royal Manas National Park** (p165) and the border town of **Gelephu** (p165).

● Dedicate a few days to the valleys of **Bumthang** (p157), where you can stretch your legs on numerous day hikes, explore Buddhist temples, hunt for souvenirs and taste the offerings of Jakar's **Swiss Farm** (p153). In Tang valley, visit eerie **Membartsho** (p159), the 'Burning Lake' where Pema Lingpa performed miracles.

JUNE	**SEPTEMBER**	**OCTOBER**	**DECEMBER**
Monsoon rains disrupt flight schedules and roads. In Bumthang, the **Nimalung tsechu** (p158) is followed by the one-day **Kurjey tsechu** (p151).	As the rainy season recedes and the skies clear, Bumthang hosts the **Tamshing Phala Choepa** (p158) and the **Thangbi Mani Festival** (p154).	Peak tourist season heralds more festivals in Bumthang: the **Jakar tsechu** (p151), the **Jampey Lhakhang Drup** (p151) and the Prakhar tsechu.	The cold begins to bite and snow can block passes, while down in Trongsa a three-day tsechu sees very few tourists.

TRONGSA

THIMPHU ✪   ● Trongsa

Trongsa town, centred on its impressive, strategically positioned dzong, is smack in the middle of the country, at the junction of the main roads to Punakha, Bumthang and Gelephu. Trongsa Dzongkhag, the region governed by Trongsa Dzong, with its links to the royal Wangchuck dynasty, covers an area of 1810 sq km. The steep and heavily forested countryside ranges from below 1000m to over 5000m, and encompasses the diverse Jigme Singye Wangchuck National Park.

Trongsa is a sleepy and pleasant town, lined with traditional whitewashed shops decorated with pot plants and prayer wheels. The town received a large influx of Tibetan immigrants in the late 1950s and early 1960s, and Bhutanese of Tibetan descent run most of the shops here. Most visitors limit themselves to a stop in Trongsa en route to Bumthang, while a few will head south towards Zhemgang, Gelephu and Royal Manas National Park.

TOP TIP

The route between the windswept town of Wangdi (Wangdue Phodrang's colloquial name), in western Bhutan, and Trongsa crosses the Black Mountains over the Pele La (3420m) before entering the broad, heavily cultivated Mangde Chhu valley. The area near Pele La is one place you might see grazing yaks from the road.

DAVE G. HOUSER/ALAMY STOCK PHOTO ©

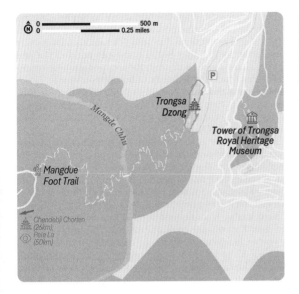

MANGDUE FOOT TRAIL

From the viewpoint and eponymous cafe there's a walking trail inviting fit and adventurous types to hike to the dzong along the Mangdue Foot Trail. This is a short but tough two-hour track that drops steeply down to a traditional *baa zam* (cantilevered bridge) over the Mangde Chhu before ascending equally steeply to the western or southern door of the dzong. The western door is often closed, and it may be hard for someone to hear your frantic knocking. Head south where the southern door (and public toilets) are usually open. Your driver will drive ahead to the dzong and should ensure one of the doors is unlocked for your arrival.

A Challenging Hike: Curious Chendebji Chorten

PELE LA TO TRONGSA

It takes about two hours or less to drive the 68km to Trongsa from Pele La. The road weaves and drops through a landscape carpeted with a strange dwarf bamboo called *cham*. This bamboo never gets large enough to harvest for any useful purpose, but its young shoots are a favourite food of grazing yaks and horses. A further descent takes you into the evergreen forests of the Longte valley, passing below the village of **Longte**.

For those wanting to stretch their legs, an easy 30-minute hike follows an ancient trail from the pass down to Longte. A longer and more interesting trail climbs from behind Longte through thick forest and over a pass to drop into the Phobjikha valley near Khumbhu Lhakhang (four hours). These and other walks can be done with your guide while your driver waits at a prearranged pick-up point.

The road passes **Rukubji** village at the end of a huge alluvial fan believed to represent the body of a giant snake. Surrounding the village, a cluster of houses and a monastery are extensive fields of mustard, potato, barley and wheat.

 WHERE TO EAT BETWEEN PELE LA & TRONGSA —————————

Tushita Café
About 9km from east of Pele La, this cosy cafe offers fine valley views and makes a worthy lunch stop. **$**

Norbu Yangphel Hotel
Roadside hotel in Sephu offering a decent lunch stop and a chance to sample *juru jaju* (river moss soup). **$**

Willing Waterfall Café
Great coffee and food, superb setting, with magical evening meals by a firepit with a floodlit waterfall. **$$**

AN EXCURSION FROM TRONGSA

If you have a spare half-day in Trongsa or really want to get off the beaten track, consider driving and then hiking up to **Taphey Goemba**, a meditation retreat north of Trongsa. It was built by the first king of Bhutan around the meditation site of 18th-century practitioner Ngawang Tsamphel.

From Trongsa take a farm road north to Yuling village to visit its surprisingly ornate lhakhang, then backtrack to take a road up to the car park, a 30-minute hike below Taphey Goemba. A further hour's hike uphill from the goemba takes you to Singye Tang, on the ridgeline, for fine Himalayan views north all the way to Gangkhar Puensum (7570m).

Entering a side valley, the road drops to **Sephu** (2610m), also known as Chazam, next to a bridge spanning the Nikka Chhu. Local artisans produce and sell bamboo baskets here beside the road. Upper Sephu is the end point of the epic 24-day Snowman trek through the remote Lunana district.

The road follows the Nikka Chhu to two chortens (stone monuments) that mark the river's confluence with the Nyala Chhu. It is then a gentle, winding descent to the village of **Chendebji**, recognisable by a cluster of traditional houses and a yellow roof lhakhang.

Two kilometres beyond Chendebji village is **Chendebji Chorten**, at an auspicious river confluence and a great place for a picnic lunch. The large white chorten is patterned after Swayambhunath in Kathmandu and was built in the 19th century by Lama Shida, from Tibet, to cover the remains of an evil spirit. The proper name of this structure is Chorten Charo Kasho; it is the westernmost monument in a 'chorten path' that was the route of early Buddhist missionaries.

From Chendebji Chorten the road turns into the broad Mangde Chhu valley. At Tashiling village, the **Tashichholing Lhakhang** is home to the Gayrab Arts & Crafts Training Institute. Inside is an impressive 9m-tall statue of Chaktong Chentong, a 1001-armed version of Chenresig (Avalokiteshvara, the Bodhisattva of Compassion).

Passing the 720MW Mangdechhu hydroelectric dam and power station, you eventually get a view of Trongsa and its imposing whitewashed dzong that appears to be suspended at the head of the valley. A **viewpoint** next to a small chorten in the centre of the road offers a great place for a photo stop (evening light is best) and a cup of tea. The dzong looks almost close enough to touch but it is still a 14km drive away!

To reach Trongsa, detour into the upper reaches of the Mangde Chhu, cross the often-raging river at the Bjee Zam, passing an attractive waterfall and a highly recommended cafe, before pulling into town.

A Majestic & Strategic Dzong

UNIFYING POWER OF ARCHITECTURE

The imposing **Trongsa Dzong**, perched high above the roaring Mangde Chhu and encircled by the brooding Black Mountains, is perhaps the most spectacularly sited dzong in Bhutan. The rambling assemblage trails down the ridge and is connected by a succession of alley-like corridors, wide stone stairs and beautiful paved courtyards. The southernmost part of the dzong, **Chorten Lhakhang**, is the location of the first hermitage, built in 1543.

🛏 WHERE TO STAY IN TRONGSA

Yangkhil Resort
Quality rooms on garden terraces facing the dzong. Cosy rooms have comfortable beds and balconies. **$$**

Tashi Ninjey Hotel
It's the only tourist-grade hotel in the town itself. The views of the Trongsa Dzong are superb. **$$**

Willing Resort
Out of town, with a bird's-eye view of the dzong, this five-star hotel sports luxurious rooms and dining venues. **$$$**

Chendebji Chorten

Construction was initiated by Ngagi Wangchuck (1517–54), the great-grandfather of Zhabdrung Ngawang Namgyal. He came to Trongsa in 1541 and built a *tshamkhang* (small meditation room) after discovering self-manifested hoof prints belonging to the horse of the protector deity Pelden Lhamo. Trongsa ('New Village' in the local dialect) gets its name from the retreats, temples and hermit residences that grew up around the chapel.

The dzong was built in its present form in 1644 by Chhogyel Mingyur Tenpa, the official who was sent by the Zhabdrung to bring eastern Bhutan under central control. It was enlarged at the end of the 17th century by the *desi* (secular ruler), Tenzin Rabgye. The dzong was severely damaged in the 1897 earthquake, and repairs were carried out by the *penlop* (governor) of Trongsa, Jigme Namgyal, father of Bhutan's first king.

Trongsa Dzong is closely connected to the royal family. The first two hereditary kings ruled from this dzong, and tradition still dictates that the crown prince serve as Trongsa *penlop* before acceding to the throne.

The dzong's strategic location gave it great power over this part of the country. The original trail between eastern and western Bhutan used to run directly through the dzong itself.

INSIDE TRONGSA DZONG

The dzong's official name is Chhoekhor Raptentse Dzong, and it is also known by its short name of Choetse Dzong. There are 23 separate lhakhangs in the dzong, though what you get to see depends on which keys are available. Most of the existing fine decoration was designed during the rule of the first king, Ugyen Wangchuck.

Rooms to visit include the atmospheric northern *kunrey* (assembly hall) and the impressive **Jampa Lhakhang** next door, with a two-storey Maitreya (Jampa) statue. The southern **Mithrub Lhakhang** houses the funerary chorten of Ngagi Wangchuck. Feel for the footprints worn into the wooden floor by one overly enthusiastic prostrator.

 WHERE TO STAY & EAT IN TRONGSA

Norbu Linka Resort
Enormous hotel with valley, rather than dzong, views. Rooms are arranged in a separate block to amenities. **$$**

Tendrel Resort
Out of town, and out of sight of the dzong, but with decent rooms and a pleasant dining room and bar. **$$**

Norling Hotel
This concrete local inn in the bazaar has a back restaurant that's a decent place for a local lunch. **$**

"XPY/GETTY IMAGES ©

TRONGSA TSECHU & MONK MIGRATION

One of the oldest, yet least visited festivals, in Bhutan is the three-day Trongsa Tsechu. It runs from the ninth to the 11th day of the 11th lunar month, so it can fall in December or January. The vibrant and animated masked dances in honour of Guru Rinpoche are held in the narrow, northern courtyard of the Trongsa Dzong. The festival culminates in the unveiling of a *thondrol* (a giant *thangka* – a painted or embroidered religious picture) depicting the eight manifestations of Guru Rinpoche.

The Trongsa *rabdey* (district monk body) migrates in colourful fashion, these days using cars and buses, between winter (Trongsa) and summer (Bumthang) residences, just as the main *dratshang* (central monk body) does between Thimphu and Punakha.

Tower of Trongsa Royal Heritage Museum

An Eclectic Museum of Druk Monarchy

ROYAL AND SACRED TREASURES

The watchtower *(ta dzong)* overlooking Trongsa Dzong houses the excellent **Tower of Trongsa Royal Heritage Museum**. The five floors of displays tell the history of the monarchy through such varied treasures as the 500-year-old jacket of Ngagi Wangchuk, the second king's saddle and a copy of the famous raven crown.

As you ascend the floors look for the radio given by American Burt Todd, a friend of the third king who visited Bhutan in the 1950s (the first American to do so) and set up Bhutan's postal system. Other treasures include a fine photo of the kings of Bhutan and Sikkim in Kolkata (Calcutta) in 1905, and a beautiful 1926 document declaring an oath of allegiance to the monarchy.

The most sacred religious item is a copy of the *Padma Kathang,* Guru Rinpoche's biography discovered by Pema Lingpa underneath the Jokhang Temple in Lhasa. There are two lhakhangs inside the *ta dzong;* the top-floor Gesar Lhakhang is dedicated to the 19th-century *penlop* of Trongsa, Jigme Namgyal.

There are sweeping views from the roof, plus a souvenir shop and a ground-floor cafe providing refreshments.

GETTING AROUND

It's easy and pleasant to walk around Trongsa – especially if you start high and finish low! After you have visited the Tower of Trongsa follow the stone staircase down to the road. Continue through Trongsa town checking out the local shops, including the Lemo Yoezer Bakery and the vegetable market, before descending all the way to the magnificent dzong.

BUMTHANG

THIMPHU ✪   ● Bumthang

The Bumthang region encompasses four major valleys: Chhume, Chokhor, Tang and Ura. Because the dzongs and the most important temples are in the large Chokhor valley, it is commonly referred to as the Bumthang valley.

There are two versions of the origin of the name Bumthang. The valley is supposed to be shaped like a *bumpa,* the vessel of holy water that is usually found on the altar of a lhakhang. *Thang* means 'field' or 'flat place'. The less respectful translation relates to the particularly beautiful women who live here – *bum* means 'girl'.

Jakar (Chamkhar) is the major trading centre and town of the Bumthang region. Well serviced with resorts and hotels, this will most likely be your base for several days as you visit the surrounding valleys. There is a strong up-valley wind from the south every afternoon, which makes Jakar nippy in the evenings.

TOP TIP

The 68km run between Trongsa and Jakar, the main town in Bumthang, is one of the easier and more interesting drives in Bhutan because it passes numerous villages and goembas as it winds through the Chhume valley. With stops you could easily fill an entire day on this lovely drive.

RICHARD I'ANSON/GETTY IMAGES ©

Jakar (p151)   147

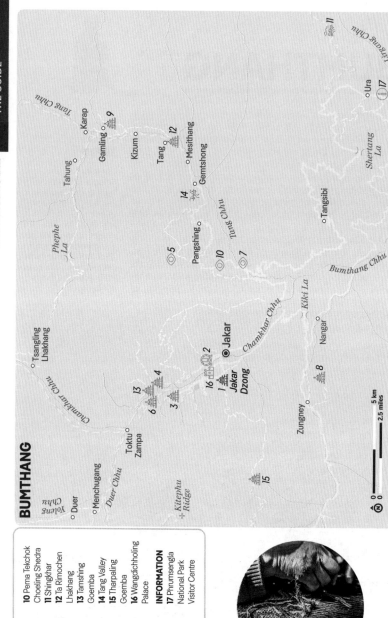

BUMTHANG

HIGHLIGHTS
1 Jakar Dzong

SIGHTS
2 Bumthang Brewery
3 Jampey Lhakhang
4 Konchogsum Lhakhang
5 Kunzendrak Goemba
6 Kurjey Lhakhang
7 Membartsho
8 Nimalung Goemba
9 Ogyen Chholing

10 Pema Tekchok Choeling Shedra
11 Shingkhar
12 Ta Rimochen Lhakhang
13 Tamshing Goemba
14 Tang Valley
15 Tharpaling Goemba
16 Wangdichholing Palace

INFORMATION
17 Phrumsengla National Park Visitor Centre

Weaving *yathra*

Chorten, Yotong La

Buddhist Buildings & Textile Tradition

TRONGSA TO JAKAR

Leaving Trongsa the highway zigzags steeply up a ridge to reach a chorten and an array of prayer flags indicating the **Yotong La** (3425m). The old trade route to eastern Bhutan parallels the modern road as it crosses the pass.

Over the pass you enter the **Chhume valley** at Gaytsa (Gyatsa). On a hill a few hundred metres to the north of Gaytsa is **Buli Lhakhang**, built by Tukse Chhoying, the son of Dorji Lingpa (1346–1405) and renovated with assistance from the American Himalayan Foundation. The three-day Buli tsechu in February kicks off with an evening *mewang* (fire ceremony) that dates back to pre-Buddhist times.

The large **Tharpaling Goemba**, visible on a cliff to the northeast of Buli, was founded by the Tibetan Nyingma (Dzogchen) philosopher and saint Longchen Rabjampa (1308–63). The goemba has several temples and more than 100 monks. It's possible to visit here by driving 10km up a sealed road or by trekking over the hill from Jakar. Above Tharpaling, at about 3800m, is the hermitage of **Choedrak**, and further uphill is the **Zhambhala Lhakhang**, named after the popular god of wealth, where pilgrims ask for boons.

YATHRA

Hand-spun, hand-woven woollen cloth with patterns specific to Bumthang are called *yathra*. They mostly have geometric designs, sometimes with a border. Three strips may be joined to produce a blanket-like rain cover called a *charkep*.

In earlier days *yathra* were often used as shawls or raincoats to protect against the winter cold. They were once made from wool from Tibet; nowadays some of the wool is imported from New Zealand, while most is sourced locally.

Since Bhutan does not have the carpet-weaving tradition of Tibet, *yathra* pieces have often served as rugs. Today a *yathra* is fashioned into a *toego*, the short jackets that women often wear over the *kira* (women's traditional dress) in cold weather.

🛏 WHERE TO STAY BETWEEN TRONGSA & JAKAR

Chumey Nature Resort
Peaceful, luxurious retreat surrounded by fields, trails and pine forests. Organic food and Buddhism courses. **$$**

Valley Resort
Rooms boast an enclosed balcony and clean spring water piped to the bathroom. **$$**

Hotel Jakar View
This brightly painted hotel has 15 traditionally decorated rooms, a cosy dining room and a terrace with a firepit. **$$**

WANGDICHHOLING PALACE

The palace of Wangdichholing was built in 1857 on the battle-camp site of the *penlop* of Trongsa, Jigme Namgyal. It was the first palace in Bhutan that wasn't designed primarily as a fortress. Namgyal's son, King Ugyen Wangchuck, the first king of Bhutan, was born in Wangdichholing and chose it as his principal residence. The entire court moved from here to Kuenga Rabten each winter in a procession that took three days. Wangdichholing was also for a time the home of the third king, before he moved the royal court to Punakha in 1952.

The sizeable building has been used as a *lobra* (monastic school) in recent times; however, the restored edifice now houses a cultural museum.

Jakar Dzong

At Yamthrak, a paved road branches off 3.5km to **Nimalung Goemba**, an important Nyingma monastery founded in 1935. A 15-minute walking trail leads downhill through whispering pines from a line of eight stupas below the main chapel to **Prakhar Lhakhang**. Another two minutes' walk, across a small suspension bridge, brings you to the highway, and hopefully your waiting car.

Back on the main road, a short 500m walk from the Yamthrak junction leads to the **Chorten Nyingpo Lhakhang**, a 16th-century chapel whose main relic is a statue of the Zhabdrung's father, Tenpa Nyima (1567–1619). In the grounds look for the white throne from which Tenpa is said to have preached for three years.

Five minutes further on, stop at the **Druk Yathra** craft shop at Zungney village to watch weavers and dyers in action and browse the souvenirs. Adjacent to the shop is the tiny **Zungney Lhakhang**, said by locals to have been built by Tibetan king Songtsen Gampo.

The highway follows the valley and continues directly to Ura, while the road to Jakar turns off and climbs to Kiki La, a crest at 2860m. Once over the ridge, the road descends into the Chokhor valley.

 WHERE TO STAY SOUTH OF JAKAR

Yozerling Lodge
Family-run place 2.5km from town. Pine-clad deluxe rooms have a *bukhari* (wood stove) and an electric heater. **$$**

Wangdicholing Resort
This well-run resort with reputable dining is on a bluff overlooking the Chokhor valley. **$$**

Yu-Gharling Resort
This bold, traditional-style hotel overlooking the valley is almost as luxurious as it is enormous. **$$**

The Heart & Soul of Bhutan

JAKAR – HUB OF BUMTHANG

Jakar (Chamkhar) is a bustling town at the foot of the impressive Jakar Dzong. Most of the shopfronts are relatively new, having been rebuilt after fires that destroyed much of the town in 2010. Many of the businesses, those in the temporary-looking single-storey buildings, are in the process of shifting to **Dekyiling**, just 1.5km north.

The impressive **Jakar Dzong** commands views over much of the Chokhor valley from its ridgetop position. The current structure was built in 1667. Its official name is Yuelay Namgyal Dzong, in honour of the victory over Tibetan ruler Phuntsho Namgyal's troops. An unusual feature here is that the *utse* (central tower) is situated on an outside wall, so there is no way to circumambulate it.

According to legend, when the lamas assembled in about 1549 to select a site for a monastery, a big white bird rose suddenly in the air and settled on a spur of a hill. This was interpreted as an important omen, and the hill was chosen. Jakar Dzong roughly translates as 'castle of the white bird'.

The main entrance leads into a narrow courtyard surrounded by administrative offices. The *utse* is on the east side of the courtyard, and beyond that is the monks' quarters. At the west end of the dzong is a slightly larger courtyard, also surrounded by administrative offices. Behind here is a half-round *ta dzong*. A walled passage leads down the hill to a nearby spring – a feature that ensured water could be obtained in the event of a long siege. The three-day **Jakar tsechu** takes place in October or November

Legacies of Guru Rinpoche

WESTERN SIDE OF CHOKHOR VALLEY

The road that leads up the western side of the valley connects a string of interesting temples, which are connected in one way or another to the visit of Guru Rinpoche to Bumthang in 746. Mountain biking is a great way to link up the monasteries and continue over to the east bank. You can walk, drive or ride from Jampey Lhakhang over Do Zam's road or suspension bridge.

Jampey Lhakhang

Jampey Lhakhang is believed to have been built in 659 by the Tibetan king Songtsen Gampo, on the same day as Kyichu Lhakhang in Paro, to subdue a Tibetan demoness (this temple is said to pin her left knee). The temple was visited by Guru

---

MAJOR FESTIVALS OF THE CHOKHOR VALLEY

Jampey Lhakhang Drup
From the 15th to the 18th of the ninth lunar month (October or November), one of the most spectacular festivals in Bhutan, the Jampey Lhakhang Drup, is staged outside the Jampey Lhakhang. After the masked lama dances, the lhakhang hosts a *mewang* (fire blessing connected to fertility rites), when pilgrims jump through a burning archway. Another late-night rite is the naked *tercham* (treasure dance), usually performed at midnight.

Kurjey Tsechu
The popular Kurjey tsechu is held in June and includes a masked dance that dramatises Guru Rinpoche's defeat of Shelging Kharpo. A *thondrol*, called Guru Tshengye Thondrol, depicting the eight manifestations of Guru Rinpoche, is unfurled in the early morning before the dances, which are performed by the monks from Trongsa.

 WHERE TO STAY IN JAKAR

Jakar Village Lodge
Below the dzong, with spotless rooms and some of the best local and international food in Bumthang. **$$**

Swiss Guesthouse
Bucolic and historic guesthouse with great food and hospitality, surrounded by orchards and overlooking the valley. **$$**

Kaila Guesthouse
A genuinely welcoming option featuring a sunny courtyard and a wing of rooms boasting sumptuous Tibetan carpets. **$$**

HIKING IN THE CHOKHOR VALLEY

Road and bridge construction means it's possible to drive all the way to Ngang Lhakhang, but it's a much nicer walk (of about two hours) from Thangbi Goemba along the true left bank of the river. Walk along the road to a small *khonying* (traditional stupa-style gateway), visit the nearby rock painting and traditional water mill and then cross the bridge over the Chamkhar Chhu at Kharsa. You can detour to explore the 17th-century ruins of Draphe Dzong, a 30-minute walk from Ngang Lhakhang. There's also a half-day hike to Luege Rowe from Thangbi. A long day hike over the Phephe La to Ogyen Chholing Manor in the Tang valley also begins here, on what is called the Bumthang Cultural Trek (p211).

Rinpoche and was renovated by the Sindhu Raja. It's the one place in the valley that feels truly ancient.

Inside the main Jampey (Jampa) Lhakhang are three stone steps representing three ages. The first signifies the past, the age of the historical Buddha, Sakyamuni. This step has descended into the ground and is covered with a wooden plank. The next age is the present, and its step is level with the floor. The top step represents a new age. It is believed that when the step representing the present age sinks to ground level, the gods will become like humans and the world as it is now will end.

The central figure in the ancient inner sanctum is Jampa, the Buddha of the future, with his feet on an elephant. This is the oldest part of the oldest chapel in Bhutan. The entry to the chapel is protected by iron chain mail made by Pema Lingpa. Look up into the alcove above the entry to see a statue of Guru Rinpoche. He sat in this alcove and meditated, leaving behind a footprint. It is said that under the lhakhang there is a lake with several *terma* – sacred texts and artefacts hidden by Guru Rinpoche.

The inner *kora* (circumambulation) path around the chapel is lined with ancient murals depicting 1000 Buddhas. On the right side of the wooden wall divider is an image of Kimlha, the goddess of the home.

On the northern side of the *dochey* (courtyard) lies the **Kalachakra Temple** (Dukhor Lhakhang). The animal-headed deities on the walls are the demons that confront the dead during the 49 days of *bardo* (the state between death and rebirth). The **Guru Lhakhang** on the south side of the courtyard features statues of Guru Rinpoche, Tsepame and Chenresig.

Kurjey Lhakhang

To the north of Jampey is Kurjey Lhakhang, an active and important temple complex named after the body *(kur)* print *(jey)* of Guru Rinpoche.

The **Guru Lhakhang** is the oldest of the three temples at Kurjey Lhakhang and was built in 1652 by Mingyur Tenpa when he was *penlop* of Trongsa. Tucked just below the eaves is a figure of a snow lion with a *jachung* (also called *garuda*) above it, which represents the famous struggle between Guru Rinpoche (appearing as the *jachung*) and the local demon, Shelging Kharpo (as the snow lion).

At the entrance to the lower-floor **Sangay Lhakhang** is a small rock passage; Bhutanese believe that in crawling through this narrow tunnel you will leave your sins behind. The upper-floor sanctuary is the holiest in the complex. There are 1000

🛏 **WHERE TO STAY IN JAKAR**

Gongkhar Hotel
The excellent Gongkhar boasts great food, spacious rooms with *bukharis* and views of the dzong. **$$**

River Lodge
Overlooking the valley, this lodge offers a spa with hot-stone bath, organic food and homemade jam. **$$**

Tashi Yoezerling Guesthouse
On the hill overlooking town with a cosy wood-lined dining room with a wood-fired heater. **$$**

CYRILLE REDON/SHUTTERSTOCK ©

Jampey Lhakhang (p151)

small statues of Guru Rinpoche neatly lined up, plus statues of Pema Lingpa and Drolma (Tara). The main statue in this sanctuary is again of Guru Rinpoche, flanked by his eight manifestations and eight chortens. Hidden behind this image is the **meditation cave**, where he left his body imprint. The far wall has images of Guru Rinpoche, his manifestations, his 25 disciples and various other figures connected with the Guru.

Ugyen Wangchuck, the first king of Bhutan, built the second temple, the **Sampa Lhundrup Lhakhang**, in 1900, when he was *penlop* of Trongsa. At the entrance are paintings of the Guardians of the Four Directions and of various local deities who were converted to Buddhism by Guru Rinpoche. The white ghostlike figure on the white horse above the doorway to the right is Shelging Kharpo; also here are local protectors Yakdu Nagpo (on a black yak) and Kyebu Lungten (on a red horse). Inside the temple is a towering 10m statue of Guru Rinpoche. A smaller image of the Guru sits facing towards Tibet with a defiant stare.

The third building in the complex was built by Ashi Kesang Wangchuck, queen to the third king, in 1984 under the guidance of Dilgo Khyentse Rinpoche. Interior murals illustrate various monastic rules and regulations, including strict dress codes.

BUMTHANG'S FAMOUS SWISS FARM

A mature development project established in 1969 by Fritz Maurer, the Swiss Farm introduced cheesemaking, brewing, European honeybees, farming machinery and fuel-efficient wood stoves to Bhutan. It also operated the country's first tourist guesthouse.

An outstanding legacy of the project is Bhutan's celebrated beer, Red Panda. It's possible to tour the state-of-the-art **Bumthang Brewery**, where you will learn about the brewing of the Swiss-style unfiltered weiss beer, before sampling the product in the adjacent **Panda Beer Garden Cafe**. The brewery tour price includes one bottle of Red Panda beer. To purchase locally made Swiss-style cheese and beer for a top-notch Bumthang picnic, head to the nearby **Yoser Lhamo Shop**.

Mountain Resort
This stylish hotel has modern interpretations of traditional stone and wood. Rooms are mini suites. **$$**

Hotel Ugyen Ling
Owned by one of Bhutan's biggest travel agencies. Above-average accommodation and a multicuisine restaurant. **$$**

Rinchenling Lodge
Spacious rooms, an excellent restaurant and a hot-stone bath are features of this family-run lodge. **$$**

EATING OUT IN JAKAR

If you stay in Jakar for more than one night you may get the opportunity to venture away from your hotel dining room and the buffet meal, either to a local restaurant or another hotel. Ask about sampling local specialities such as *puta* (buckwheat noodles) and *khule* (buckwheat pancakes).

Bumthang's rivers are famed for their trout and, despite Buddhist prohibitions on the taking of life, fresh fish occasionally appears on hotel dinner plates. You will also find small shops offering pizza and espresso coffee in the bazaar. A further possible option is to book a romantic meal at one of the five-star resorts.

MORTEN FALCH SORTLAND/GETTY IMAGES ©

Tamshing Goemba

Thangbi Goemba

Thangbi Goemba, 3.5km north of Kurjey Lhakhang, was founded in 1470 by Shamar Rinpoche and, after a dispute, was taken over by Pema Lingpa. The main chapel of the Dusum Sangay (past, present and future Buddhas) is entered under another of Pema Lingpa's famous chain mails. *Gomchen* (lay or married monks) attend here, celebrating a *mani* (prayer) festival and fire ceremony in the middle of the eighth lunar month (October).

Ngang-yul

A bumpy 10km drive up the Chokhor valley from Thangbi Goemba is the small region known as Ngang-yul (Swan Land). The site was visited by Guru Rinpoche, although the present **Ngang Lhakhang** was built in the 15th century by Lama Namkha Samdrup, a contemporary of Pema Lingpa. The interior contains some lovely statues and paintings. The primary statue is of Guru Rinpoche, flanked by early Buddhist missionary Shantarakshita and Tibetan king Trisong Detsen. The upper *goenkhang* (chapel dedicated to protective deities) features statues of the 'Tsela Nam Sum' trinity of Tsepame, Namse and Drolma, with Chenresig standing to the left. The statue of Guru Rinpoche to the right was fashioned by Pema

BUMTHANG CULTURAL TREK

The **Bumthang Cultural Trek** (p211) can be done in a single day, hiking from the Chokhor valley to the Tang valley, or you can make it a two-day camping trek.

WHERE TO EAT IN JAKAR

Panda Beer Garden Cafe
Adjacent to the Bumthang Brewery, this cosy cafe serves excellent pizzas, Swiss-style fondue, cakes and espresso. **$$**

Café Perk
Espresso, cakes, milkshakes and masala chai. Menu includes pancakes, pasta and grilled sandwiches with fries. **$$**

Bumthang Pizza
Local pizza joint with veg and non-veg pizzas plus a bar. Bhutanese varieties include beef and mushroom. **$**

Lingpa himself. Protector deities lurk in the shadows. Hanging from the rafters are masks used in the three-day **Ngang Bi Rabney**, a festival organised in the middle of the 10th month (December).

Relics of Pema Lingpa

EASTERN SIDE OF CHOKHOR VALLEY

One way to visit the eastern side of the Chokhor valley is to walk a couple of hundred metres north from Kurjey Lhakhang, then follow a path east to cross a prayer-flag-strewn footbridge. Note, however, that the road bridge and associated road widening has impacted this walk. From the bridge you can see a natural rock formation named **Do Zam**, said to be the remains of a stone bridge that was built by a goddess trying to meet Guru Rinpoche, but destroyed by a demon.

The major influence in the temples on this side of the valley was Pema Lingpa, the great *terton* (discoverer of *terma*) of the 16th century.

Tamshing Goemba

Formally the Tamshing Lhendup Chholing (Temple of the Good Message), Tamshing Goemba was established in 1501 by Pema Lingpa and is the most important Nyingma goemba in the kingdom. Pema Lingpa built the unusual structure himself, with the help of *khandromas* (female celestial beings), who, it is claimed, made many of the statues. On the inner walls are what are believed to be original unrestored images that were painted by Pema Lingpa, though there are even older paintings underneath.

The entrance to the lhakhang is via a courtyard lined with monks' quarters. Upon entering the inner courtyard, directly in front is the small **Mani Dungkhor Lhakhang**, built in 1914 to hold a huge prayer wheel. Those allergic to bees be warned that an active hive has occupied the courtyard for a few years.

The main lhakhang, to your right, has an unusual design, with the key chapel screened off in the centre of the assembly hall, almost like a separate building. In the chapel are three thrones for the three incarnations (body, mind and speech) of Pema Lingpa. During important ceremonies the reincarnations sit here, although a photograph is substituted if one of the incarnations is not present.

The primary statue in the inner sanctuary is of Guru Rinpoche flanked by Jampa (Maitreya, the Buddha of the future) and Sakyamuni. This statue is particularly important because

PEMA LINGPA'S MIRACLES

The first *terma* took place when a dream told Pema Lingpa to go to where the river forms a large pool that looks like a lake. There, he saw a temple with many doors, only one of which was open. He plunged naked into the lake and entered a large cave where there was a throne, upon which sat a life-size statue of Lord Buddha and many large boxes. An old woman with one eye handed him a chest and he suddenly found himself standing at the side of the lake holding the treasure.

His second find was the most famous. When he returned to the lake, many people gathered to watch and the district's sceptical *penlop* accused him of trickery. Pema Lingpa took a lamp and proclaimed: 'If I am a genuine revealer of your treasures, then may I return with it now, with my lamp still burning; if I am some devil, then may I perish in the water'. He jumped in and was gone long enough that the sceptics thought they'd been proven right, until he re-emerged with the lamp still burning and holding treasure. The lake became known as Membartsho (Burning Lake).

OTHER LHAKHANGS OF CHOKHOR VALLEY

Sey Lhakhang
A monastic school established in 1963, also known as Lhodrak Seykhar Dratshang.

Chakhar Lhakhang
On the site of the palace of the Indian king Sindhu Raja, who first invited Guru Rinpoche to Bumthang.

Zangto Pelri Lhakhang
A short distance south of the Kurjey Lhakhang compound. It features a 3D depiction of the paradise of Guru Rinpoche.

it was sculpted by the *khandromas*. The statue's eyes are looking slightly upward, following the angels in their flight; another unique aspect of the statue is that the Guru is not wearing shoes. Above the altar are two *maksaras* (mythological crocodiles) and a *garuda*. On the walls are the eight manifestations of Guru Rinpoche, four on each side.

The upper floor forms a balcony around the assembly hall. Pema Lingpa was a short man and it is said that he built the low ceiling of the balcony to his exact height. Around the outside are 100,000 paintings of Sakyamuni. In the upper chapel is a statue of Tsepame, the Buddha of Long Life, and a collection of masks. Also here, is a statue of Pema Lingpa in a glass case fashioned by the man himself.

At one side of the dimly lit inner *kora* path within Tamshing Goemba is a cloak of chain mail made by Pema Lingpa. It sits in an unlocked glass and wood cabinet against the wall. Attesting to his metallurgy skills, the beautiful links are polished, smooth and large, and the entire cloak weighs in at a hefty 25kg. If you can hoist it on to your shoulders it is an auspicious act to carry it around the *kora* three times, including prostrating before the chapel (three times!) and getting back on your feet.

Konchogsum Lhakhang

Just 400m south of Tamshing, the towering, recently constructed and brightly painted Konchogsum Lhakhang completely envelops the restored remains of the original temple. That much smaller temple, most of which dates from the 15th century, when Pema Lingpa restored it, was almost destroyed by a butter lamp fire in 2010. Parts of the original building probably date back to a Tibetan design from the 6th or 7th century.

The old lhakhang retains its central statue of Nampal Namse (Vairocana, one of the five Dhyani Buddhas). On Vairocana's right are Chenresig and Longchem Rabjampa (founder of Tharpaling Goemba). On Vairocana's left are statues of Guru Rinpoche and Pema Lingpa (said to be a reincarnation himself of Longchem Rabjampa). There is a pedestal in front of the old lhakhang that used to be outside, but has now been internalised within the soaring walls of the new lhakhang. Upon this pedestal sat a large and ancient bell. It is said that when this bell was rung it could be heard all the way to Lhasa, Tibet. The story goes that a 17th-century Tibetan army tried to steal the bell, but it was too heavy and they dropped it, cracking the bell. The fractured bell resides in the new Kudung Chorten Lhakhang in the upper level of the new building.

EXCURSION TO PEMA SAMBHAVA LHAKHANG

North of Tamshing, a short steep climb leads to the small Pema Sambhava Lhakhang. The original lhakhang was built in 1490 by Pema Lingpa around the cave where Guru Rinpoche meditated and assumed his manifestation of Padmasambhava. The lhakhang was expanded by Jigme Namgyal, the father of the first king, and restored in the early 1970s.

There are several rock paintings here, as well as a representation of the local protector Terda Norbu Zangpo, who lurks in a corner behind the door beside a leather whip, and the cave itself is painted in rainbow colours. Ask to see the main relic, a conch shell that is said to have flown here from Do Zam.

OTHER LHAKHANGS & GOEMBAS OF CHOKHOR VALLEY

Deothang Goemba (Dawathang Goemba)
Known as the Field of the Moon. It's just north of Kurjey Lhakhang and dates from 1949.

Luege Rowe
Little-visited lhakhang at the far northern end of the valley offers a fine half-day hike.

Shugdrak
A 10-minute hike and a series of ladders leads pilgrims to this sacred Guru Rinpoche cave and chapel.

STEVE ESTVANIK/SHUTTERSTOCK ©

Konchogsum Lhakhang

**Sherab Dema
Village Homestay**
Uphill, just behind
Jampey Lhakhang,
you'll find this
recommended
homestay where
you can experience
homegrown
hospitality, practise
archery and enjoy a
hot-stone bath. **$$**

Balakha Farmhouse
Located beside the
Ngang Lhakhang,
this rural homestay is
simple, but you'll get a
comfortable mattress
on the floor and a
shared organic meal
with the family. **$**

**Alpine Organic
Homestays**
The homestays
available in
the villages of
Nangsiphel,
Shabjithang and
Dorjung are simple
but offer a hot-stone
bath and are available
for booking during the
Nomads' Festival. **$**

Leki Guesthouse
Leki is one of the
oldest hotels in
the valley. Textile
buffs will enjoy the
traditional dyeing
demonstration. **$$**

The modern structure is truly magnificent. Massive, brightly painted columns soar to the mandala-painted ceiling. A perimeter mezzanine features seated statues of various (mind, body and spirit) reincarnations of Pema Lingpa, and virtually every surface has been decorated with intricate murals and designs. Either side of the lhakhang are monks' quarters, signifying that this place is developing, phoenix-like, into a vibrant centre of Buddhist learning.

Walking the Bumthang Valleys

OPPORTUNITIES TO STRETCH THE LEGS

There are plenty of opportunities for day hikes in Bumthang, most of which offer a wonderful combination of remote sacred sights, wide valley views and sublime picnic spots.

The half-day hike from the Swiss Guest House in Jakar to the large **Pelseling Goemba**, 'Lotus Grove' Monastery, is all uphill (2½ hours), gaining 800m, through a mix of forest, meadows and villages, and you are rewarded with great views. A road also winds up to the monastery, so you can get picked up. For a remoter hike, drive to Pelseling and then hike over the ridge and around a side valley to **Kunzangdrak Goemba** in the Tang valley. Arrange for your vehicle to pick you up there before visiting other sights in the valley.

 HOMESTAYS IN CHOKHOR VALLEY

Pema Lhazom Farmstay
In Chokhortoe village, north of
Ngala Lhakhang in Wangchuck
Centennial National Park. It
offers hikes and birdwatching. **$**

Dorjibi Homestay Lodge
Just north of Do Zam, east of
Bumthang Chhu, offers a little
extra comfort than a traditional
farmhouse. **$**

**Ngalhakhang Aj
Heritage Farmstay**
Adjacent to Ngala Lhakhang,
northeast of Kurjey Lhakhang.
Good base for valley treks. **$**

MORE FESTIVALS IN CHOKHOR VALLEY

Nimalung Tsechu
The three-day Nimalung tsechu in June (or July) is held at Nimalung Goemba.

Tamshing Phala Choepa
This three-day festival sees *cham* dances at Tamshing Goemba in the eighth lunar month (September or October), before they relocate to nearby Thangbi Goemba for another three days of festivities.

Ngang Bi Rabney
The three-day Ngang Bi Rabney at the Ngang Lhakhang, high up in the valley can fall in November or December.

Nomads' Festival
The annual two-day Nomads' Festival is held in Nangsiphel village on the third weekend in February and features a series of traditional sports such as shot put, wrestling, archery, tug-of-war and even pillow fighting on a pole, along with mask dances. Locals set up stalls selling everything from buckwheat products to fermented cheese.

Tsha tsha (clay offerings), Membartsho

A favourite one-way walk is from Lamey Goemba over the ridge to **Tharpaling Goemba** in the Chhume valley. The first two hours are a hard uphill slog through rhododendrons and bamboo, before you finally crest a pass and descend across the bare hillsides of the Chhume valley to the Zhambhala Lhakhang, Choedrak Hermitage and, finally, Tharpaling, and your waiting vehicle.

The Secluded & Spiritual Tang Valley

REMOTE AND MYSTERIOUS

Tang is the most isolated of Bumthang's valleys. It is higher than Chokhor so there's not as much agriculture here, although in places where the soil is fertile and deep the Arcadian scenes are picture-perfect.

From Jakar it's 11km to the road that branches north up the Tang valley. This road climbs past Membartsho (1.3km from the turnoff) and the **Pema Tekchok Choeling Shedra**, a large nunnery, to reach the turnoff to the jumping-off point for the hike to Kunzangdrak. After a short descent to the river, it's 3km to **Mesithang** and 1km further to the **Ta Rimochen Lhakhang**. The road passes a picnic spot (which doubles as an archery field!) before the bridge at **Kizum** (Ki

  WHERE TO STAY IN TANG VALLEY

Ogyen Chholing Heritage House
Traditional yet comfortable rooms: authenticity, creature comforts and excellent food. **$$**

Tshewwang Choden's Homestay
Traditional-style stay with authentic meals in Ogyen Chholing village. **$**

Sangay Dawa Homestay
In the village of Tandingang, known locally as Tahung. A short hike from Ogyen Chholing. **$**

LINDSAY FEGENT-BROWN/LONELY PLANET ©

Zam), 22km from the road junction. Across the bridge, a steep road winds up to the mansion and village of Ogyen Chholing.

Membartsho

A five-minute walk from a parking spot at a bend in the road leads to a picturesque pool in a shadowy ravine of the Tang Chhu that is known as Membartsho (Burning Lake; see p155). The 27-year-old Pema Lingpa found several of Guru Rinpoche's *terma* here. It's a lovely, if slightly unsettling, spot, where nature, religion and mythology blur into one.

A wooden bridge crosses the prayer-flag-strewn gorge and offers a good vantage point over the 'lake'. Only the enlightened will spot the temple that lurks in the inky depths. The sanctity of the site is made evident by the numerous small clay offerings called *tsha-tsha* piled up in various rock niches.

Under a rock shrine with a carving of Guru Rinpoche flanked by Sakyamuni and Pema Lingpa is a cave that virtuous people can crawl through, no matter how big they are. Beware: it's quite small, and very dusty. Also, don't venture too close to the edges of the ravine for that elusive photo angle. Vegetation hides where the rock ends and a treacherous drop into the river begins. Sadly, there have been several drownings in the swift waters here.

Ta Rimochen Lhakhang

Ta Rimochen Lhakhang was built by Pema Lingpa in the 14th century to mark a sacred place where Guru Rinpoche meditated. The original name 'Tag (Tak) Rimochen' (meaning 'an impression of tiger's stripes') is derived from the vertical yellow stripes that stain the dark rock cliff behind the building.

There are handprints and footprints of the Guru and his consort Yeshe Tshogyel on the cliff face, as well as several wish-fulfilling stones, sacred symbols and even an invisible doorway. There are more footprints at the top of the steps leading to the temple. Inside the main chapel, look for a depiction of local protector Lhamo Remaley.

The two huge rocks below the lhakhang represent male and female *jachung (garudas)*. By the road you can see the roadside bathing tub of the Guru and even the buttock marks of Yeshe handprints, worn into the rock during an epic bout of tantric lovemaking.

Ogyen Chholing

From Kizum bridge it's a 3km drive to **Ogyen Chholing Manor**. The 16th-century *naktshang* (temple dedicated to a warlord or protective deity) was built by Deb Tsokye Dorji, the one-time *penlop* of Trongsa and a descendant of the

KUNZENDRAK GOEMBA

A stiff 45-minute hike up the hillside above the nunnery leads to one of the most important sites related to Pema Lingpa. He began construction of the goemba in 1488, and many of his most important sacred relics are kept here.

Walk around the back of the **Wangkhang Lhakhang** to the gravity-defying **Khandroma Lhakhang**, the meditation cave of Yeshe Tshogyel, spectacularly situated against a vertical rock face that seeps holy water. Ask to see the woodblocks and stone anvil bearing the footprint of Pema Lingpa.

Figure on 2½ hours for the return trip. There is a very rough road to the goemba but this doesn't detract from the hike (the more comfortable option).

 WHERE TO STAY IN URA VALLEY

Ura Bangpa Farmhouse
This delightful home in Ura offers authentic accommodation and meals in a clean, friendly environment. **$**

Hotel Araya Zamlha
Beside the highway above Ura, this hotel has basic pine-panelled rooms with *bukhari* and private bathrooms. **$**

Shingkhar Naktshang Heritage Farmstay
Country manor with traditional rooms, local food and hikes in surrounding countryside. **$**

Ura

HIKES AROUND SHINGKHAR & URA

There are several good hiking options in the valley. The easiest is the two-hour return hike to the cliff-hanging **Shamsul Lhakhang**. The trail starts from the dirt road 3km above Shingkhar. A longer hike leads up to the Singmi La, along the former trade route to Lhuentse, and multiday treks continue further through Phrumsengla National Park to Songme in the Lhuentse valley.

On the way back to Ura stop at **Somtrang Lhakhang**, with its courtyard megaliths and a meditation retreat in the cliffs above the village. A footpath offers a pleasant walk from here directly down to Ura village. A three-day *kangsoe* festival (in honour of the local deity) brings the place to life at the end of the ninth month (November).

terton Dorji Lingpa. The present structures, including the *tshuglhakhang* (main temple), *utse, chamkhang* (dance house), *shagkor* (servants' quarters) and *nubgothang* (guesthouse), are more recent, having been rebuilt after their collapse in an 1897 earthquake.

The family that owns Ogyen (Ugyen) Chholing has turned part of the complex into a **museum** to preserve its legacy. The fascinating and well-captioned exhibits offer real insights into the lifestyle of a Bhutanese noble family. Highlights include a book of divination, a *dakini* dance costume made of bone and the revelation that petrified yak dung was one of the ingredients for Bhutanese gunpowder. Particularly interesting is the section on the once-thriving trade with Tibet, describing how Bhutanese traders would take tobacco, English cloth, rice, paper and indigo to trade fairs over the border in Lhodrak, to return laden with bricks of Chinese tea, gold dust, salt and borax (an ingredient in butter tea). The living quarters have been renovated into excellent guest accommodation as **Ogyen Chholing Heritage House**.

Instead of leaving by road the way you came, consider making the one-hour walk back down to Kizum bridge via the charming **Choejam Lhakhang**, with its *kora* path and room full of festival masks, and the **Narut (Pelphug) Lhakhang**, built around a sacred cave enclosing a Guru Rinpoche footprint and a shrine to the local protector Garap Wangchu.

 OTHER HIKES IN BUMTHANG

Thangbi Goemba to Ngang Lhakhang
A pleasant, mostly flat, three-hour hike along the south-bank trail of the Chamkhar Chhu.

Drak Choeling Retreat
A 1½-hour uphill hike from Pema Sambhava Lhakhang that takes you to this silent retreat (don't disturb the hermits).

Luege Rowe
A charming half-day hike to a remote, little-visited lhakhang that feels untouched by time.

Bumthang's Eastern & Enigmatic Valley

JAKAR TO URA VALLEY

The road to the village of Ura crosses the bridge to the east of Jakar, then travels south along the east bank of the Chamkhar Chhu, winding around a ridge past the turnoff to the Tang valley. As the road climbs, look back at excellent views up the Chokhor and Chhume valleys.

The road climbs to a chorten, then finally crosses the **Shertang La** (3590m), also known as the Ura La. Just before the pass you'll get a view of Gangkhar Puensum (7570m) to the northwest and the yellow-roofed lhakhang of Shingkhar village below.

It's then a long descent into the Ura valley. The direct way down on foot from the pass makes for a nice hourlong walk into Ura village. You can also tackle this trail on a mountain bike. A couple of kilometres before the turnoff to the village of Ura, which lies below the highway, is the turnoff to Shingkhar.

The village of **Shingkhar** is 9km up a side road and over the ridge from Ura. The **Rinchen Jugney Lhakhang**, on a hill just above the village, was founded by the Dzogchen master Longchen Rabjampa (1308–63). The village's central **Dechen Chholing Goemba** is headed by Shingkhar Lama, whose predecessor featured prominently in the Bhutanese novel *The Hero with the Thousand Eyes* by Karma Ura. The central lhakhang has its floorboards exposed to show the stone teaching throne of Longchen. The protector deities are appropriately fierce. The **Shingkhar Rabney** (festival), held at the Dechen Chholing Goemba in the ninth month (October), does not see the tour groups that often crowd out Ura, and features an unusual yak dance.

Ura is one of the most interesting villages in Bhutan. There are about 40 closely packed houses along cobblestone streets, and the main **Ura Lhakhang** dominates the town, giving it a medieval atmosphere. In cold weather Ura women can still be seen wearing a sheepskin shawl that also serves as a blanket and a cushion.

A few hundred metres beyond Hotel Araya Zamlha (towards Mongar) is the start of the **Ura–Geyzamchu Walking Trail**, a 9km, five-hour hike crossing the Wangthang La pass and rejoining the main road at Geyzam Chhu. It's a demanding but rewarding walk through rhododendron, pine forests and alpine meadows along an old trade route. For information and a local guide visit the **Phrumsengla National Park Visitor Centre** or ask at Hotel Araya Zamlha.

MAJOR FESTIVALS OF URA

Ura Yakchoe
The annual Ura Yakchoe has gained notoriety as a festival that changes date at the last minute. If you decide to visit for the festival, usually held in May, it's wise to allow a couple of days' leeway. The three days of masked dances usually start on the 12th day of the third lunar month with a procession carrying an image of Chana Dorji from the nearby Gaden Lhakhang down to the main lhakhang. The eve of the festival sees the frantic brewing of *sinchhang* (a spirit distilled from millet, wheat or rice) and late-night exorcisms.

Matsutake Festival
Ura is the centre of Bhutan's matsutake mushroom (*sangay shamu* in Dzongkha) production, a fact celebrated with recipes, local stalls and other fungi-related fun in August's Matsutake Festival.

GETTING AROUND

Bumthang's Bathpalathang Airport is on the east bank of the Chamkhar Chhu in Jakar. It operates highly weather dependent Druk Air flights to/from Paro and Yongphula Airport (Trashigang). Timetables change seasonally depending on demand. Taxis congregate south of the bazaar next to the local bus stand. The Dragon Ride counter at Dragon Handicrafts in Jakar rents out mountain bikes, which is a great way to get around Chokhor valley's main sights.

ZHEMGANG
& SARPANG

THIMPHU ✪

Zhemgang

Sarpang

The two *dzongkhags* of Zhemgang and Sarpang lie on the southern border of central Bhutan. These regions see very few tourists, even though Gelephu is connected to Paro by regular flights and has decent road access. Perhaps all this will change in time as Gelephu is anticipated to be the site for a major new city and international airport. The region around Zhemgang was once a collection of tiny principalities, collectively known as Khyeng, and only absorbed into Bhutan in the 17th century.

For tourists the highlights revolve around the extraordinary botanical wonderland from subtropical to temperate rainforest that blankets the equally extraordinary topography. The scene is therefore set for superb birdwatching and other wildlife encounters in and around Royal Manas National Park, where intrepid wildlife enthusiasts can experience an area of unsurpassed biodiversity.

TOP TIP

A road branches south at Trongsa following the Mangde Chhu. A junction at Wangduegang signals the turnoff to Zhemgang, while continuing along the main road leads to Tingtibi. Here the road splits again for either Royal Manas National Park or Gelephu. A quicker, alternative route links Gelephu to Wangdue Phodrang and the west, via Dhamphu.

LINDSAY FEGENT-BROWN/LONELY PLANET ©

Golden Langur

GOLDEN LANGURS

As you drive south, keep an eye out for troops of golden langurs swinging in the trees right beside the road. Langurs are elegant, arboreal monkeys with graceful limbs, extraordinarily long tails and a charismatic presence.

Three species of langur make a home in Bhutan's forests. The common grey or Hanuman langur is found west of Pele La; the capped langur is found east of the Manas Chhu in eastern Bhutan; and the famous golden langur is only found from the Punak Tsang Chhu in the west to the Manas Chhu in the east. Not surprisingly, its distinctive feature is its lustrous blonde-to-golden coat. Also around Zhemgang are troops of mixed capped and golden lineage.

Journey to Southern Jungles

TRONGSA TO TINGTIBI VIA ZHEMGANG

The highway south of Trongsa initially follows the Mangde Chhu, winding in and out of various side valleys, and passing numerous access roads leading to the Mangdechhu Hydroelectric Project. It's an interesting drive, passing several huge waterfalls, and the bountiful rice terraces of the Mangde Chhu valley. Potential stops on the route south include the palaces of Kuenga Rabten and Eundu Chholing.

Kuenga Rabten, the winter palace of the second king, Jigme Wangchuck, is 23km (one hour) south of Trongsa. The first storey of the U-shaped building was used to store food; the second was the residence of royal attendants and the army; and the third housed the royal quarters and the king's private chapel. Part of this floor has been converted into a library, storing books from the National Library. Sandwiched between the king's and queen's quarters is the **Sangye Lhakhang**, with statues of Sakyamuni, the Zhabdrung and Guru Rinpoche. The entire complex was undergoing extensive renovation in 2023.

Further down the valley is **Yundrung (Eundu) Chholing**, the winter palace of the first king, Ugyen Wangchuck. The

 WHERE TO STAY IN PANBANG

Marang Jungle Lodge
Comprising comfortable tents mounted on platforms plus a communal dining area. Hot showers available. **$$**

Royal Manas Eco Lodge
On a sweeping bend of the Mangde Chhu, with four rooms in two cottages, each with a private hot-water bathroom. **$$**

Ogyen Zilnon Inn
Comfortable, air-con and fan-cooled, brightly painted rooms in nearby Thinleygang village. **$$**

LINDSAY FEGENT-BROWN/LONELY PLANET ©

Lehleygang

building belongs to a local Dasho (nobleman) but is looked after by the monastic body, and tourists are welcome. The 2nd-floor *goenkhang* has a highly venerated chorten of Pema Lingpa (always under wraps), a fabulous collection of arms and two fearsome bronze soldiers.

South of Eundu Chholing the road continues past the villages of Lungtel and Taksila, before descending to the bridge at **Tongtongphey**, which marks the start/end point of the Nabji trek. Past Koshela and Pangzum villages the road swings round the unstable Riotala cliffs, opening up views of Nabji and Korphu villages across the river.

At Wangduegang the Zhemgang bypass continues ahead to offer a direct route to Gelephu (114km). Turn left here to take the road up to Zhemgang (20km).

The sleepy *dzongkhag* centre of **Zhemgang** is a natural place to break the trip and try a local lunch. The surprisingly impressive dzong dates to the 12th century and is home to about 70 monks and several statues of the valley protector Dorji Rabten. An annual tsechu here in March sees few international tourists. The picturesque old town, still bearing the original name of Trong, is worth a look. Wander through its cluster of stone houses along a narrow paved central street to visit its charming lhakhang.

After leaving Zhemgang the road joins the main highway at the bridge across the Mangde Chhu. Over the bridge and 1km past the town of Tingtibi is the turnoff to Gonphu, Panbang and access to Royal Manas National Park.

 WHERE TO STAY IN GELEPHU

Gold Fish Resort
Recommended hotel with spacious villas and rooms, multicuisine restaurant, outdoor bar and mini waterworld. **$$**

Hotel Kuku Grand
Comfortable, spotless and modern hotel with good amenities on the northern approach to town. **$$**

Lhaazaay Suites
Suites are certainly large but not luxurious, and there's a multicuisine restaurant and bar. **$$**

Incredible Wildlife at Royal Manas National Park

A TRANSNATIONAL CONSERVATION AREA

The drive from Tingtibi to Panbang, as the road meanders beside the swift-flowing Mangde Chhu, is a real delight. About 3km before the village of Bobsar there are peculiar 'hanging gardens' of bamboo and Himalayan screw pine clinging to the riverside cliffs. Around 10km before reaching Panbang the road passes the beautiful twin waterfalls of **Lehleygang**. Keep an eye out here for capped langurs, darker-coated cousins of golden langurs.

Royal Manas National Park is home to a wide variety of animals, including elephants, water buffaloes, leopards, between 30 and 50 tigers, clouded leopards, civets, rhinoceroses and more than 360 species of birds. The park abuts the Manas National Park in Assam in India, forming an important transnational conservation area.

November to March are the best months to visit. Summer is extremely hot and some of the accommodation closes from June to August. There are several tsechus in the region in the 10th Bhutanese month (November).

Crossing to the Plains

GELEPHU AND THE BORDER WITH INDIA

The large, but hardly bustling, border town of **Gelephu** is the gateway to south-central Bhutan. It's a pleasant enough town but, for now, is just a place to overnight before leaving or entering Bhutan.

If you find yourself with time to kill, visit the weekend market, spin the prayer wheels at the large Buddha statue beside the football ground or visit the large distillery operated by the army welfare division. The **Nyimalung Tratsang**, 1km north of town, is the winter residence for monks from Nyimalung Goemba in the Chhume valley.

ACTIVITIES IN THE NATIONAL PARK

Tourism is still in its infancy at Royal Manas National Park. Your Bhutanese agent can arrange rafting, trekking, fly-fishing and wildlife guides through the **River Guides of Panbang**. This local outfit can also arrange cultural shows and village visits to witness the local Khenpa culture, including Bon festivals.

In addition to the short raft trip down the Manas Chhu between Panbang and Manas Range (the park headquarters), one-, two- and three-day river expeditions can be arranged. Longer walks within the national park require hiring a park guide and may require elephants for transport and security. Visitors should be aware that animal-welfare groups advocate against riding elephants due to health concerns for the animals.

 GETTING AROUND

Druk Air flies from Paro (direct or via Jakar) to Gelephu airport, west of town. Good, sealed roads run north to Trongsa, either bypassing or via Zhemgang, and northwest to Wangdue Phodrang via Sarpang and Damphu.

If/when the border reopens to non-Indian foreigners you can organise to take your Bhutanese vehicle to Guwahati (five hours) in India. A potentially simpler transport option is to hire an Indian taxi, which your Bhutanese guide will help arrange. Whether leaving or entering India, don't forget to get an Indian immigration stamp at the easily missed Indian Foreigners Checkpoint at Deosiri, 10km from the Bhutan border.

Unannounced transport strikes *(bandhs)* in Assam can cause potential havoc with travel schedules, although in recent years *bandhs* have become less frequent. The border officials receive very short notice of *bandhs*, so you may only be made aware of one when you reach the gate and find it closed. The only thing to do is to return to Gelephu. Most *bandhs* last 12 hours, but may last up to 48 hours.

Above: Kuri Chhu valley (p177). Right: *Kushutara* (brocade weavings), Khoma (p177)

EASTERN BHUTAN

BUDDHIST PILGRIMAGES, BIRDWATCHING AND TEXTILES

The wild and rugged east of Bhutan sees far fewer tourists than the more accessible western regions and so remains a frontier for travel in Bhutan.

Those few intrepid travellers venturing east are immediately rewarded with a feeling of adventure: impenetrable forests, high passes and quite a few daunting moments on mountain roads. Moreover, there are traditional villages and towns little influenced by tourism, as well as great dzongs (fort-monasteries) and mysterious temples, empty apart from silent statues and chanting monks. Many travellers to the east are lured by the magnificent forests – lush havens inhabited with rare and unique bird and wildlife and internationally renowned for birdwatching. The east is also unrivalled in traditional arts and crafts, and 'textile tourism' is comparatively well developed. Much of the population in the east lives in tiny settlements secreted high above roads or in isolated valleys; the region is also home to many ethnic groups, some comprising fewer than 1000 people.

In ancient times, eastern Bhutan was ruled by a collection of separate petty kingdoms and was an important trade route between India and Tibet. The most important figure in this region's history was Chhogyel Mingyur Tenpa. When he was *penlop* (governor) of Trongsa (1647–67), he led his armies to eastern Bhutan to quell revolts in Bumthang, Lhuentse, Trashigang, Mongar and Zhemgang. His efforts brought eastern Bhutan under the rule of the *desi* (secular ruler of Bhutan) and went a long way towards the ultimate unification of the country.

LINDSAY FEGENT-BROWN/LONELY PLANET ©

THE MAIN AREAS

MONGAR	LHUENTSE	TRASHIGANG
Restful highway stop near world-class birdwatching. **p172**	Textile traditions and a great Guru statue. **p176**	An attractive town that's crossroads of the East. **p179**

Lhuentse, p176

The ancestral home of Bhutan's royal family, and famous for its weaving and textiles and the world's largest statue of Guru Rinpoche.

CAR & MOTORCYCLE

Bhutan's main east–west highway intersects at Mongar, from where you can continue east along the highway to Trashigang or take the road heading north towards Lhuentse. In Trashigang roads fan out north to Trashi Yangtse, east to Sakteng and Merak, and south to the border with India at Samdrup Jongkhar.

AIR

Yongphula Airport is about an hour's drive from Trashigang. It hosts domestic flights to/from Paro via (Jakar) Bumthang. Flight schedules are frequently interrupted by capricious mountain weather, so it pays to have a plan B.

WALKING

Generally lower altitudes keep it hot and steamy through late spring to summer. Additionally, monsoon rains cascade down from June to August. This means most walks in the east are kept to day hikes or relatively short treks, such as Merak to Sakteng.

CHINA (TIBET)

Dungkhar

LHUENTSE

Rodang La

BUMTHANG

Lhuentse

Tangmachu

Ungaar

Jakar

Shertang La

Gorgan

Fawan

Autsho

Shershong

Thrumshing La

Thrumshing La National Park

Phrumsengla National Park

Sengor

Yong Khola

Rewan

Kori La

Bridung La

Mongar

Nimgong

MONGAR

ZHEMGANG

PEMAGATSH

Naitola

Panbang

Nganglam

Manas Camp

SARPANG

INDIA (ASSAM)

TOP: LINDSAY FEGENT-BROWN/LONELY PLANET ©, RIGHT: LINDSAY FEGENT-BROWN/LONELY PLANET ©

Find Your Way

Eastern Bhutan remains a rugged and adventurous region and one of the most awesome road trips you'll ever experience. Here you will discover little-visited religious shrines, culturally diverse villages, bird-filled forests and stunning landscapes.

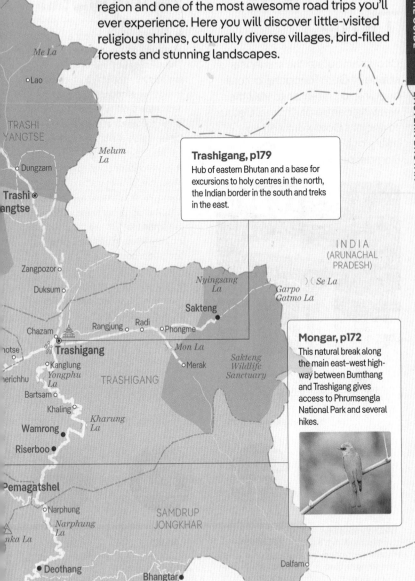

Me La

○ Lao

TRASHI YANGTSE

○ Dungzam

Trashi angtse ◉

Melum La

Trashigang, p179
Hub of eastern Bhutan and a base for excursions to holy centres in the north, the Indian border in the south and treks in the east.

INDIA (ARUNACHAL PRADESH)

Zangpozor ○

Duksum ○

Nyingsang La

Garpo Gatmo La

) (*Se La*

Sakteng

Chazam ○

Rangjung ○   Radi ○   ○ Phongme

...otse ○

※ **Trashigang**

Mon La

Mongar, p172
This natural break along the main east–west highway between Bumthang and Trashigang gives access to Phrumsengla National Park and several hikes.

○ Kanglung

Yongphu La

○ Merak

Sakteng Wildlife Sanctuary

...erichhu ○

Bartsam ○

TRASHIGANG

Khaling ○

Kharung La

Wamrong ●

Riserboo ●

Pemagatshel

○ Narphung

Narphung La

...nka La △

SAMDRUP JONGKHAR

● **Deothang**

Bhangtar ●

Dalfam ○

Samdrup ◉ **Jongkhar**

○ Darranga

Ⓝ 0 ———— 20 km
0 ———— 10 miles

169

Plan Your Time

Circumambulate the immense statue of Guru Rinpoche before heading to Lhuentse to visit the weaving centre of Khoma. Detour to ancient Gom Kora and go hiking or birding in Phrumsengla, Bomdeling or Sakteng parks.

LINDSAY FEGENT-BROWN/LONELY PLANET ©

Drametse Goemba (p181)

Three Days in Eastern Bhutan

● From Bumthang take the exhilarating drive over the **Thrumshing La** (3750m; p173) towards Mongar. Stay for a couple of nights in **Mongar** (p172) and dedicate a day trip to **Taki La** (p178), to look up at the world's tallest statue of Guru Rinpoche.

● Next continue north to remote **Lhuentse** (p176) to visit its ridgetop dzong. While returning to Mongar, make a brief detour to the village of **Khoma** (p177) to see the intricate weaving performed on backstrap looms.

● The next day in Mongar can be filled with a couple of **short hikes** (p175) around the town, calling on various monasteries or lhakhangs (temples).

Seasonal Highlights

Late February to March is a good time to visit for comfortable temperatures, festivals and spring blooms. Late spring and summer are hot and humid, though this is the best time for birdwatching.

FEBRUARY
Bhutanese celebrate the new year, Losar, between mid-January and March. **Trashi Yangtse** hosts a three-day tsechu (dance festival).

MARCH
Gom Kora (p185) holds a tsechu that attracts hundreds of Bhutanese, many of whom circumambulate the sacred rock at night.

APRIL
The weather warms and rhododendrons flower. Tourists are scarce. **Chorten Kora** (p186) hosts two festivals that attract pilgrims from Arunachal Pradesh.

STEVE ESTVANIK/SHUTTERSTOCK ©, LOTHAR KURTZE/ALAMY STOCK PHOTO ©, AMAR THAPA/500PX/GETTY IMAGES ©

Five Days to Travel Around

● On the way to Mongar from Bumthang, hikers and birdwatchers will want to stop the car and spend a full day tackling one of several walks in **Phrumsengla National Park**. Wildlife-watching enthusiasts will also want to overnight at **Yong Khola** (p173) where a comfortable hotel hosts birders from around the world. You can tick off elusive species on evening and predawn excursions.

● A couple of nights in **Trashigang** (p179) will allow time for a full day's excursion to **Trashi Yangtse** (p186) via the sacred and ancient lhakhang at **Gom Kora** (p185) and the riverside stupa at **Chorten Kora** (p186).

If You Have More Time

● Commit a few days to the forests and trails around **Mongar** (p172). From Mongar, head north to **Lhuentse** (p176) and spend a night in a local homestay in **Khoma** (p177). Sample local cuisine, including the fiery *arra* (spirit distilled from rice) and wake to the crowing of cockerels and the clack of backstrap looms, and don't forget to purchase a memento of the *kushutara* (brocade weaving).

● Using **Trashigang** (p179) as a base, you can head out to **Merak** (p184) to tackle a trek north to **Trashi Yangtse** (p186) via **Gom Kora** (p185). Begin the journey home via the airport at **Yongphula** (p187) or the Indian border at **Samdrup Jongkhar** (p187).

JUNE

Monsoon rains play havoc with flight schedules and the east's fragile mountain roads. Waterfalls, such as **Namling** (p174), are simply spectacular.

OCTOBER

Peak tourist season has arrived, though the east is quiet and it's a good time to find peace on the trails.

NOVEMBER

Clear weather, though nippy nights. Three-day tsechus in **Mongar** and **Trashigang** (p182) occur simultaneously.

DECEMBER

The cold begins to bite, and snow can block passes. Way up in **Lhuentse** (p178) a three-day tsechu (p178) sees very few tourists.

171

MONGAR

The Mongar district is the northern portion of the ancient region of Khyeng. Shongar Dzong, Mongar's original dzong, is in ruins, which can be easily seen from the highway and explored with a bit of trailblazing. The new dzong in Mongar town is not as historically significant as Shongar, though it hosts a tsechu in winter that sees very few tourists.

Many travellers spend a night in Mongar before continuing to Trashigang or Lhuentse. While here the pleasant old bazaar is worth a stroll. It features a row of traditional stone buildings decorated with colourful wooden facades, potted plants and prayer wheels. A large prayer wheel, near the central clock tower and exercise park, attracts reverential old-timers catching up on local news and the day's last rays of sunlight. Modern Mongar is represented by the concrete towers, each one housing a general-produce store on the ground floor, behind the old bazaar.

TOP TIP

It takes about seven hours to travel between Jakar and Mongar. The road crosses two high passes and skirts numerous sheer drops on what is one of the most spectacular drives in the country. During winter the Thrumshing La is occasionally closed for a day or two during heavy snowfall.

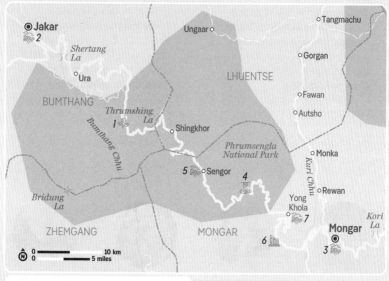

SIGHTS
1 In Situ Rhododendron Garden
2 Jakar
see 3 Mongar Dzong
3 Mongar Town
4 Namling Waterfall
5 Sengor
6 Shongar Dzong
7 Yong Khola

LINDSAY FEGENT-BROWN/LONELY PLANET ©

Mongar

Rinzin Thinley,
manager and chef,
Trogon Villa, Yong
Khola. *trogonvilla.com*

Time of Year
Spring (mid-February
to April), with mating
and nesting activity,
or October and
November.

Time of Day
From 5.30am (6.30am
in winter) to 11am, and
after 3.45pm, once
the heat of the day is
noticeably retreating.

Equipment & Clothing
Wear dull greens,
browns and beiges –
brightly coloured birds
don't like competition
– and bring good
binoculars (at least
8x42) and a camera.

Where to Go
The best spot is
Jainala, a short drive
away, from where you
can wander through
broadleaf forest.
Nearby is a farm road
heading to Tshamang
village through
the Drangmaling
Community Forest
where over 50 bird
species have been
observed.

A Dramatic Drive, Historical Ruins & Birding Heaven

JAKAR TO MONGAR

It takes about seven hours to cover the epic drive from Jakar to Mongar. Three kilometres before Thrumshing La there is a small park that features over 20 species of rhododendron. It's possible to follow the trail inside the **In Situ Rhododendron Garden** and hike up through the forest for 40 minutes to the pass. If you have a keen interest in rhododendrons and are here between late March and May, it's often possible to get a park ranger to accompany you and point out the different species; mention this to your guide in advance and ask at the national park office in Ura.

As you approach the pass, and if you are lucky enough to visit on a clear day, watch for a view of Gangkhar Puensum (at 7570m it is often cited as the world's highest unclimbed mountain). A chorten and prayer flags adorn the **Thrumshing La** (3750m), 85km from Jakar, and the border of Mongar Dzongkhag; you are now officially in eastern Bhutan.

 WHERE TO EAT & STAY BETWEEN JAKAR & MONGAR

Kuenzang Hotel & Bar
Roadside hotel in Sengor with set lunches for tourists and local dishes such as *ema datse* (chillies with cheese). **$**

Hotel Tshewangmo
In Sengor, producing a variety of dishes for lunch. Cycling groups utilise the basic accommodation. **$**

Trogon Villa
Located at Yong Khola and aimed at birdwatchers. Comfortable rooms, excellent food and a cosy restaurant. **$$**

LINDSAY FEGENT-BROWN/LONELY PLANET ©

Namling waterfall

SHONGAR DZONG

On the road to Mongar, near Menchugang village, is a view of the ruined Shongar Dzong. There's not much to see – some stone walls almost hidden by trees – but this is believed to have been one of the earliest and largest dzongs, possibly built as early as 1100. Like Trongsa, Shongar was powerful because the dzong was ideally situated to control movement between eastern and western Bhutan.

You can hike to the dzong in around 20 minutes on a sweaty trail where your companions are birds and butterflies. Your combatants, on the other hand, are leeches, stinging nettles and thorny acacias. Do we dare imagine that the same passion that restored Drukgyel Dzong could be retold at Shongar Dzong? Watch this space!

The road now switches back and forth descending through an ancient fir forest. At about 3000m, 20km from the pass, the route emerges from the trees and enters the pastures of the Sengor valley. The settlement at **Sengor** has a few houses near the road, although the main part of the village, about 20 houses, is in the centre of the valley below.

The next stretch of road is the wildest in Bhutan. Five kilometres beyond the Sengor valley the road begins a steep descent into the Kuri Chhu valley, clinging to the side of a cliff, with numerous waterfalls leaping out onto the road. The frequent fog and cloud on this side of the pass make it difficult to see what's below – for which you should be profoundly grateful, since often, there's nothing.

Thirteen kilometres past Sengor a turnout offers views towards the **Namling waterfall**, which plunges from beneath the road and is spectacular and scary after monsoonal rainfall. There are several chortens on this stretch – erected as memorials to the almost 300 Indian and Nepali labourers who died constructing the road.

WHERE TO STAY IN MONGAR

Wangchuck Hotel
Wangchuk dominates the accommodation scene here with 32 spacious rooms, good food and a delightful setting. **$$**

Druk Zhongar Hotel
Well-run, friendly hotel with comfortable rooms equipped with TVs and fans; some have a balcony. **$$**

Hotel Druk Zom
Local hotel with 10 basic rooms. There's a bright, multicuisine restaurant-cafe that serves espresso coffee. **$**

About 17km from Namling, after a long descent that traverses the side of a cliff, the road reaches safer ground. At **Yong Khola** it emerges into a large side valley of the Kuri Chhu, a lush semitropical land of bamboo, ferns, leeches and excellent birdwatching.

At **Kuri Zampa** (570m) you finally hit the valley floor – an amazing descent of 3200m from the pass. Step out of your vehicle and breathe in the thick syrupy air before frantically stripping off three layers of clothing. On the east side of a prayer-flag-strewn bridge is a large concrete chorten that is patterned after Bodhnath in Nepal; it is said to contain relics from the original Shongar Dzong. Beside the bridge is a deserted factory that used to extract oil from the wild lemongrass that is so abundant here.

A well-constructed road leads downstream to the town of **Gyalpozhing** and the Kuri Chhu power scheme, beyond which a road leads further downstream to Nganglam on the Indian border. Meanwhile, the road to Mongar, and further east, climbs through chir pine forest up the eastern side of the Kuri Chhu valley.

Stretching the Legs

HIKES AROUND MONGAR

If you have a half or full day spare in your itinerary, there is some fine off-the-beaten-track hiking in the hills south of Mongar. The following route offers ridge walks, sweeping valley views and remote Buddhist retreats and lhakhangs (temples) in a three-quarter-day hike.

From **Yakgang Lhakhang** drive or hike uphill for 45 minutes (take the shortcuts past the chortens to avoid the dirt road) to the ridgetop monastery at **Phongchu La**. There are expansive views down to the Kuri Chhu and the lushly forested Kheng region to the south, while the monastery itself has some interesting puppets of local protector deity Dorji Gyeltsen.

From Phongchu La it's 25 minutes downhill to tiny **Senlung Goemba**. The main chapel is often locked but there's an unusual personal meditation tent at the entrance.

A steep climb of 40 minutes through forest leads you past two chortens to the ruins surrounding **Jaiphu Lhakhang**. The main route continues along the ridge from Jaiphu Lhakhang to Shami (Sainu) Goemba, then continues 20 minutes further to the road pass at **Phurji Laptsa**, and your waiting car.

For an easier 2½-hour walk, do it in the opposite direction, starting at Phurji Laptsa and getting picked up at Phongchu La.

HIKING & BIRDING AROUND MONGAR

The wild landscape between Thrumshing La and Shongar Dzong offers several opportunities for adventurous hiking. Robust birdwatchers will love the three-hour hike from Thrumshing La down to Sengor through beautiful, bird-filled old-growth forest. The two-day walk from Sengor to Yong Khola also takes you through one of the best birdwatching spots in Bhutan and many birding groups base themselves at Yong Khola or the nearby Norbugang campsite.

Another good hiking and birding option is to follow the steep, day-long hiking trail from Latong La down to Menchugang, via Saling and Shongar. In general, September to November and February to March are the best times to hike in this region.

GETTING AROUND

Mongar is conveniently located on the main east–west highway between Bumthang and Trashigang and is near the turnoff north to Lhuentse. It's a great place to rest and recover from a long and twisting drive and to simply wander the streets or mountain trails.

LHUENTSE

THIMPHU ✪

● Lhuentse

Formerly known as Kurtoe, the isolated district of Lhuentse is the ancestral home of Bhutan's royal family. Although geographically in the east, it was culturally identified as central Bhutan, and the high route over Rodang La was a major trade route until the road to Mongar was completed. Despite the roads and motorised transport, the feeling of remoteness and isolation here is palpable to this day. The dzong in Lhuentse, commanding a spur and overlooking the snaking Kuri Chhu valley, is one of the most picturesque in Bhutan.

Among the many mountains that the road and the Kuri Chhu weave through is one that had a shelf excavated to provide a base for the world's tallest statue of Guru Rinpoche. This colossal homage to the celebrated saint of Bhutan occupies a grand throne and temple complex that is a must-see on the way to or from Lhuentse.

TOP TIP

Lhuentse is 63km from the junction at Gangola and around a three-hour drive from Mongar. It's a dramatic trip, frequently taking you alongside cliffs high above the river valley. Since you follow the main valley it's generally a comfortable, straightforward ride – as long as there haven't been any recent landslides.

TRAVELIB/ALAMY STOCK PHOTO ©

Lhuentse Rinchentse Phodrang Dzong (p178)

KHOMA VILLAGE

If you're interested in weaving, and even if you're not, it's worth making the drive up to this traditional weaving village. The village produces some of Bhutan's most sought-after and expensive *kushutara* (brocade weaving); almost all the 30 or so houses in the village have traditional backstrap looms set up on their porches.

The weavings are so elaborate that they resemble embroidery and are generally used as *kiras* (women's traditional dress), though bags and other smaller pieces are produced for sale. The village is internationally known in textile circles and comparatively wealthy. You can easily arrange a Bhutanese-style lunch (if on a day trip) or an overnight homestay in the village.

Following the Kuri Chhu

MONGAR TO LHUENTSE

It is 12km from Mongar to the junction of the Lhuentse road at Gangola, where locals sell packets of cornflakes, oranges and peanuts. The Lhuentse road winds around the hill to Chali and Palangphu and then crosses the unstable Dorji Lung slide area (and its protective chortens) to descend to the banks of the Kuri Chhu at Rewan.

After passing a large, white Tibetan-style chorten surrounded by 108 smaller chortens, the road reaches the extensive cornfields and languid riverside village of **Autsho** (920m). On the river you may spot Assamese macaques among the boulders, capped langurs in the overhanging trees and

 WHERE TO EAT & STAY BETWEEN MONGAR & LHUENTSE

Puensome Bakery	**Phayul Resort**	**Homestay of Chhimi Yuden**
In Mongar, the place to load up on pizza, doughnuts, apple pie, fruit cake and biscuits. **$**	This riverside hotel in Autsho is a great spot for lunch, a masala tea break or an overnight stop. **$$**	This place in Khoma is always modernising. Plentiful food and *arra* (spirit distilled from rice), plus a weaving centre. **$$**

INSIDE GURU RINPOCHE STATUE

Inside this enormous and highly decorated statue are three levels of chapels. Note that the statue of Guru Rinpoche on the entrance floor has an open mouth and it looks like he is about to speak. Upstairs are three dioramas of Zangto Pelri, Guru Rinpoche's celestial abode. The top chapel has a central altar featuring statues of five bodhisattvas topped by a Buddha with a female consort in *yabyum,* the union of wisdom and compassion. If the door to access the inside chapels is locked ask your guide to ring the phone number posted on the northern door to summon the monk with the key.

Guru Rinpoche statue, Taki La

black cormorants diving for fish. It's a worthy refreshment or overnight stop.

As you ascend, the Kuri Chhu valley begins to widen. The road crosses to the west bank of the river at Thinleypang where there is an intersection; go straight ahead for Lhuentse, or turn left to climb 14km to **Taki La** (1762m), and the colossal 45m-high **Guru Rinpoche statue**, via the village of **Tangmachu**. The statue claims to be the tallest Guru statue in the world, beating a similarly Herculean rival in nearby Sikkim, at a cost of over US$2 million. It's certainly an impressive if incongruous sight way up here in the mountains, and it hosts several colourful festivals.

Back on the road to Lhuentse, there's eventually a view of **Lhuentse Dzong**, which dominates the head of the valley. Just before Lhuentse an intersecting road leads to a bridge across the Kuri Chhu, and past a large chorten and cremation ground at the confluence with the Khoma Chhu. This is the road to **Khoma village** (4km).

As you approach **Lhuentse**, there is an excellent view of the **Lhuentse Rinchentse Phodrang Dzong**, as it is correctly known, perched dramatically atop a bluff. Seeing very few tourists, the various lhakhangs inside the dzong are well worth a visit – if you can find the monk with the keys. Several festival drums stand guard just outside the atmospheric *goenkhang* (chapel dedicated to protective deities). Beyond the dzong is a **dratshang** (college), built to house the monastic community. The **Lhuentse tsechu** is held in December or January and sees very few tourists because of Lhuentse's remoteness. It's worth driving up to the Royal Guesthouse, simply for the views down to the dzong and towards the snowy peaks at the head of the Kuri Chhu valley.

Birthplace of a King

BEYOND LHUENTSE TO DUNGKHAR

A road runs from Lhuentse for 40km to the small village of **Dungkhar**, named because the ridge upon which it sits is shaped like a conch *(dungkhar).* Pema Lingpa's son Kuenga Wangpo settled here, and it is through him that Bhutan's royal family, the Wangchucks, trace their ancestry to the Kurtoe region. Jigme Namgyal, father of the first king, was born here in 1825 and left home when he was 15 to eventually become Trongsa *penlop* and the 51st *desi.* The renovated 16th-century **Dungkhar Naktshang**, sitting above the village, houses the government *gewog* (lowest administrative level) offices. A tsechu is held here on the same days as the one held at Lhuentse Dzong. Just below the village is the unassuming birthplace of Jigme Namgyal.

GETTING AROUND

You can easily visit Lhuentse as a day trip from your base at Mongar. Alternatively, overnight in one of the professionally run homestays in the village of Khoma. Another accommodation option is the delightful Phayul Resort at Autsho.

TRASHIGANG

Trashigang (Auspicious Mountain) is the heart of eastern Bhutan and a crossroads that was once the centre of important trade with Tibet. It is one of Bhutan's more attractive and interesting towns, well worth a wander, and is the natural base for excursions north, south and east. The charming town and dzong rest at the foot of a steep wooded valley, with the tiny Mithidang Chhu channelling right through the centre of town. Apart from the dzong, Trashigang's focal point is a tiny plaza that curves around a prayer wheel.

Not a lot of tourists make it to Trashigang, but many Canadian teachers worked here in the past and the people of Trashigang are well used to Westerners. While tourist-grade accommodation is limited, there is no shortage of local bars and you're bound to find at least one amusing place to drink and meet the locals.

TOP TIP

The journey from Mongar to Trashigang is easier and less exhilarating than the trip from Jakar to Mongar, but you'll still need about 3½ hours to cover the 91km between the two towns. To avoid the drive back west, consider exiting at Samdrup Jongkhar (check to see if the border is open) or flying back to Paro from Yongphula.

LINDSAY FEGENT-BROWN/LONELY PLANET ©

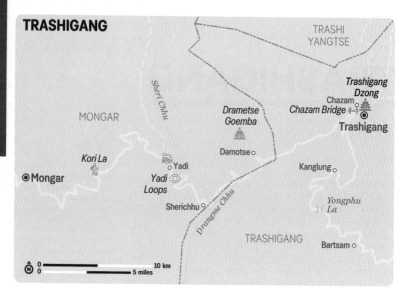

TRASHIGANG

'A' TREASURE HUNT

Below Yadi, a secondary road branches off the highway for 17km to **Shershong** (Serzhong) village and the two- or three-day pilgrimage trek to **Aja Ney**. The 'A' of Aja is a sacred letter and 'ja' means 'one hundred'. Guru Rinpoche placed 100 letter As on rocks here, and for devotees it's like a spiritual treasure hunt: the more you see the more merit you gain. Those without sin usually find the most.

Towards the Kori La

MONGAR TO KORI LA

Leaving Mongar, the road climbs past fields of corn and the *shedra* (Buddhist college) and Zangto Pelri Lhakhang at Kilikhar. Swinging into a side valley, you enter a forest of rhododendrons adorned with orchids.

About 3km past Kilikhar a paved side road leads 2km down to **Wengkhar Lhakhang**, founded by the third Zhabdrung near the site of his birthplace. Clothes and relics of the Zhabdrung are displayed here on the 10th day of the third lunar month.

At **Chompa**, a trail leads up for 1½ hours or so to the photogenic and little-visited cliff-side retreat of **Larjung (Larjab Drakar Choeling) Lhakhang**. Rather than return the same way, it's possible to continue on foot to the Kori La. The path isn't obvious, so it's a good idea to arrange a guide in advance; this can be done at the Coffee Café at the pass.

About 1km further is the **Kori La** (2400m), heralded by an array of prayer flags, a small *mani* (carved mantra) wall, and a building containing hundreds of butter lamps. If these are lit, step inside for instant warmth but note the lack of

---

 WHERE TO EAT BETWEEN MONGAR & TRASHIGANG

Coffee Café
At Kori La you can get a cup of instant coffee or tea and a packet of biscuits. **$**

Monmaya Restaurant & Bar
You can grab Bhutanese and Nepali dishes or a masala tea here by the roadside in Yadi. **$**

Monkey Shoulder Café
Just off the highway in Zalaphangma (Monkey Shoulder). It's well set up for passing trade. **$$**

oxygen. The adjacent Coffee Café can produce a hot instant coffee or tea with biscuits. The forest surrounding the pass is good for birdwatching.

Nearby is the start of the **Kori La–Golishing Nature Trail**, a former trade route that traverses 2.75km (45 minutes) of pleasant downhill forest trail before ending at a side road, 3km from the main road, where your driver can pick you up.

Beyond the Kori La

KORI LA TO TRASHIGANG

The highway drops from the pass into the upper reaches of the extensive Manas Chhu basin, switchbacking down through broadleaf forests to the charming private lhakhang near the village of **Naktshang**.

The road continues its descent to the substantial village of **Yadi** (1480m), where several local restaurants can supply a decent meal or hot drink.

Beyond Yadi are numerous switchbacks, nicknamed the **Yadi Loops**, which lead down through a forest of sparse chir pine with an understorey of fragrant lemongrass, dropping 350m in 10km. There's a good viewpoint where you can see the road weaving down the hill; photos taken from here often appear in books and brochures to illustrate just how circuitous Bhutan's roads are.

After more switchbacks, the road crosses a bridge painted with the eight Tashi Tagye symbols and continues for 10km to **Sherichhu** (600m). Climb out of the Sherichhu valley to a chorten and cross a ridge to meet the large Drangme Chhu, which flows from the eastern border of Bhutan. The road winds in and out of side valleys for 12km to Thungdari, 71km from Mongar, where a side road leads to **Drametse Goemba**.

Back down on the main road you'll catch glimpses of Trashigang Dzong high above the south bank of the Drangme Chhu.

After passing a Public Works Department (PWD) camp at Rolong, the road reaches a 90m-long bridge at **Chazam** (710m). This place was named after the original chain-link bridge here, said to have been built by the Tibetan bridge builder Thangtong Gyalpo in the 15th century (*cha* means 'iron', *zam* means 'bridge'). The large building that formed the abutment of the old bridge has been partially restored and turned into a lhakhang just a short distance upstream

DRAMETSE GOEMBA

The biggest and most important monastery in eastern Bhutan, Drametse is an 18km, 40-minute detour off the main road at Thungari. The monastery was founded in 1511 by the granddaughter (some say daughter) of Pema Lingpa, Ani Chhoeten Zangmo, in a place she named Drametse, which means 'the peak where there is no enemy'.

Today the monastery has about 100 monks and *gomchen* (lay or married monks) and is famous as the home of the Nga Cham drum dance that features in many tsechus; it was proclaimed a Masterpiece of the Oral and Intangible Heritage of Humanity by Unesco in 2005. Visit Drametse on your way to Trashigang or Mongar and find accommodation and meals in these two regional centres.

 WHERE TO STAY IN TRASHIGANG

Lingkhar Lodge
A charming collection of well-appointed boutique cottages surrounded by bird-filled gardens and fruit trees. **$$**

Druk Deothjung Resort
Rooms are large and comfortable, with views of the valley. It is the most popular place to stay. **$$**

Rangshikar Homestay
In a noble family's ancestral house. Rooms are simple, yet comfortable, and the traditional meals are generous. **$$**

TRASHIGANG DZONG

Trashigang Dzong rests on a thin promontory overlooking the confluence of the Drangme Chhu and the Gamri Chhu. It was built in 1667 by Mingyur Tenpa, Bhutan's third *desi*. The entire eastern region was governed from this dzong from the late 17th century until the beginning of the 20th century.

Inside are a half-dozen lhakhangs. The 1st-floor *goenkhang* features paintings of a yeti, while another chapel is dedicated to the deity Choegi (Yama) Gyelpo, the wrathful aspect of Chenresig. Many lama dances are performed in Trashigang to appease Yama, especially during the three-day tsechu in November/December, which concludes with the unveiling of a large *thangka* (religious picture) and the displaying of a statue of Guru Rinpoche.

Trashigang

of the new bridge. Look for the ruins of watchtowers on the ridge above the old bridge.

The road switchbacks up towards **Trashigang**, passing the turnoff to Samdrup Jongkhar before continuing 3km to Trashigang, well hidden in a wooded valley.

A large prayer wheel sits in the centre of Trashigang's tiny plaza. The covered pedestal holding the prayer wheel is a favourite resting place. Restaurants, bars and a bakery and handicraft shop surround the plaza.

GETTING AROUND

From Trashigang it's 280km by road to Bumthang (roughly two days' travel), 350km to Trongsa and 550km to Thimphu (three days). Other options to consider, to avoid backtracking all the way west, are crossing into India at Samdrup Jongkhar or flying to Paro. The domestic Yongphula airport is about an hour's drive from Trashigang and hosts weather-dependent flights to/from Paro via Bumthang's Bathpalathang Airport.

Beyond Trashigang

Trashigang is your base for exploring the Sakteng Wildlife Sanctuary, Gom Kora and Trashi Yangtse, or to exit Bhutan via Samdrup Jongkhar.

Most people heading out this way are trekking to and between the twin villages of Merak and Sakteng, each the centre of its own secluded valley within the 741-sq-km Sakteng Wildlife Sanctuary. The two villages are home to the Brokpas, a semi-nomadic ethnic group, traditionally yak herders by trade.

The drive from Trashigang to Trashi Yangtse takes about two hours of driving time, but you should budget extra time to visit Gom Kora on the way. There's lots to see en route and it's a great day trip from Trashigang. Even if you don't have time to drive all the way to Chorten Kora and Trashi Yangtse, do make the effort to take the short trip to Gom Kora.

TOP TIP

Merak and Trashi Yangtse can be visited as day trips from Trashigang. The only reason to head to Samdrup Jongkhar is to exit Bhutan.

FOTOFRITZ16/GETTY IMAGES ©

Gom Kora (p185)   183

MIGOI, THE BHUTANESE YETI

The Bhutanese name for the yeti is *migoi* ('strong man'), and they are believed to exist throughout northern and northeastern Bhutan. The *migoi* is said to be covered in hair that may be anything from reddish-brown to black, but its face is hairless, almost human. It is similar to the yetis of Nepal and Tibet in that the breasts of the female are large and sagging, and both sexes have an extremely unpleasant smell.

But Bhutanese *migoi* are special because they have the power to become invisible, which accounts for the fact that so few people have seen them. Another feature that helps them escape detection is that their feet may face backwards, confusing people who try to follow them.

Migoi on postage stamp

Journey Further East

TRASHIGANG TO MERAK

Merak and Sakteng were closed to foreigners from 1995 to 2010 to protect the traditional culture of the area from undue global influence. After the ban was lifted numerous roads have been carved into this region, so it is not as secluded as it once was. You can now easily drive to Merak from Trashigang and back in a day. While the roads have potentially shortened the trekking routes, this is by no means the end of trekking in the region, or a reason not to visit. The **Merak–Sakteng trek** was always primarily a cultural trek: it's a chance to visit the Brokpas in their homelands and experience village life, and this is still the prime reason to visit. Day hikes and side trips to several lhakhangs and goembas can be arranged and the Brokpas have their own unique festivals in honour of their protective deity, Aum Jomo.

A road heading east descends from Trashigang to the banks of the Gamri Chhu at 820m and stays on the south side of the river, passing through a flat flood-prone area. The chorten in the middle of the floodplain provides divine protection against floods. Shortly afterwards is the village of **Lungtenzampa** (Prophecy Bridge), which had its eponymous bridge wiped out in a flood!

The road crosses the small Kharti Chhu and makes a short climb to **Rangjung** at 1120m. An elaborate chorten dominates the charming centre of town, which is worth a stroll. Above the town is the **Rangjung Yoesel Chholing Goemba**, a large Nyingma monastery founded in 1990 by Garub Rinpoche. *Cham* (religious ritual dancing) ends a 10-day *drupchen* (festival) in the 12th month (January).

The road continues east, climbing through terraces to **Radi** (1570m), famous for its local rice. At **Khardung** village a road heads southeast towards the **Mon La** (3278m), entering **Sakteng Wildlife Sanctuary** after 30km, and on to **Merak** (55km). If you are staying overnight, your Bhutan agent will organise a full camping set-up to use at the official campgrounds, or you might stay in one of several homestays. Apart from the Brokpas, the sanctuary's most famous residents are the *migoi* (yetis), for whom the sanctuary was allegedly established in 2002, and red pandas.

WHERE TO STAY IN MERAK & TRASHI YANGTSE

Merak Homestay
Simple, basic and friendly accommodation in the heart of Merak. It's also known as Ngaden Farmhouse. **$**

Kamaling Hotel
The sole tourist hotel in Trashi Yangtse, with a restaurant, bar and modern rooms. **$$**

Bomdelling Wildlife Sanctuary Guesthouse
The visitor centre has four simple rooms with private bathrooms and shared kitchen. **$**

LEO MCGILLY/SHUTTERSTOCK ©

Views along the Merak–Sakteng trek

Buddhist Kora

TRASHIGANG TO GOM KORA

From Trashigang follow the switchbacks down to the bridge over the Drangme Chhu at **Chazam**. From Chazam, the road winds its way above the west bank of the river to **Gom Kora**, only 45 minutes (22km) from Trashigang.

The correct name for the site is Gomphu Kora. Gomphu denotes a sacred meditation site of Guru Rinpoche and *kora* means 'circumambulation'. Pilgrims circumambulate the goemba throughout the night during the **tsechu** on the 10th day of the second lunar month (March/April).

The central figure in the temple is Guru Rinpoche. To the right is Chenresig, in his 1000-armed aspect. Sacred objects, including a *garuda* 'egg', a footprint of the Guru and one of his consort Yeshe Tshogyel, are locked in a glass cabinet.

Within the grounds is a fantastical large black rock. It is said that Guru Rinpoche was meditating in a small cave when a demon in the shape of a cobra suddenly appeared. The Guru, alarmed, stood up quickly, leaving the impression of his pointed hat at the top of the cave, and then transformed himself into a *garuda,* leaving the imprint of his wings nearby.

TEXTILES OF THE EAST

Just 1.5km past Rangjung is **Pema Lhundup Handicrafts**, a private house turned weaving centre that sells beautiful, embroidered cloth, shawls and scarfs made from *bura* (raw silk – literally 'insect fibre') or *sechu* (spun silk) by women from the surrounding villages, including Tzangkhar. *Kiras* vary in price from Nu 18,000 to 100,000, while silk scarves are around Nu 200 to 25,000. The knowledgeable owners, Phuntso Choden and her mother Namgyal Pelden, offer displays on spinning and weaving. Weaving enthusiasts can also visit Tzangkhar from a turnoff by a hairpin loop just before Radi (Km 23). Many of the women here are weavers and you can buy silks directly from them.

WHERE TO SHOP IN TRASHI YANGTSE

Wood Turning & Laquering Cluster
Cooperative selling beautiful *dapas* (bowls) turned from woods including rhododendron.

National Institute for Zorig Chusum
Arts and crafts institute where you can watch the students at work and purchase art.

Thinley Dendup General Shop & Handicraft
Stocks textiles, *dapa*, oboes, brass butter lamps and other religious paraphernalia.

185

FRAMALICIOUS/SHUTTERSTOCK ©

Chorten Kora

MEET THE BROKPAS

The Brokpas of Merak and Sakteng trace their origins from Tshona in southern Tibet. They are a culturally distinct ethnic group recognisable by their unique dress. Most notable is their *shamo*, a beret-like black hat made from the chest hair of a yak, with spider-like tentacles descending from its edges to channel away rainwater. Women wear a red-and-white-striped silk dress called a *shingkha*, while men wear a red wool jacket known as a *tshokhan chuba*.

Most practise transhumance, moving with their yaks between the highlands in summer and lower pastures in winter. As they travel down to Phongme, Radi and Trashigang in winter they trade their stocks of *chora* (fermented cheese), butter and dried meat in exchange for salt, tea and grains.

Following the Kulong Chhu

GOM KORA TO TRASHI YANGTSE

The drive from Gom Kora to Trashi Yangtse follows the Kulong Chhu, affording great views of the river and a multihued tapestry of vegetation on the opposite bank. Keep an eye out for troops of capped langurs right beside the road.

Three kilometres before Trashi Yangtse, the original **Trashi Yangtse Dzong** appears on a promontory. Built by Pema Lingpa, it now houses the town's community of monks.

The orderly settlement of **Trashi Yangtse** occupies a large bowl-shaped valley in one of the furthest corners of the kingdom, 550km from Thimphu.

Chorten Kora is patterned on the great stupa of Bodhnath in Nepal. It was constructed in 1740 by Lama Ngawang Loday in memory of his uncle, Jungshu Phesan, and to subdue local spirits. The story behind the chorten is that Lama Ngawang Loday went to Nepal and brought back a model of Bodhnath carved in a radish. He had it copied here so that people could visit this place instead of making the arduous trip to Nepal. The reason that Chorten Kora is not an exact copy of Bodhnath is because the radish shrank during the return trip.

During the first month of the lunar calendar (February or March) there is an auspicious *kora* held here, where people gain merit by walking around the chorten. It is celebrated on

---

 WHERE TO STAY IN SAMDRUP JONGKHAR

Druk Mountain Hotel
Modern hotel with welcoming staff, spacious rooms with bathrooms, multicuisine restaurant and bar. **$$**

Hotel Menjong
Comfortable though worn rooms with private bathrooms. There's a multicuisine restaurant and a separate bar. **$$**

TD Guesthouse
North of the town centre, TD has eight rooms, each with two double beds, TV and private bathroom. **$$**

two separate dates (the 15th and 30th days of the lunar month). The first date (Dakpa Kora) is for the people from the Dakpa community in Arunachal Pradesh. The second kora (Drukpa Kora) is for the Bhutanese, who attend the local fair and witness the unfurling of a *thondrol* (huge *thangka*).

On the northwestern outskirts of Trashi Yangtse, the **Bomdeling Wildlife Sanctuary Visitor Centre** has a small museum with some vaguely interesting displays on the natural history of the 1520-sq-km sanctuary. While the amateurishly stuffed wildlife adds little value, the friendly staff can advise on hiking and homestay options in the sanctuary.

Exiting to India

TRASHIGANG TO SAMDRUP JONGKHAR

The only reason to make this meandering, roller-coaster drive, of at least six hours, through southeastern Bhutan is to enter or leave it via Assam, India, although at the time of research the border was temporarily closed to non-Indian foreigners. The road from Trashigang climbs past the improbable hilltop Yongphula airport to cross the **Yongphu La** (2190m), offering you a last glimpse of the Himalaya.

Beyond **Khaling**, the road climbs again to the head of a rhododendron-filled valley to cross the **Kharung La** at 2350m. There's a short descent through crumbling hills, then another climb to another pass at 2430m. Curling around the valley, the road descends to **Wamrong** (2130m), the best place for lunch. As you further descend you get glimpses of the Assam plain before encountering the day's most dangerous section of road, the **Menlong Brak** (*brak,* or *brag,* means cliff in Sharchop). The fragile road is adorned with prayer flags, prayer plaques and chortens in a bid to appease the confluence of topography and physics.

The road eventually hits the valley floor with a thud, as a farewell statue of Guru Rinpoche marks the end of the Himalayan foothills. The road curves through the final ripples of the continental collision zone, passing the cursory checkpoint at **Pinchinang**, 4km or so before Samdrup Jongkhar.

The highway enters **Samdrup Jongkhar** from the north, passing the small modern dzong before crossing a bridge and veering left into the surprisingly neat and compact bazaar. If you continue south instead of turning left, you will hit the border. A Bhutanese-style gate decorated with a dragon bids you farewell as you collect your passport exit stamp and cross into the heat and chaos of India.

CROSSING THE BORDER: SAMDRUP JONGKHAR TO GUWAHATI

The border was closed to non-Indian foreigners at the time of research. Bhutan Immigration, at the border, is open 24 hours every day. Here you will get a passport stamp if entering or leaving Bhutan. The Indian Foreigners Checkpoint, where you get stamped in or out of India, is at Darranga, 5km south of the border, and is also open 24 hours. It is essential to bring a photocopy of your Indian visa and passport information pages.

Both Bank of Bhutan and Bhutan National Bank in Samdrup Jongkhar will change ngultrum into Indian rupees. In theory you are required to have your original exchange receipt, passport copy and an application form, available in the banks. But your guide can also do it hassle free.

GETTING AROUND

It is possible for your Bhutanese driver to take you to Guwahati (three hours from Samdrup Jongkhar), but the difficulties for Bhutanese on Indian roads, even at the best of times, is tremendous. That's not to mention occasional political problems in Assam resulting in strikes *(bandhs)* that can close the border. The cheaper and usually hassle-free way to get to Guwahati is to arrange an Indian taxi with your hotel in Samdrup Jongkhar. Alternatively, take a taxi to Rangiya, where there are numerous train options east or west across India.

ALEX TREADWAY/GETTY IMAGES ©

Above: Flags on the Laya trek (p205). Right: Snow leopard

TREKKING ROUTES IN BHUTAN

EXPLORE THE WILD BEAUTY OF THE 'OTHER' HIMALAYA

Bhutan's trekking routes take you past 7000m Himalayan giants and over high passes into some of the remotest corners of the high Himalaya.

Almost two-thirds of Bhutan still lies beyond the reach of any road. Composed of rugged Himalayan summits, high passes, pristine forests, turquoise lakes, rolling yak pastures, traditional villages and a healthy sprinkling of exotic wildlife from takins to snow leopards, this is one of the world's best-preserved (and least-explored) mountain landscapes.

Bhutan offers a wide range of treks, from tough high-altitude expeditions reaching the base camps of snowcapped Himalayan giants to relaxing community-based village trails linked by subtropical forest. And with walks ranging from two days to one month, there's a trek for everyone.

The remarkable thing about trekking in Bhutan is how often you have the epic views, pristine forests and lakes to yourself. Many trekking routes see fewer than 100 foreign trekkers annually and even Jhomolhari sees fewer than 1000 per year; that's less than the number visiting the Everest region in a week. This alone makes the mandatory organised camping-style treks worth the cost in many people's eyes.

Perhaps the best part of all is that you can trust your Bhutanese tour agent, guide and cook to take charge of every conceivable camping chore, leaving you to simply relax, enjoy the trail and soak up the extraordinary scenery. Shangri-La indeed.

THE MAIN AREAS

JHOMOLHARI & THE PARO VALLEY	BEYOND JHOMOLHARI & THE PARO VELLY	CENTRAL & EASTERN TREKS
Bhutan's most accessible and popular treks. p194	Remoter, higher and tougher. p204	Little-trekked cultural routes. p210

Other Treks
Bumthang Cultural Trek (p211)
Owl Trek (p211)
Rodang La Trek (p212)
Nabji Trek (p212)

Laya Trek, p205
An extension of the Jhomolhari trek, combining diverse flora and fauna with the culturally interesting Laya region.

Jhomolhari Trek, p199
Bhutan's premier trek offers spectacular views of 7314m Jhomolhari from a camp at Jangothang, with views nearby of Jichu Drake.

Soi Yaksa (Jhomolhari Loop) Trek, p203
All the amazing views of Jhomolhari, plus spectacular views of Jichu Drake from the Tshophu lakes and three high passes.

Saga La Trek, p198
Short overnight trek linking the Haa and Paro valleys, with fine distant views of Jhomolhari from its high point.

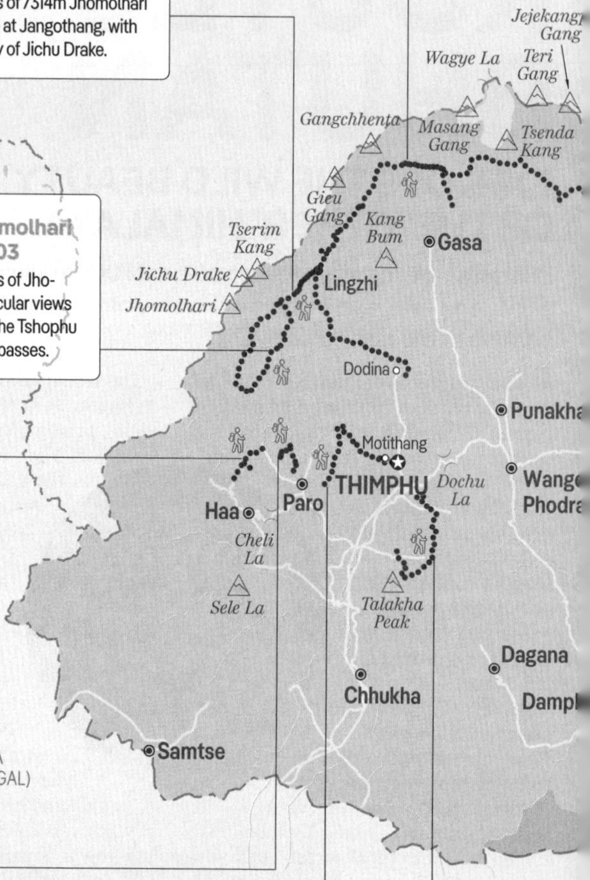

Bumdrak Trek, p196
A short trek that takes in half a dozen temples, including famous Taktsang (the Tiger's Nest), with an overnight at a luxurious camp.

Druk Path Trek, p195
One of the most scenic and popular treks in Bhutan, following a wilderness trail past remote mountain lakes between Paro and Thimphu.

Jejekang Gang
Wagye La
Teri Gang
Gangchhenta
Masang Gang
Tsenda Kang
Gieu Gang
Kang Bum
Gasa
Tserim Kang
Jichu Drake
Lingzhi
Jhomolhari
Dodina
Punakha
Motithang
THIMPHU
Dochu La
Wange Phodra
Haa
Paro
Cheli La
Sele La
Talakha Peak
Dagana
Dampl
Chhukha
INDIA (WEST BENGAL)
Samtse

Find Your Way

All tourists to Bhutan have their own transportation, so getting to and from the trailhead will be arranged by your agency. Changes in schedule due to weather or illness are not uncommon, so be prepared to be flexible.

CHINA
(TIBET)

Zongophu Gang
(Table Mountain)

gphu / Kulha
ng △ Gangri

Chisangang Ri △

△ Chura
Gang

za △ △△
Kangri! Melunghi!
Gang
Gangkhar
Puensum

Wangchuk
Centennial
Park

Gokthong
La

Snowman Trek, p206
The ultimate trekking challenge to Lunana and beyond – it's hard, risky and expensive, with 50% of trekkers failing to reach their destination.

●Lhuentse

Yotang
La
○Duer
○Kizum

Trashi ●
Yangtse

INDIA
(ARUNACHAL
PRADESH)

○Sephu
Jakar ●

Trongsa ●

Thrumshing
La

Thrumshing La
National Park

Phrumsengla
National
Park

Trashigang ●

Rangjung
○

Sakteng

Phongme

Merak

Black
△ Mountain

Mongar ●

Zhemgang ●

Jigme Singye
Wangchuck
National Park

Pemagatshel ●

Narphung
La

△
Tunka
La

Samdrup
Jongkhar ●

**Dagala Thousand
Lakes Trek, p208**
A short trek near Thimphu that takes you to a little-visited collection of high-altitude lakes and mountain views.

INDIA
(ASSAM)

**Merak–Sakteng
Trek, p213**
Lots of cultural interest here, with village stays in unique Brokpa communities, and trekking through pristine *migoi* (yeti) habitat.

0 ——— 50 km
Ⓝ 0 ——— 25 miles

Plan Your Time

Whether you opt for a two-day or two-week trek, be sure to add on several days to see Bhutan's main sights. Time your trek with a festival and you'll have the perfect Bhutan itinerary.

Dagala Thousand Lakes Trek (p208)

TREK	DAYS	DIFFICULTY
Druk Path Trek	6	medium-hard
Bumdrak Trek	2	medium
Saga La Trek	2	easy
Jhomolhari Trek	7	medium-hard
Soi Yaksa (Jhomolhari) Loop	6	medium
Laya Trek	10	medium-hard
Snowman Trek	24-26	hard
Dagala Thousand Lakes Trek	5	medium
Owl Trek	2-3	medium
Nabji Trek	3-4	easy
Merak–Sakteng	2-7	medium

Seasonal Highlights

In general, the second half of October and mid-April are the best times to trek in Bhutan, though this is also peak tourism season. Late April and early November are excellent alternatives.

FEBRUARY

Temperatures are low but the Druk Path, Bumdrak and Saga La treks are often feasible by the end of the month.

MARCH

Treks below 4000m are possible, for example to Jhomolhari base camp or Merak–Sakteng, but high passes are still snowed in.

APRIL

Excellent conditions and spring blooms, though lesser-trekked passes can still be closed if there has been heavy or late snow.

MAXIMUM ELEVATION	TREKKING SEASON	OTHER INFORMATION	PAGE
4235m	Feb-May, Sep-Dec	Popular trek from Paro to Thimphu via mountain lakes and temples	p195
3900m	mid-Feb-May, Sep-Nov	Short, luxurious trek that visits the Tiger's Nest	p196
4000m	mid-Feb-May, Sep-Nov	Overnight route from the Haa to Paro valleys, with views of Jhomolhari	p198
4930m	Apr-Jun, Sep–mid-Nov	Classic route to spectacular views of 7314m Jhomolhari peak	p199
4890m	Apr-Jun, Sep-Nov	Jhomolhari views, lovely mountain lakes and three passes	p203
5005m	Apr-Jun, mid-Sep-mid-Nov	Extension of the Jhomolhari trek to take in the remote villages of Lingzhi and Laya	p205
5320m	Sep-Oct	The ultimate trekking challenge through Lunana	p206
4520m	Apr, Sep-Oct	Peaceful trek near Thimphu, passing many high-altitude lakes	p208
3870m	Mar-May, Oct-Dec	Follow yak herders' trails to panoramic views and remote retreat centres	p211
1635m	Oct-Mar	Low-altitude cultural trek through the villages of the Monpa people	p213
3480m	mid-Mar-May, Sep-Nov	Cultural trek into one of the most culturally interesting parts of the remote east	p213

MAY
Warmer temperatures are comfortable in the high valleys of Jhomolhari, Laya and Lingzhi, with more chance of snow-free passes.

OCTOBER
The best month for mountain views and the only feasible time for the Snowman trek. The **Royal Highlander Festival** hits Laya.

NOVEMBER
Cold nights but crisp, sunny days are common. Bring extra clothes for the second half of the month and avoid high passes.

DECEMBER
Too cold for high-altitude treks, with passes snowed in, but possible for the Druk Path trek, Owl trek or multiday hikes in Bumthang.

JHOMOLHARI &
THE PARO VALLEY

Western Bhutan is home to Bhutan's most popular trekking routes. Jhomolhari is the main focus, mostly for its relatively easy access and its spectacular views of several 7000m peaks. Two routes stand out here: the full trek from Jhomolhari via the remote region of Lingzhi to the roadhead north of Thimphu, and the shorter Soi Yaksa loop via the spectacular Tsophu Lakes and three high passes.

Bhutan's most popular trek is the Druk Path, from Paro to Thimphu, which combines mountain lakes with monasteries and retreat centres in a relatively short walk. For the most time-efficient taste of the trails, hike from Haa to Paro on the Saga La trek, or combine Bumdrak with a visit to the Tiger's Nest. Add in easy access to trailheads, plus the country's most impressive sights and its biggest festivals, and the choice is clear.

TOP TIP

Try to time your trek with one of the west's colourful festivals. Mid-October brings the Jhomolhari Festival to Dangochang, and a week later is the more interesting Royal Highlander Festival in Laya. Prime trekking season also coincides with April's Paro tsechu and October's Jakar tsechu and Jampey Lhakhang Drup, both in Bumthang.

PASCAL BOEGLI/GETTY IMAGES ©

Jangothang (p201)

DRUK PATH TREK

Druk Path Trek

WALK FROM PARO TO THIMPHU

Linking the major sights of the Paro and Thimphu valleys via a series of scenic high-altitude lakes, the Druk Path is the most popular trek in Bhutan. The main draws are remote meditation retreats, alpine scenery and the convenience of easy access, without losing days of your trip driving to trailheads.

The trek has a longer season than most in Bhutan, but snow can block higher sections in late autumn and early spring. Most people walk the route in six days, but fit walkers can do it in five by combining the last two days. Superhumans can even run the trek in a single day: an old punishment for Bhutanese soldiers was a forced one-day march along this route.

Some agencies offer a shortened version of this trail called the Tsaluna trek, which descends to Tsaluna village and trailhead from either Jangchhu Lakha (four days) or Jimilang Tsho (five days).

Most groups start walking after lunch from **Damche Gom** (2985m), high above Paro Dzong, from where it's a two-hour climb through forest to the **Jili La** (3540m). Well-acclimatised

TREK STATS

Duration 6 days
Max elevation 4235m
Difficulty Medium
Season February to May, September to December
Start Above Paro
Finish Motithang
Summary This popular trek climbs past remote lakes and mountain monasteries, before dropping into the Thimphu city limits. Trekking days are short, but the relatively high altitudes make it moderately strenuous.

JILI DZONG

The small 16th-century Jili Dzong (also spelled Jele or Jela) sits on an important site. It was the residence of Ngawang Chhogyel (1465–1540), the cousin of Lama Drukpa Kunley, and the Zhabdrung is said to have meditated and been visited by the protective deity Pal Yeshe Goenpo here, before heading down to Paro to defeat an invading Tibetan army. The impressive main lhakhang contains a large statue of Sakyamuni that's almost 4m high.

If you're not trekking the Druk Path, it's possible to visit Jili Dzong as a day hike from Paro. An adventurous alternative continuation is along the roller-coaster ridgeline from Jili Dzong to Dongkala, via Dochorten Goemba and Benri Lhakhang (p103).

groups can even combine days one and two, walking as far as Rabana in one day. The first night's camp is just below historic **Jili Dzong**.

From the dzong, day two descends to a saddle, before climbing to great views of Paro, the Bemang Rong valley and, hopefully, Jhomolhari in the distance. The trail crosses to the east side of the ridge, offering views of Gimena village and goemba, before climbing to a saddle and yak pasture of **Jangchhu Lakha** (3760m), with camping options at often-boggy **Tshokam** (3770m) or the yak herders' camp of **Rabana** (3890m), surrounded by rhododendrons.

There are two trails to Jimilang Tsho on day three, with most groups choosing the high trail for its better views of 7314m Jhomolhari and 6989m Jichu Drake (or Drakye). An hour after Rabana you crest the minor **Langye Ja La** (Ox Hump Pass; 4070m), where you can climb 50m to the hilltop for impressive 360-degree views. A second pass offers more views of Jhomolhari. After a lunch stop on the next saddle, climb around the ridge to a chorten for a final view of the peak. A steep 30-minute descent leads to pleasant camping at the far shore of **Jimilang Tsho** (Sand Ox Lake; 3885m), which is stocked with trout.

The next day the trail climbs through rhododendrons to a ridge, then descends and follows the ridge to prayer flags overlooking small **Janye Tsho**. Descend to a yak herders' camp near the lake at 3880m before climbing again to a ridge at 4150m, with views of **Simkotra Tsho**, where you'll likely camp at 4100m.

Day five requires a long climb past three false summits, before descending to a herders' camp at **Labana** (4110m), beside a shallow lake. There's a final longish climb to the **Labana La** (4235m), before descending to a minor pass at 4210m, where there are views of the distant Dochu La. A final 4090m pass opens up views of the entire Thimphu valley and possibly Gangkhar Puensum in the far distance. It's worth taking a side trail for 20 minutes southeast down to **Thujidrak Goemba**, a remote meditation centre that clings to the side of a rock face at 3950m.

Continuing past Thujidrak, you'll soon reach the meditation cells and lhakhangs (temples) of **Phajoding Goemba** (3640m), scattered across an open, grassy hillside. Darkness brings the bright city lights far below you and the feeling that you have arrived back at the edge of the world.

The final day is 1130m of descent, so keep your trekking poles handy. You can choose to route left via **Chhokhortse Goemba** to the BBS broadcasting tower at Sangaygang, or right on the steeper trail to **Motithang**. The delights of Thimphu await.

PHAJODING MEDITATION CENTRE

Phajoding Goemba (p71) was founded in the 13th century by Tibetan master Phajo Drugom Shigpo and has several interesting lhakhangs. It's a popular day hike from Thimphu, climbing up via a pass and temple at Pumola.

Bumdrak Trek

TASTER TREK IN STYLE

This short overnight trek has much to recommend it: great views of the Paro valley, gorgeous sunsets over the mountains of Haa towards Sikkim, an interesting cliff-face

BUMDRAK TREK

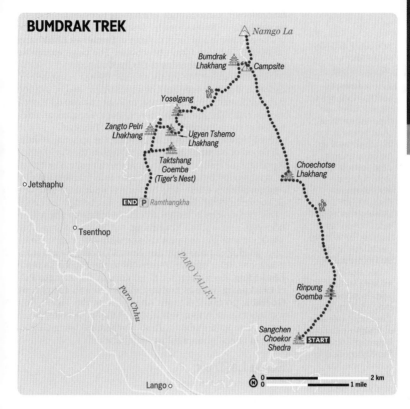

Namgo La

Bumdrak
Lhakhang
Campsite

Yoselgang

Zangto Pelri
Lhakhang
Ugyen Tshemo
Lhakhang

Taktshang
Goemba
(Tiger's Nest)

○ Jetshaphu

END [P] Ramthangkha

Choechotse
Lhakhang

○ Tsenthop

PARO VALLEY

Paro Chhu

Rinpung
Goemba

Sangchen
Choekor
Shedra   START

Lango ○

Ⓝ 0 ――――――――― 2 km
0 ――――――――― 1 mile

pilgrimage site, little-visited chapels above Taktshang Goemba and the spectacular Tiger's Nest itself.

The semi-permanent camping accommodation at Bumdrak is the most luxurious in Bhutan, complete with sunloungers, gas heaters and wooden beds, but this is not an easy stroll. It's all uphill for the first day, taking you up to almost 4000m, and all downhill on the second day, so you have to be in decent shape to enjoy this trek. Depending on how your agent has arranged the trek, you will likely just carry a daypack with what you need for an overnight.

The trek starts from **Sangchen Choekor Shedra** (2900m), a Buddhist college home to 150 students, 600m above the valley floor. The first day is only a four-hour walk, so you could do some sightseeing in the morning and have a hot packed lunch at the *shedra* before heading off. The trail heads left by an area of burnt forest and again below the Rinpung Goemba meditation centre.

Continue climbing through blue pine, oak and rhododendron forest until you see **Choechotse Lhakhang** (3640m), a steep hourlong climb above you. The statue of Denpa here is said to have once saved the valley from a measles epidemic. The trail climbs briefly up to two sets of prayer flags (3780m)

TREK STATS

Duration 2 days
Max elevation 3900m
Difficulty Medium
Season Mid-February to May, September to November
Start Sangchen Choekor Shedra
Finish Ramthangkha
Summary A short but steep hike that gives a top-down perspective on the famous Tiger's Nest.

197

ACCLIMATISATION HIKES FROM JANGOTHANG

If you are doing the Soi Yaksa loop, hike up the main valley past the last stone house, cross the bridge, turn left and continue up the valley towards Jichu Drake, keeping to the right of the terminal moraine. Eventually you'll reach a viewpoint by a side valley but you can continue further to two glacial lakes right at the foot of the peak.

If you are not following the Soi Yaksa loop itinerary, make a half-day trip to the stunning twin lakes of **Tshophu**, with Jichu Drake and Jhomolhari framed magnificently behind them. Take the first bridge in the main valley, climb to the top of the ridge and continue up the valley to the end of the second lake.

TREK STATS

Duration 2 days

Max elevation 4000m

Difficulty Easy

Season Mid-February to May, September to November

Start Talung village/ Makha Zampa bridge

Finish Balakha, upper Paro Valley

Summary Monasteries, villages and superb views of Jhomolhari are the highlights of this easy trek.

before levelling out through a charming forest of larch, silver fir and juniper (known locally as *tsendhen*). Just beyond here is a large pasture and the first views of **Bumdrak Lhakhang** (3900m), 1¼ hours from Choechotse. The large **campsite** (3860m) lies just to the side of the lhakhang.

The cliff-hugging 17th-century hermitage has a dramatic location, said to have been built on a spot frequented by 100,000 *dakinis* (female celestial beings); *bum* means '100,000', *drak* means 'cliff'. The main deity here is Dorje Phagmo, an emanation of Guru Rinpoche's consort Yeshe Tshogyel.

If you have the time and energy, make the optional 45-minute ascent of **Namgo La** (the 'Pass as High as the Sky') behind Bumdrak; the trail starts just behind the campsite. The 4100m peak is crowned by a collection of prayer flags marking a *durtoe* (sky-burial site), where dead babies are brought for sky burial. For dawn views climb the low ridge just behind the camp.

Day two descends 1260m so can be tough on the knees. It's a one-hour walk to **Yoselgang**, the 'Shining Summit', at 3300m, where you can visit the assembly hall with its beautiful woodblock print depicting Guru Rinpoche's eight manifestations. It's a further 10 minutes to the **Ugyen Tshemo Lhakhang**, then a further 15 minutes to the **Zangto Pelri Lhakhang**, with its fantastic views down to **Taktshang Goemba**, 20 minutes away. After visiting the Tiger's Nest you join the main tourist trail downhill for 1½ hours to the car park at Ramthangkha. Grab lunch at Taktsang Cafe en route or at restaurants below Ramthangkha.

Saga La Trek

SHORT WALK OVER A HISTORIC PASS

The overnight Saga La trek follows the traditional route taken by Haa farmers on their annual trips to plant rice in the Paro valley. Each day is really a half-day's walk, so you can easily fit in some sightseeing at either end, preferably at Yangthong or Jangtey monasteries in Haa, and Drukgyel Dzong in Paro, or you could even do the trek in one long day if you are fit.

From Talung village it's just two hours' walk, gaining 425m, to the main campground at **Khadey Gom** (3450m), with two other possible campsites a little further.

The next day it's a 45-minute ascent to the **Saga La** (3700m) up a series of eroded horse trails. There are some views of Jhomolhari (7314m) and Jichu Drake (6989m) peaks, as well as views west towards the border with Tibet, but if the weather is clear, it's worth hiking south along the ridge for an hour to a hilltop series of stone walls and a better viewpoint.

Back at the pass it's a steep 45-minute descent to **Dongney Tsho** pasture on a trail that can be very muddy. After a two-hour descent from the summit you finally reach a large pasture by **Chodeyphu village** (2900m), which offers a fine place to camp if you want to turn this into a leisurely two-night trek. You can detour to explore the village or descend directly on a dirt logging road for 45 minutes, past the Himalayan Keys Resort, to reach the main Paro valley road at **Balakha**, not far from Drukgyel Dzong.

SAGA LA TREK

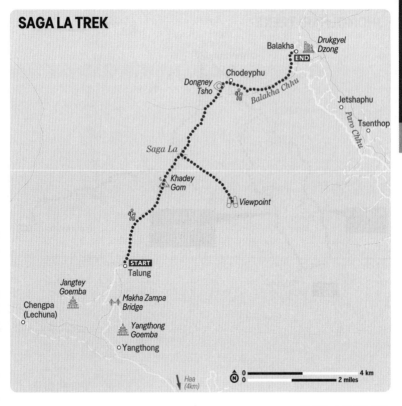

Balakha   Drukgyel Dzong
END

Chodeyphu

Dongney Tsho

Balakha Chhu

Jetshaphu

Tsenthop

Paro Chhu

Saga La

Khadey Gom

Viewpoint

Jangtey Goemba

Chengpa (Lechuna)

Makha Zampa Bridge

START
Talung

Yangthong Goemba

Yangthong

Haa (4km)

N   0 —————— 4 km
0 —————— 2 miles

Jhomolhari Trek

BHUTAN'S MOST POPULAR TREK

The Jhomolhari trek is to Bhutan what the Everest Base Camp route is to Nepal: a trekking pilgrimage. With three major treks routing via Jhomolhari, the first section of this walk is the busiest in the country.

The first two days of the trek follow the upper Paro Chhu valley to Jangothang, climbing gently but relentlessly, with a few short, steep climbs over side ridges. It then crosses a high pass and visits the remote village of Lingzhi, then crosses another pass before making its way towards Thimphu. The last three days of the trek cover a lot of ground.

Be prepared for a few downsides amid the undeniable scenic splendour. Power pylons now run the entire distance from Sharna to Lingzhi, following the exact route of the trek. There's more plastic waste along the trail than any other trek. And nights can be very cold, especially above Jangothang, so bring down gear.

Get an early start from Paro to give yourself enough time to drive the 1½ hours to the trailhead. The trail starts by the bridge at Sharna (2890m), just past the army checkpoint at Gunitsawa.

TREK STATS

Duration 7 days
Max elevation 4930m
Difficulty Medium–hard
Season April to June, September to mid-November
Start Sharna Zampa
Finish Dom Shisa/Dolam Kencho
Summary Bhutan's showcase trek offers a spectacular view of the 7314m Jhomolhari from a high camp at Jangothang.

JHOMOLHARI TREKS

Goyul

Tserim Kang

Lingzhi Dzong

Chha Shi Thang

Lingzhi

Mo Chhu

Thuptu Chhu

0   10 km
0   5 miles

Jhomolhari 2

Jhomolhari

Jichu Drake

Chhokam Tsho

Army Camp

CHINA
TIBET

Jangothang (4080m)

Nyile La

Yeli La

Mechiphu Chhu

Dangochang

Takethang

Soe

Paro Chhu

Tshophu

Khedo Tsho

Army Camp

Bhonte La

Thangthangka

Soi Yaksa

Dhumzo Chhu

Shodu

Wang Chhu

Barshong

Dom Shisa

Tremo La

Sey Dzong

Jhomolhari Trek

Thombu Shong

Takhung La

Soi Yaksa (Jhomolhari Loop) Trek

Dolam Kencho **END**

Shing Karap

Thombu La

Thombu Chhu

Sharna Zampa

Gomiron Chhu

Gunitsawa

START/END

Paro Chhu

Chobiso

Do Chhu

Cheri Chhu

Dodina

Sangatung

Mitshi Zampa

Langrithang

Dechenchoeling

Chang Zampa

Drukgyel Dzong

Tshokam

Labana

Chodeyphu

Phume La

Motithang

THIMPHU

Lingzhi Dzong

Paro to Jangothang

DAYS 1–3

Day one is a long, hard day with lots of ups and downs, made worse by the rock-hopping required. Tough soles are a real advantage here. After about two hours, you will reach **Shing Karap**, a stone house and clearing at 3110m. Further ahead is a stone-paved trail leading left to Tremo La (don't take this). This is the old invasion and trade route from Phari Dzong in Tibet, and still looks well beaten since it's used by army caravans to ferry rations to the border post.

After taking the right branch and crossing a side stream, climb over a little ridge, then descend and cross the Paro Chhu on a wooden cantilever bridge. The route now goes up and down a rocky trail through forests of birch and fir, followed by blue pine, maple and larch.

After crossing the Paro Chhu three times you'll see a white chorten on the opposite side of the river across a bridge. Don't cross it, or it'll take you up the Ronse Ghon Chhu towards Soi Yaksa, the campsite on Day 4 of the Soi Yaksa (Jhomolhari Loop) trek.

A 15-minute walk from the bridge is a large meadow with Jhomolhari looming majestically at the head of the valley. This is **Thangthangka** (3610m), with permanent toilets, a small stone kitchen shelter for your crew and a Bhutanese-style house selling beer. Camp fires are not allowed.

ALEX TREADWAY/GETTY IMAGES ©

Wake up early for good views of Jhomolhari, as they soon disappear behind a ridge as you start walking. After less than an hour your guide will need to register your group at an army camp.

Eventually, the trail turns sharply right at a whitewashed *mani* (carved mantra) wall, just before a white chorten, and then climbs gently alongside a beautiful section of river, as ancient juniper trees start to appear. You are now entering yak country. Above the trail is the village of Soe, though you cannot see it until you are beyond it.

One hour beyond Soe is **Takethang** (3940m), a cluster of stone houses on a plateau near a cremation site. The villagers grow barley and a large succulent plant called *kashaykoni* that is fed to yaks during winter.

The trail heads straight across the plateau, eventually arriving at the administrative centre of **Dangochang**, with its large white chorten, school, clinic, national park ranger office and government guesthouse. From here, it's a gentle uphill past a naturally arisen phallus-shaped stone to three hilltop chortens just before the camp at **Jangothang** (4080m), with its spectacular view of Jhomolhari. As with yesterday's camp there is a stone toilet block and a small kitchen shelter.

Jangothang is the most popular campsite in Bhutan and you are unlikely to have it to yourself. The name (meaning 'land of ruins') derives from the remains of a small fortress that sits atop a rock behind the campsite. Despite often being called Jhomolhari 'Base Camp', Jangothang has never actually been used as base camp by any summit expedition. It's important to figure in an acclimatisation day in Jangothang. If you are having problems with the altitude here, consider returning.

Jangothang to Lingzhi

DAY 4

On day four head up the main valley past the last stone house, as a spectacular view of Jichu Drake (6989m) opens up. Cross the log bridge, then start up a steep traverse. Soon the top of Jhomolhari appears over the ridge above the camp at Jangothang. The snow peak in the middle is Jhomolhari 2 (6942m).

At 4470m, the trail leads left and enters a large east–west glacial valley with numerous moraines. Apart from a few small gentians, only grass, tundra and small juniper bushes grow here. Past a false summit with a cairn at 4680m, the trail approaches the ridge and you can see Jichu Drake to the northwest. The final push is up a scree slope to **Nyile La** (4870m), three to four hours from camp. You can climb higher to the northwest, where you'll see Jhomolhari 2 and Jichu Drake on one side, and Tserim Kang (6789m) on the other. Nyile La is frequently very windy, so descend quickly through scree to a stream on the valley floor for an excellent lunch spot.

The trail now heads north, contouring along the hillside high above the valley. Eventually you will see an army camp near the river below; the white tower of Lingzhi Dzong is visible in the distance. Past a lookout at 4360m, the trail descends into the large Jaje Chhu valley, switchbacking through rhododendrons and birches to a yak pasture on the valley floor. Jichu Drake and Tserim Kang tower over the head of the valley and you can see some remarkable moraines on their lower slopes. The camp is

OFF THE BEATEN TREK

Trek in splendid isolation on these lightly trekked alternative trails.

Nub Tshona Pata Trek
Five- to seven-day wilderness loop onto the high alpine plateau northwest of Haa. The trail crosses half a dozen passes (maximum 4255m), with the third night at Tshona Pata Tsho. The region is connected to Sherab Mebar, the *terton* (treasure finder) who revealed Buddhist texts here.

Naro Six Passes Trek
Connects the first five days of the Jhomolhari trek (to Lingzhi) with the last two days of the Druk Path trek, via the remote Ledi La and Yusa La passes, for a nine-day total.

Gangkhar Puensum Base Camp Trek
A nine-day trek from Jakar to the base of the world's highest unclimbed mountain (7570m).

MY FAVOURITE TREKS

Steve Berry, managing director of Himalayan trekking specialist Mountain Kingdoms, shares his favourite treks, gained from four decades' experience of trekking in Bhutan. *@MKingdoms*

Lunana Snowman
The longest, toughest and most remote trek in Bhutan. Just a handful of villages amid stupendous high mountain scenery with a trail out through largely uncharted terrain. Magnificent!

Rodang La
This trek reveals the lesser-known eastern side of Bhutan with much cultural interest, plus great birding and even the chance to encounter a yeti crossing the Rodang La.

Druk Path
My favourite short trek – in just five days you'll pass a haunted temple, sacred lake and hermit retreat, meet yak herders and enjoy fabulous Himalayan views.

Hiker above Sol Yaksa valley

at **Chha Shi Thang** (4010m) near a large stone community hall used by both Bhutanese travellers and trekking groups. **Lingzhi** is up the obvious trail on the opposite side of the Jaje Chhu.

If you take a spare day here, you can visit the interesting village and dzong at Lingzhi (also spelt Lingshi) or make an excursion to **Chhokam Tsho** (4340m) near the base camp of Jichu Drake. It's useful to rest up for the following strenuous trek day.

Lingzhi to Dolam Kencho
DAYS 5–7

Day five is a long and tiring walk of 22km, gaining and losing over 900m in elevation. Climb towards a white chorten on a ridge above the camp, then turn south up the deep Mo Chhu valley, crossing numerous side streams and then the numerous channels of the Mo Chhu itself after three hours. Climb steeply to cross into a large side valley, then climb up the headwall, zigzagging through rocks to a large cairn atop the trek's highpoint, **Yeli La**, at 4930m. The trail here is carved into a rock cliff and is quite narrow. From the pass, on a clear day, you can see Jhomolhari, Gangchhenta (Great Tiger Mountain; 6840m) and Tserim Kang (6789m).

Descending to a hanging valley after passing a small lake at 4830m, the trail tracks the outflow from the lake to descend into another huge valley with a larger lake, **Khedo Tsho**, at 4720m. Watch for grazing blue sheep. The trail then crosses the upper reaches of the Jaradinthang Chhu and descends along the valley, following the river southwards to a chorten at 4150m, where it turns eastwards into the upper Wang Chhu valley. After a log bridge, the trail traverses a narrow, sandy slope to a camping spot at **Shodu** (4080m), just at the treeline.

From Shodu start day six by crossing the river past an abandoned army camp to traverse under steep yellow cliffs with meditation caves carved into them, where the Zhabdrung supposedly spent some time. Down a steep stone staircase, the trail reaches the river, crossing it six more times in the next three hours. Eventually the route climbs gradually for one hour to **Barshong**, where there is a dilapidated community hall and the ruins of a small dzong. There is a designated camp below the ruins at 3710m, but many groups extend today's walk for 45 minutes to **Dom Shisa** ('Where the Bear Died'). It won't be long before vehicles can reach Barshong.

The next day it's a short walk to **Dolam Kencho** (3230m), a pleasant meadow where you can meet your vehicle for the rough drive down to Thimphu.

Soi Yaksa (Jhomolhari Loop) Trek

SPECTACULAR MOUNTAIN VIEWS AND HIGH PASSES

If you fancy seeing the amazing views of Jhomolhari and Jichu Drake up close, but want to avoid the tiring slog all the way to Lingzhi, this trek is for you. While it's possible to return from Jangothang to Sharna Zampa by the same route taken on the way up, this alternative route over three high passes is much more rewarding.

For the first three days follow the Jhomolhari trek description (p200). From Jangothang, the trail crosses the Paro Chhu to climb 300m up the side of the hill to a large cirque nestling the stunning twin lakes of **Tshophu** (4380m). Look back for fabulous views of Jhomolhari, Jhomolhari 2 and Jichu Drake. The trail then climbs high above the eastern side of the second lake, across a scree slope to crest a ridge. From here, it descends into a hidden valley, before climbing steeply to the **Bhonte La** (4890m), the highest point on this route.

Descending from Bhonte La, the route traverses a scree slope, and then winds down a ridge to switch back over 1000m into the **Soi Yaksa** valley (also known as the Dhumzo Chhu valley), a beautiful setting for a camp at 3800m with rocky cliffs, wildflower meadows, a few nomadic settlements and a waterfall at the end of the valley.

Day five gradually climbs through forests of birch and oak to eventually leave the treeline behind. Dropping to a meadow with a chorten and a *mani* wall, you could make a quick detour to the ruins of the **Sey Dzong**, in a side valley nearby. Otherwise, you can simply continue ahead from the *mani* wall, cross the stream on a wooden bridge, and follow the trail up the hillside into a small side valley, before emerging onto a ridge. At a junction take the right path (left takes you to the Lalung La and Drukgyel Dzong). After an hour you reach the **Takhung La** (4520m), with spectacular views of Jhomolhari, Jichu Drake, Tserim Kang and, if you are lucky, formidable Kanchenjunga (8586m), far away on the western horizon. Meander down to yak herders' huts and your camp at **Thombu Shong** (4180m).

The next morning (day six) climb through a garden of wildflowers and rhododendrons to finally cross the **Thombu La** (4380m). Pause for a last good look at Kanchenjunga and Drakye Gang (5200m), among other peaks, before bracing yourself for a brutal descent of 1800m in three hours to reach the army camp at **Gunitsawa** (2730m). Before you know, it you are back in a car driving to Paro.

TREK STATS

Duration 6 days

Max elevation 4890m

Difficulty Medium

Season April to June, September to November

Start/finish Sharna Zampa

Summary The shorter version of the main Jhomolhari trek goes to the Jhomolhari base camp at Jangothang, returning via several high lakes and three passes.

Beyond Jhomolhari & the Paro Valley

Remoter, higher and tougher, the trekking routes beyond Lingzhi are for true Himalayan connoisseurs; this is not the place for your first trek.

Lining the remote mountain border with Tibet are some of the most beautiful, remote and isolated corners of Bhutan. Turquoise glacial lakes glitter at the base of graceful 7000m peaks here, and the wild valleys that tumble off the curving glaciers are linked by a series of high passes that offer epic high-altitude views. There are almost no villages here, only yaks, blue sheep, marmots and, just maybe, the odd snow leopard or two.

Physical and logistical challenges abound. But if you are up for big adventure in a corner of the world glimpsed by only a handful of other travellers, the remote regions of Lingzhi, Laya and Lunana rank as some of the most magical in Bhutan.

TOP TIP

Bring two of everything you might conceivably need, because you can't count on getting any other supplies along these remote treks.

PASCAL BOEGLI/GETTY IMAGES ©

Narethang (p207)

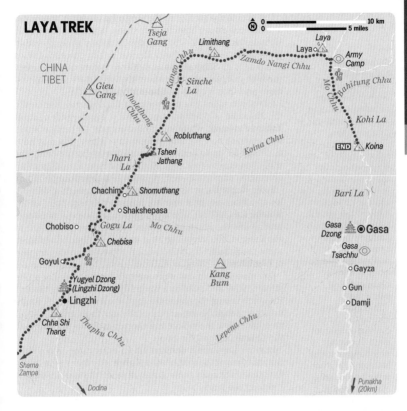

LAYA TREK

Tseja Gang
Limithang
Laya
Laya
Army Camp
CHINA TIBET
Gieu Gang
Kango Chhu
Sinche La
Zamdo Nangi Chhu
Mo Chhu
Bahitung Chhu
Jholethang Chhu
Robluthang
Koina Chhu
Kohi La
Tsheri Jathang
END Koina
Jhari La
Chachim
Shomuthang
Bari La
Shakshepasa
Chobiso
Gogu La
Mo Chhu
Gasa Dzong
Gasa
Chebisa
Gasa Tsachhu
Goyul
Gayza
Yugyel Dzong (Lingzhi Dzong)
Kang Bum
Lingzhi
Gun
Chha Shi Thang
Thuphu Chhu
Lepena Chhu
Damji
Sharna Zampa
Dodina
Punakha (20km)

0   10 km
0   5 miles

Laya Trek

CULTURAL INTEREST AND MOUNTAIN SPLENDOUR

This trek takes you into the remote and isolated high country bordering Tibet, introducing you to the intriguing culture of Laya and allowing you to cross paths with takins, Bhutan's national animal. If you're lucky, you might also spot the exotic blue poppy, Bhutan's national flower.

The single best month for trekking in Laya is probably April. A fine way to end this trek is to time it with Laya's two-day **Royal Highlander Festival** in the third week of October.

The trek begins in the Paro valley and follows the same route as the Jhomolhari trek for the first four days to Lingzhi (p199), before heading further into the mountains.

Once in Lingzhi (4080m) it's worth visiting the ridgetop **Yugyel Dzong**, built to control trade over the Lingzhi La, between Punakha and the Tibetan town of Gyantse. Lingzhi village has a few houses, a school and a post office. The region is renowned for its medicinal herbs.

An hour from Lingzhi the trail gradually descends to Goyul at the base of some dramatic rock walls, and then climbs and descends into the spectacular Chebisa valley, with a frozen waterfall at its head. **Chebisa** (3880m) is your camp for the night.

TREK STATS

Duration 10 days
Max elevation 5005m
Difficulty Medium-hard
Season April to June, mid-September to mid-November
Start Sharna Zampa
Finish Koina
Summary This extension of the Jhomolhari trek adds on a stop in the far-flung village of Laya. It offers diverse flora and fauna and a good opportunity to spot blue sheep and even takins.

205

LAYA

Spread out over a hillside near the Tibetan border, Laya is one of the highest and remotest villages in Bhutan, considered by many to be a *bae-yul* (Buddhist hidden land). The surroundings form the country's primary yak-breeding area, with many villagers living in black yak-hair tents in their summer pastures. Villagers raise turnips and mustard and produce a crop of wheat or barley each year before winter.

The Layaps have their own language, customs and distinct dress. The women wear conical bamboo hats, known as *zham*, with a bamboo spike at the top, held on by a beaded band. They dress in black woollen jackets with silver trims and long woollen skirts and wear lots of silver jewellery, including silver teaspoons.

MOUNTAIN FUN & GAMES

Laya's **Royal Highlander Festival** (p126) is the biggest event in the Layap year and is increasingly popular with foreign tourists, many of whom hike up from the road head and overnight in one of Laya's many homestays.

Day six climbs steeply to the **Gogu La** (4440m), where you should keep an eye open for blue sheep, bearded vultures and Himalayan griffons. Ups and downs follow through cedar, rhododendron, fir and birch forests, finally descending to a lunch spot at **Shakshepasa** (3980m), before a steep uphill through yak pastures high above the valley floor leads to pastures and then a camp at **Shomuthang** (4220m).

Day seven takes you past views of 6526m Kang Bum up to the **Jhari La** (4750m) and then down to the riverside camp of **Tsheri Jathang**, which acts as a sanctuary for herds of takin who migrate here for four months in summer. You may have to detour for up to an hour to avoid disturbing the herd. The trail then climbs to a crest and traverses a side valley to an overnight camp in the rocky meadow of **Robluthang** (4160m).

From Robluthang it's a tough climb up through a side valley and moraine, past marmot holes to the high point of the **Sinche La** (5005m), where the snow-covered peak of Gangchhenta fills the northern horizon. Descend past a moraine to the Kango Chhu, cross the river twice and climb to a plateau above the Zamdo Nangi Chhu and the lovely riverside campsite of **Limithang** (4140m), with Gangchhenta towering overhead.

Day nine is a half-day walk through forests, crossing a side stream twice and passing a waterfall to reach **Laya** (3840m). It's worth taking the rest of the day to explore the valley. Zhabdrung Ngawang Namgyal passed through Laya, and in a small meadow below the village is a chorten with the footprints of the Zhabdrung and his horse.

Leaving Laya you'll descend via an army camp into a tight canyon to reach the road head at **Koina** after four or five hours. Eventually the road from Gasa will reach the army camp but it could take years.

Snowman Trek

THE ULTIMATE BHUTAN TREK

Bhutan's Snowman (or Lunana Snowman) trek is often described as the world's hardest trek. The combination of distance, altitude, remoteness and unreliable weather certainly makes for a tough and uncertain trek, but just as big a hurdle for many is the cost. Even with the current temporary Sustainable Development Fee (SDF; see more p33) discounts for longer trips, it's hard to do this trek for less than US$10,000. More people have summited Everest than have completed the Snowman trek.

Over 3½ weeks the route takes you across 11 passes right across the roof of Bhutan, past its most scenic peaks, lakes and mountain communities, through the isolated regions of Lingzhi, Laya and Lunana, to end in Bumthang or Trongsa. It's the ultimate Bhutan trek.

If this sounds too easy for you, consider signing up for October's **Snowman Race**, a five-day, 203km ultra-marathon from Gasa to Bumthang along the route of the Snowman trek; it's often described as the world's toughest race.

If you plan to trek this route, it's essential to check your emergency evacuation insurance. If you get into Lunana and snow blocks the passes, the only way out is by helicopter, a costly

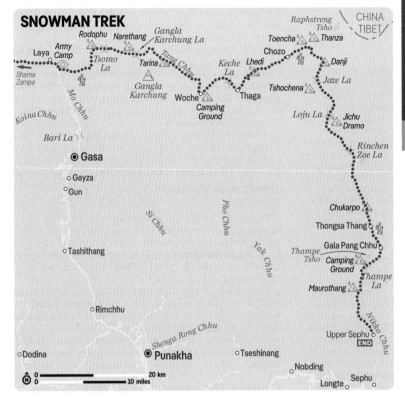

way to finish an already expensive trek.

The window for the Snowman trek is narrow, from late September to mid-October; after the main monsoon rains, but before snow closes the high passes. Start too late and you run the risk of being stuck between two snow-bound passes. Don't plan a summer trek; this is a miserable place to be during the monsoon.

Jhomolhari to Danji

DAYS 1-18

The first nine days of the trek follow the route of the Laya trek (p205), via Jhomolhari and Lingzhi, followed by a rest day in Laya. The route then climbs to **Rodophu** (4160m) for a night, before climbing through meadows over the **Tsomo La** (4900m), with its views towards Tibet, and then across a high barren plateau to a camp at **Narethang** (4900m) below the 6395m peak of Gangla Karchung.

Day 13 starts with an hourlong climb to the 5120m **Gangla Karchung La**, with Kang Bum (6526m) to the west, and Tsenda Kang (6481m), Teri Gang (7300m) and Jejekangphu Gang (7100m) due north. There are breathtaking views of the glacial lakes of Teri Gang, 1km below you. A steep, slippery descent then drops you down into the U-shaped valley of the Tang Chhu, which you descend to good campsites at **Tarina**.

TREK STATS

Duration 24–26 days
Max elevation 5320m
Difficulty Hard
Season September to October
Start Sharna Zampa
Finish Upper Sephu or Dur

Summary Bhutan's infamous Snowman trek to Lunana is the country's toughest challenge. Fewer than half the people who attempt this trek eventually finish it, either because of problems with altitude or heavy snowfall on the high passes.

Bhutan's Trans-Bhutan Trail is the country's longest walk, leading for 403km from Haa in the west to Trashigang in the east, and built with the support of the fifth king, who is a keen hiker. Consisting mainly of existing walking paths and a restored network of ancient trails, it sticks largely to Bhutan's middle hills, offering an unparalleled cultural hiking experience.

Some sections can be walked staying in hotels and homestays, but to do the full walk requires a camping crew. The entire route requires an investment of around 30 days (and at least US$12,000), but it's easy to bite off a more manageable chunk. See the the Western Bhutan chapter (p81) for some of the best day hikes.

Rinchen Zoe La, Snowman Trek

The next day continues to descend past waterfalls and then swings steeply into the high side valley of **Woche**, the first village in Lunana, at 3940m.

On day 15 it's up and over the 4650m **Keche La**, with its excellent views of Jejjekangphu's triple peak, down the Phu Chhu valley to Thaga and then northeast upstream to **Lhedi village** (3700m). Expect strong winds here in the afternoon. Day 16 follows the river past **Chozo** village and dzong, through yak pastures and glacial sand to climb to your camp in Toencha or **Thanza**, in front of the immense 3000m vertical wall of Zongophu Gang (Table Mountain; 7100m). Take a rest day in Thanza, hiking up to surrounding glacial lakes such as Raphstreng Tsho. Day 18 climbs gently to a camp at yak meadows in **Danji**, where blue sheep are often spotted.

Thanza to the Trailhead

DAYS 19-26

There are several alternative endings from here. One of the most popular is to continue southeast from Danji for a week via the Gophu La, Gangkar Puensum Base Camp and Seke La, to **Duer tsachhu** (hot springs) and then over the Gutong La and Jule La passes, to end at **Duer** in the Bumthang valley for a total of 25 or 26 days.

Alternatively, it's six days over the Jaze La, Loju La and Rinchen Zoe La to camp at beautiful **Thampe Tsho**. You then climb the 11th (!) and last pass of the trek, **Thampe La** (4600m), to sacred **Om Tsho**, where Pema Lingpa found a number of *terma* (sacred hidden texts and artefacts), to then descend the Nikka Chhu to Maurothang and finally **upper Sephu**, to join the Wangdue Phodrang to Trongsa highway.

Dagala Thousand Lakes Trek

HIGH PLATEAU AND LAKES

If you like the idea of walking for five days in gorgeous mountain scenery without bumping into another trekker, look no further than this lake circuit south of Thimphu. Better still, it's not particularly demanding (despite a few steep climbs), and most trekking days are short.

Your driver will drop you in Geynikha village, a 29km drive south from Thimphu, from where it's a short hike down to the Geynitsang Chhu to reach the suspension bridge at **Geynizampa**. Some companies use this as the first overnight stop, exploring local villages in the afternoon.

The trail from Geynizampa was once a major trading route between Thimphu and Dagana, though today it's used mostly by yak herders and woodcutters. A long initial climb leads to an outstanding viewpoint at 3220m, then eases up to a right turn atop the ridge. Veer off the main trail to reach the campsite at **Gur**, surrounded by yak pastures at 3290m.

On day two a long, stiff climb is followed by a long, gentle climb, in and out of side valleys to the **Pangalabtsa** pass (a *labtsa* is a pass) at 4250m, where there is a spectacular view of the Dagala range. This is prime yak country, with numerous herders' camps scattered across the broad Labatamba valley. Descend to the valley floor and then climb to your camp at 4300m near **Utsho**, a beautiful high-altitude lake.

DAGALA THOUSAND LAKES TREK

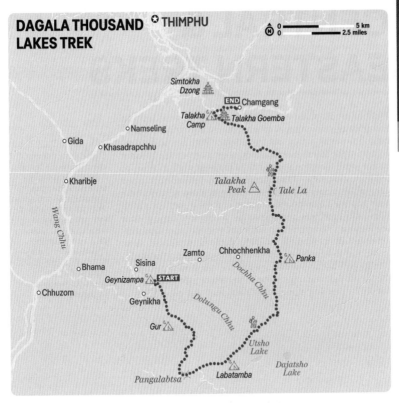

The area around the lakes bursts with alpine wildflowers in September. There are numerous other pretty lakes in the vicinity, and you could easily add on an extra day here to explore them and hike up to **Jomo** peak (5050m).

Day three climbs along the western side of Dajatsho lake to a saddle with good mountain views at 4520m, then descends past herders' camps, before climbing over three ridges and descending to the campsite at **Panka** (4000m). Water is scarce here in spring, so you may have to camp 20 minutes below.

Day four climbs steeply to the **Tale La** (4180m), from where you descend 1100m through a mixed forest of spruce, birch, juniper, rhododendron and then bamboo to reach a campsite near the 15th-century goemba at **Talakha** (3080m). The views from here up the Thimphu valley are stupendous, and you should be able to see the Buddha Dordenma on the west side of the valley. The monastery's *goenkhang* (protector chapel) is adorned with weaponry captured from Assamese separatists in southern Bhutan.

If your driver has a 4WD, you can end the trek at Talakha. Alternatively, walk down to meet your driver at Chamgang in about three hours. On your way back to Thimphu, stop at stately Simtokha Dzong (p79), one of the most impressive sights in the southern part of the valley.

TREK STATS

Duration 5 days

Max elevation 4520m

Difficulty Medium

Season April, late September to October

Start Geynizampa

Finish Talakha or Chamgang

Summary A peaceful trek near Thimphu to a number of lovely, high-altitude lakes (though not quite as many as the name suggests).

CENTRAL & EASTERN TREKS

Trekking in central and eastern Bhutan is typically a trek between and among remote villages, offering the chance to experience local cultures with strong ties to tradition. With the possible exception of the Merak-Sakteng trek, central and eastern Bhutan do not share the same popularity as the west when it comes to trekking, and trails and infrastructure are not as well maintained – though that does add to the sense of adventure. All treks have been impacted by road construction and some previously multiday treks have been reduced to just a couple of days, or even one long day. Nevertheless, if you want to spend more time trekking, your agent and guide should be able to extend the trek along traditional foot trails and alternative routes to avoid the roads.

Treks such as the Bumthang Cultural Trek, Rodang Latrek or the Merak-Sakteng trek can be shortened or extended depending on the time you have available and your wishes.

TOP TIP

Coincide your trek with one of the several festivals in Bumthang and/or the eastern and southern *dzongkhag* (administrative districts). The spring and autumn trekking seasons feature the Ura Yakchoe, Jakar tsechu, Jampey Lhakhang Drup and Ngang Bi Rabney, among others. In the east, there's the Gom Kora, Mongar and Trashigang tsechus.

LEO MCGILLY/SHUTTERSTOCK ©

Views along the Merak–Sakteng Trek (p213)

Bumthang Cultural Trek

CHOKHOR VALLEY TO TANG VALLEY

This trek has changed due to the construction of roads and many people now do the trek in a single day, starting early from **Jakar** and driving to **Ngang Lhakhang** or staying at homestay accommodation in Ngang Lhakhang before the walk. Trekkers are rewarded with the option of interesting and luxurious accommodation at **Ogyen Chholing Manor** at the end of the walk. The walk is short but packs in a tiring 750m climb to the **Phephe La** (3360m).

If you want to make it a two-day camping trek, it is possible to start from **Thangbi Goemba**, walk up the true left bank of the Chamkhar Chhu and camp at **Sambitang**, about a 30-minute walk from Ngang Lhakhang. There is a second camping spot and a farmstay at **Tandingang** (Tahung) at the far end of the trail, but most groups continue to nearby Ogyen Chholing, now that it is connected by road.

Owl Trek

CHOKHOR VALLEY TO CHHUME VALLEY

Keen to sample some 'nightlife' out in the mountains? Consider walking the Owl rrek, a route exploring the Bumthang region that owes its name to the hooting of owls that can be heard at campsites through the night. A two-or three-day itinerary, the Owl trek starts at either Chutigang or Menchugang village (5km north of Toktu Zampa) and ends at either Tharpaling Goemba or Jakar Dzong.

The original trail goes from Menchugang, just north of Jakar, and includes a 1½-hour climb to Chutigang. Some itineraries also visit Duer village at the start of the trek. There is, however, a road leading to **Chutigang** (2685m) and this is where most itineraries start. The trail follows the valley of the Drangngela Chhu, in a southerly direction. The gentle climb leaves behind the ubiquitous blue pine to enter a forest of giant fir trees adorned with old man's beard, while drifts of snow announce increasing elevation as you approach **Shona campsite** (3240m), the night's camp.

The climb out of Shona is gentle. After about two hours a string of prayer flags and a stiff breeze welcomes you to **Rang La** pass (Drangela; 3595m). Views to the southeast encompass Gaytsa and Chhumey valley below the snowy peaks of the Black Range. Here the trail turns east to follow the ridge as it ascends through winter yak pasture to the exposed campsite at **Kitephu** (3870m). If there is insufficient water your crew will want to press on for 1½ hours to make camp above **Tharpaling Goemba**. From here you have the choice of meeting your vehicle, descending on foot via Samtenling Lhakhang to Domkhar in the Chhume valley, or climbing back over the ridge behind Tharpaling to descend through forest to Jakar.

TREK STATS

Duration 1 day

Max elevation 3360m

Difficulty Medium

Season March to May, September to November

Start Ngang Lhakhang

Finish Ogyen Chholing

Summary Delightful forests and interesting lhakhangs and villages at the start and end make this a good option if you fancy a challenging day walk with flush toilets at either end.

TREK STATS

Duration 2–3 days

Max elevation 3870m

Difficulty Medium

Season March to May, October to December (though spring can be muddy)

Start Chutigang

Finish Tharpaling Goemba

Summary Dense rhododendron and fir forests make way for exposed, elevated winter yak pastures, with a panoramic view of Himalayan peaks from Kitephu. A short but moderately challenging and moderately high trek along old yak herders' trails.

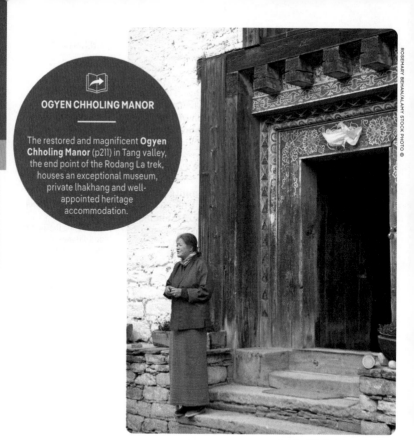

ROSEMARY BEHAN/ALAMY STOCK PHOTO ©

OGYEN CHHOLING MANOR

The restored and magnificent **Ogyen Chholing Manor** (p211) in Tang valley, the end point of the Rodang La trek, houses an exceptional museum, private lhakhang and well-appointed heritage accommodation.

Ogyen Chholing Manor (p211)

TREK STATS

Duration 6–8 days
Max elevation 4160m
Difficulty Medium–hard
Season October to November
Start Ogyen Chholing
Finish Trashi Yangtse
Summary This trek across eastern Bhutan is tough and involves a tremendously long, steep descent.

Rodang La Trek

ADVENTUROUS FORMER TRADE ROUTE

Ever since a highway was rolled out to connect its end points, this once-important trade route has remained largely untrodden by locals. But its inclusion as part of the Great Himalayan Trail (greathimalayatrail.com) has somewhat revitalised this trail. Its high difficulty level should be a draw for more adventurous types. You can add a day onto this trek by starting in Ngang Lhakhang and adding on the Bumthong Cultural Trek.

The long climb to Rodang La takes two days. Above Ogyen Chholing, at the start, the trail is rutted with cattle hoof prints and can be slippery. **Rodang La** (4160m) is subject to closure because of snow, and is best hiked in October, early November or late spring. The trek crosses the road near Lhuentse (p176), which breaks up the continuity of the trekking experience and offers a chance to visit the remote dzong or shorten the trek.

Roads are nibbling away at the trail in four different directions, so check with your agent to see how developments have affected the trek.

Nabji Trek

PIONEERING CULTURE TREK

If you're looking for a low-altitude winter trek, or if village life, birdwatching and family interactions are more important than mountain views, the Nabji trek could well be your cup of tea.

This trail pioneered community-based tourism in Bhutan, whereby local villagers are employed on a rotating basis to offer services and amenities such as porterage, village tours, cultural shows and food at campsites along the route. Campsite fees go into a community fund to support education, conservation and tourism development.

The trailheads of this winter trek are on the road between Trongsa and Zhemgang, and the trek itself offers a chance to spot some exotic local creatures such as the golden langur, the rufous-necked hornbill and the crested serpent eagle, among others.

As with so many treks in Bhutan, road building is gnawing away at both ends of the trek, and you will probably find yourself walking on farm roads at some stages. Depending on how much walking on roads is desirable, you may end the trek at Nabji or Nimshong. This trek can easily be done in the opposite direction.

TREK STATS

Duration 3–4 days
Max elevation 1635m
Difficulty Easy
Season October to March
Start Tongtongphey
Finish Nimshong
Summary A low-altitude trek passing through the land of the isolated Monpa people.

Merak–Sakteng Trek

SECLUDED EASTERN CULTURE

This trek in the far-eastern corner passes through the **Sakteng Wildlife Sanctuary**, an unspoilt and delicate ecosystem that's home to the endangered snow leopard and red panda, the Himalayan black bear, the Himalayan red fox and perhaps even the legendary *migoi* (yeti). The region is also home to the isolated Brokpa people, one of the Himalaya's most interesting ethnic groups.

As with so many trekking routes in Bhutan, roads are encroaching upon these routes. A road reaches Merak and another, north of the Gamri Chhu, reaches Sakteng. Homestays are available in both villages. Alternative foot trails and campsites are being developed to avoid the bulk of the new roads and you should enquire about these with your agent.

The most popular option is to begin at **Damnongchu**, though it's possible to start the trek from **Merak**. One option to avoid the bulk of the new roads is to start trekking from Merak to **Namchena**: the next day involves camping near **Tangling-Tsho**, and day three takes you over **Preng-La** pass (4267m) to reach Khaling by lunch, following the old migration route of Merak villagers.

TREK STATS

Duration 2–7 days
Max elevation 3480m
Difficulty Medium
Season Mid-March to May, September to November
Start Damnongchu or Merak
Finish Sakteng, Thakthri or Jyongkhar
Summary A star attraction offering a sneak peek into one of the most secluded regions in Bhutan.

TOOLKIT

The chapters in this section cover the most important topics you'll need to know about in Bhutan. They're full of nuts-and-bolts information and valuable insights to help you understand and navigate Bhutan, and get the most out of your trip.

Arriving
p216

Getting Around
p217

Money
p218

Accommodation
p219

Family Travel
p220

Health & Safe Travel
p221

Food, Drink & Nightlife
p222

Responsible Travel
p224

Accessible Travel
p226

LGBTiQ+ Travellers
p226

Nuts & Bolts
p227

Language
p228

Bus stand, Thimphu

✈ Arriving

The vast majority of travellers to Bhutan arrive by air at Bhutan's only international airport in Paro. Some travellers, particularly those coming from India, enter or exit Bhutan by road at Phuentsholing on the southern border with India. A number of other land borders are open only to Indian and Bhutanese travellers.

Visas

With the exception of travellers from India, Bangladesh and Maldives, visitors to Bhutan must arrange a visa online (US$40) with the Department of Immigration, either directly or through a Bhutanese agent as part of an all-inclusive tour.

SIM Cards

B-Mobile or Tashi Cell SIM cards can be purchased and topped-up at agents throughout Bhutan, including Paro Airport. Dedicated 'Tourist' SIMs for travellers can be loaded with various data bundles. B-Mobile has the best coverage out east.

Border Crossings

Crossing between Bhutan and India is relatively straightforward at Phuentsholing, south of Thimphu. At the time of research, Gelephu (central Bhutan) and Samdrup Jongkhar (eastern Bhutan) were closed to non-Indian visitors.

Wi-Fi

Wi-fi is readily available in hotels and restaurants that see regular tourist traffic in Bhutan. Elsewhere, mobile coverage is surprisingly good considering the terrain.

AIRPORTS IN BHUTAN

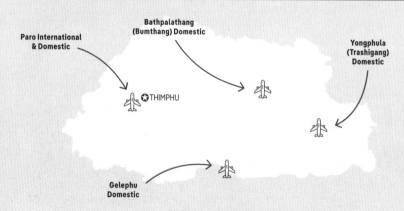

Paro International & Domestic

Bathpalathang (Bumthang) Domestic

Yongphula (Trashigang) Domestic

THIMPHU

Gelephu Domestic

ABOVE: FUSE/GETTY IMAGES ©, RIGHT: GEORGE MDIVANIAN / EYEEM/GETTY IMAGES ©

Getting Around

Most visitors will have their transport – whether by car, bus or on foot – arranged by their tour agency, and the cost is included in the price of the tour.

TRAVEL COSTS

driver & car ental
**<100km: from
Nu 3000/day
>100km:
Nu 30/km**

petrol
approx
Nu 75/litre

quality
bicycle rental
**from
Nu 2000/day**

Car or Minibus

Unless you are on a trek or take an internal flight, you will move around Bhutan by minibus, 4WD or car with a driver. It isn't possible to self-drive a hire car. For trips to central and eastern Bhutan during winter or the monsoon, a 4WD is a distinct advantage.

Drivers

The professional drivers that transport tourists around the country by cars and minibuses are among the most polite, sensible and careful drivers you are ever likely to encounter, anywhere. They know the roads intimately and, more crucially, the vagaries of local weather conditions.

TIP

The roads in Bhutan are notoriously winding – bring travel-sickness medication with you.

ROAD ACCIDENTS

Despite the low speeds and usual careful driving, accidents do occur on the narrow roads. It is important that the police establish who was at fault in any traffic accident. This means that the police must arrive and make the decision before any of the vehicles can be moved, even if the vehicles are blocking a narrow road. A relatively minor accident can stop traffic for hours while everyone waits patiently for the police to arrive from the nearest town.

**DRIVING
ESSENTIALS**

Drive on the left

Speed limit is 30km/h in towns and 50km/h outside of towns

.08
Blood alcohol limit is 0.08%

Road Conditions

The one main road from west to east, the National Hwy, is a stretch of well-maintained tarmac that meanders its way across the country, over clattering bridges, along the side of cliffs and over high mountain passes. Snow, landslides, mudflows and rockfalls present seasonal hazards that may temporarily delay you.

Air Travel

Bhutan has just a handful of domestic air services operated by Druk Air out of Paro. Schedules are changeable and highly weather dependent. Domestic airfields include Gelephu (in southern Bhutan, near the border with India), Bumthang (Bathpalathang/Jakar, central Bhutan) and Yongphula (south of Trashigang in the east).

Taxis

There's almost no need to take a taxi when you're in Bhutan. But there are local taxi services in Thimphu, Paro, Phuentsholing, Jakar and elsewhere. Most trips are charged a flat rate that is rarely open to negotiation. Taxi drivers have a habit of charging foreigners, including Indians, as much as they can – one of Bhutan's few rip-offs.

Money

CURRENCY: **NGULTRUM (Nu)**

Credit Cards

Major International credit cards are accepted at tourist-directed handicraft stores and many of the hotels in Thimphu, Paro and other larger towns, but a surcharge of up to 5% often applies to cover the fees levied by the credit-card companies. PINs must be four digits.

Changing Money

There are currency exchange counters at Paro airport, larger hotels and the banks. Most will change major international currencies, and some smaller currencies from Asia. Indian rupees are used interchangeably with ngultrums and are not officially exchanged at banks. Unspent ngultrums can be changed into US dollars on departure at exchange counters and shops.

Tipping

At your discretion, but hotel staff will appreciate a small tip for carrying your bags. Restaurant bills include service tax, and tipping is not common. It is customary to tip your guide and driver at the end of an organised trip; allow at least US$15 per day for guides, and US$10 per day for drivers.

HOW MUCH FOR...

dzong or museum entry
free to Nu 2500

a hot-stone bath
from Nu 2000

a bright red wooden phallus
Nu 300– 30,000 (depending on the size)

 Buy Art

If you plan to make a major purchase, for example textiles or art, consider bringing US dollars in cash. Most shops will accept this, and it can save you the hassle of exchanging a large quantity of money in advance and then attempting to change it back if you don't find the exact piece you were looking for.

LOCAL TIP

Note that the exchange rate for US dollar bills of denominations lower than US$100 is much lower than for the large bills.

MORE ON CHANGING MONEY

Tours are almost universally prepaid, so you'll only need money for drinks, laundry, souvenirs and tips. For this, bring cash as ATMs are not always reliable. Banks in Bhutan exchange US, Canadian and Australian dollars, UK pounds, euros, Japanese yen and some other Asian and Scandinavian currencies. If you missed the bank, businesses and individuals are usually happy to accept US dollars in cash and often give a better rate than the banks. Indian rupees (except Rs 2000 notes) may be used freely anywhere in Bhutan; don't be surprised if you get change in rupees. Ngultrums cannot be used in India.

Keep in mind that it's difficult to change ngultrums back into hard currency at the end of your trip so don't change too much money at the start of your trip. Most people give their unused ngultrums as a tip to their guide.

Accommodation

Homestays or Farmstays

The only accommodation available in some parts of the far east and easily the preferred option for those looking for unparalleled immersion into local culture. Here you will be fed authentic local dishes, and have the chance to participate in the cooking. Mattresses may not be as plush or as warm as a hotel, and the bathroom may be down the hall or even outside.

Tourist-Grade Hotels

Tourist-quality hotels are simple but comfortable rooms that have met a strict minimum standard. Most rooms follow the pine-clad, 'country cottage' theme, though there are also many modern exceptions. Appointments include electricity, wi-fi, telephone, TV, private bathroom and hot water. Every hotel has a restaurant that serves buffet meals when a group is in residence and offers à la carte dining at other times.

Local Hotels

Tend to be noisy and well-worn affairs. A last resort that may be your only option during a very busy tsechu (festival), or way out east where there is not an oversupply of hotels. Some local hotels can still be comfortable, though the mattresses (thin and firm) and toilet facilities (squat or with makeshift plumbing) may not be quite what you're used to.

Five-Star Hotels

Bhutan has a growing number of luxury options, including the Uma, Amankora, Six Senses, Zhiwa Ling and Termalinca resorts. For these you will be paying a substantial supplement over the standard tour fee being offered by Bhutanese agents. However, if you are travelling in the low season, you should ask for at least a 30% discount.

HOW MUCH FOR A NIGHT IN...

a homestay
US$20–30

a three-star hotel
US$40–100

a five-star hotel
from US$800

Camping

Government rules dictate that all treks in Bhutan must be arranged as fully fledged camping trips booked through a tour operator. Therefore your tent and sleeping mat, as well as the kitchen tent, dining tent, toilet tent etc, are all catered for and usually set up by the time you arrive at the camping area.

HOT-STONE BATHS

Many hotels and homestays offer a *dotsho* (traditional hot-stone bath), a simple narrow wooden box containing water warmed with fire-heated rocks. The red-hot rocks tumble and sizzle into the water behind a grill that separates the bather's skin from the scorching rocks. More traditional places add natural herbs such as artemisia. You'll need to book a couple of hours in advance for the rocks to be heated; expect to pay around Nu 2000 for the experience, double or triple this in top-end places. Bring a towel and soap in cheaper places.

Family Travel

Travelling with children here doesn't have to be financially ruinous: children aged five and under are exempt from the Sustainable Development Fee (p33), while those aged six to 12 years pay 50%. However, kids may get bored with long drives, steep walks to monasteries, buffet food and the general lack of entertainment. They will, though, be accepted by local kids and their families.

Getting Around

Child car seats and capsules are hard to find, and the minivans used for transporting tourists may not have the required seat belts or anchor points to secure a seat if you bring your own. Make all relevant enquiries before you leave home. Footpaths are either non-existent or diabolical – a pram or stroller will become an encumbrance. Consider bringing a hiking carrier for younger kids instead.

Facilities

Imported disposable nappies (diapers) are sold in larger cities, but dedicated nappy-changing facilities are very rare. On the other hand, most Bhutanese will go out of their way to assist a parent in need. Bhutan has one of the highest rates of breastfeeding in the world, but it is usually done discreetly; local people would be surprised to see a tourist breastfeeding in public.

Hotels

Most hotels can arrange an extra bed, family room or an adjoining room, but cots are scarce; bring a travel cot from home for very young children. Upmarket restaurants in larger hotels may have highchairs; they are non-existent elsewhere.

Food

Kids will soon notice the paucity of Western-style fast-food restaurants in Bhutan. Burgers and pizzas have infiltrated Paro and Thimphu, but not much further. Most kitchens can whip up potato fries and *momos* (dumplings) if the buffet has the kids rolling their eyes.

KID-FRIENDLY PICKS

Thimphu's Traffic Police (p54) Gesticulating gendarmes in Thimphu.

Archery (p53) DIY at a hotel or homestay (do you have a first-aid kit?). Alternatively, watch a tournament at, for example, Changlimithang Archery ground in Thimphu.

Buddha Dordenma (p78) A huge, huge Buddha that you can explore inside and out.

Guru Rinpoche, Taki La (p178) Ditto Bhutan's favourite saint, way out east.

Khuru Conceivably safer than bows and arrows, Bhutanese darts is darts on steroids. Lots of fun and will hone skills, but remember that first-aid kit.

THE GREAT OUTDOORS

The long drives, dzongs (fort-monasteries), lhakhangs (temples) and museums can be a bit testing on kids' patience, but luckily there are lots of activities available in the great outdoors that should interest them. There are hikes that can be done in a day (eg Taktshang Goemba, p96), or longer treks (p189) that involve camping (and maybe yaks!). Rafting is another activity that doesn't have to be as scary as it may sound. There are very gentle rafting trips available in Punakha (p117) and Royal Manas National Park (p165). Of course, if white-water adventure is what you are after, this too can be arranged.

Health & Safe Travel

INSURANCE

Although few people have problems in Bhutan, a travel insurance policy is a prerequisite to obtaining a visa and it must be in place when you make the application. Make sure it is comprehensive, covering theft, medical problems and evacuation. Policies should also cover costs if you are forced to cancel your tour because of flight cancellation, illness, injury or the death of a close relative. This can protect you from major losses, given Bhutan's prepayment conditions (p32).

Vaccinations & Infectious Diseases

Specialised travel-medicine clinics can give specific recommendations for you and your trip, or visit your usual doctor before you travel. Most vaccines don't produce immunity until at least two weeks after they're given, so get your jabs four to eight weeks before departure.

The only vaccine required by international regulations is for yellow fever. Proof of vaccination will only be required if you have visited a country in the yellow-fever zone within six days prior to entering Bhutan.

Medical Kit

Recommended items for a personal medical kit: antifungal cream, antibacterial cream, antibiotic for skin infections, antibiotics for diarrhoea, antihistamine, antiseptic, DEET-based insect repellent, diarrhoea treatment, first-aid items (scissors, bandages, gauze, thermometer, sterile needles and syringes, safety pins and tweezers), painkillers and sunscreen.

TAP WATER

Never drink tap water in Bhutan. Bottled water is generally safe – check the seal is intact at purchase. Most hotels provide perfectly safe purified water for guests. There are several options for purifying your own water while trekking: boiling, chemical purification and water filtration.

Malaria

Malaria is present in Bhutan but the risk to travellers is small, unless you will be spending time in rural southern Bhutan. Seek expert advice as to the most appropriate course of prophylaxis.

HIGH ALTITUDE

If you are going to altitudes above 3000m you should get information on preventing, recognising and treating acute mountain sickness (AMS). AMS is a notoriously unpredictable condition and can even affect people who are accustomed to walking at high altitudes. AMS has been fatal at 3000m, although most fatalities occur above 3500m.

Food, Drink & Nightlife

Chillies

The Bhutanese love chillies, so much that some dishes consist entirely of chillies and are often accompanied by chilli-infused condiments! The mouth-scorching local meals will bring tears of joy to the eyes of chilli lovers, though don't expect the aromatically spiced dishes typical of the subcontinent. These can only be found in the Nepali-influenced south of Bhutan or at an Indian restaurant.

HOW TO...

Dine in Hotels & Restaurants

Due to the unique nature of travel in Bhutan, restaurant opening hours have little meaning. Almost all tourists will have breakfast in their hotel and guides will prearrange lunch and dinner in restaurants or hotels, which will normally offer a buffet or set meal at whatever time your guide determines.

The food in hotels is often the best in town, but if you want to sample local restaurants, especially in Thimphu or Paro, you or your guide can arrange it. For pre-paid tours the tour operator should pay for all your restaurant meals. The possible exceptions include the several upper-end restaurants in Thimphu and the dining rooms in five-star hotels. Also, you may end up paying for a casual visit to a cafe for espresso coffee and snacks. In almost all restaurants it's a good idea to order an hour or more in advance if you are ordering from a menu – or wait forever for your meal. Also, don't be surprised if many of the offerings are not available.

Since most travel in Bhutan is via an all-inclusive package, most of your meals will be in the form of a hotel buffet comprising continental, Indian, Chinese and one or two toned-down Bhutanese dishes. The buffets and set meals put on by tourist hotels are typically not packed with the same chilli firepower as local dishes.

MENU DECODER

arra homemade spirit distilled from barley, wheat or rice

barthu noodles

bja sha maroo chicken in garlic and butter sauce

chhang beer made from rice, corn or millet, pronounced chung

chugo dried yak cheese

dal lentil soup

ema datse chilli with cheese sauce

hogey salad of cucumber, Asian pepper, red chilli, spring onion and tomato

kewa datse potatoes with cheese sauce

khule buckwheat pancakes

momo steamed dumpling filled with meat or cheese

nakey fiddlehead fern fronds

no sha huentseu stewed beef with spinach

olo choto literally 'crow beak', a hooked-shaped broad bean

phak sha laphu stewed pork with radish

phak sha phin tshoem pork with rice noodles

puta buckwheat noodles

shamu datse mushrooms with cheese sauce

sip fried, beaten corn

sud-ja Tibetan-style tea with salt and butter

thukpa noodles, often served in a broth

tsampa roasted-barley flour

zao fried rice

Drinks

Tea (sweet, Indian-style chai or a teabag) and coffee (predominantly of the instant variety) are drunk throughout Bhutan and are readily available. For espresso and quality tea you'll need to head to the cafes of Thimphu or, away from Thimphu, an upmarket hotel. Bottled beer, wine and spirits are readily available throughout the country, while many places like to make a point of introducing visitors to the local brew, *bang chhang,* and sinus-clearing firewater, *arra.*

HOW MUCH FOR...

an instant coffee
Nu 30

an espresso coffee
Nu 200

a glass of wine
Nu 500–800

a bottle/can of beer
Nu 200

dinner at a local restaurant
Nu 200–300

dinner at a hotel restaurant
Nu 500–800

dinner at a five-star restaurant
from US$100

HOW TO... Find Drinks & Nightlife

Microbreweries have arrived in Bhutan, including one beside the Tashi Namgay Resort in Paro. One of the best beers brewed in Bhutan is the Red Panda weiss beer, a tangy unfiltered beer brewed and bottled in Bumthang. On a larger scale, Bhutan Brewery produces Druk Lager and the high-alcohol (8%) Druk 11000. Imported beers, such as Singha and Tiger, are sometimes available, but the well-priced locally brewed products dominate the shelves.

Wine is readily available but it's expensive for the quality. There are imported bottled wines and, more reasonably priced, locally bottled imported wine.

Thimphu is the place for cosy bars and cocktails; elsewhere you will be mostly restricted to your hotel bar serving local and imported liquor and local beer. Local bars are closed on Tuesdays, but this doesn't usually affect tourist hotel bars. Thimphu, Paro and increasingly other towns have karaoke bars, dance clubs and live music venues.

Yak Cheese

While travelling through Bhutan and visiting local shops, look for the strings of rock-hard, dried yak cheese *(chugo)* hanging from shop rafters. Soften it in your mouth and be careful of your teeth.

STAPLES & SPECIALITIES

Beef and fish come from India or Thailand, usually flown in frozen and safe. During the summer you may be limited to chicken, or a vegetarian diet in more remote parts of the country. Yak meat is occasionally available, but only in winter.

Bhutan's national dish is *ema datse,* large green (sometimes red, but always very hot) chillies *(ema),* prepared as a vegetable, not a seasoning, in cheese sauce *(datse).* The second-most popular dish is *phak sha laphu* (stewed pork with radish). Other typically Bhutanese dishes, always served with chillies, include *no sha huentsu* (stewed beef with spinach), *phak sha phin tshoem* (pork with rice noodles) and *ja sha maru* (chicken in garlic and butter sauce). Hotel and trekking cooks make some excellent non-spicy dishes, such as *kewa datse* (potatoes with cheese sauce) and *shamu datse* (mushrooms with cheese sauce). These dishes also come with chillies, eg *shamu*

ema datse, so be careful. More seasonal are the delicious wild asparagus and unusual *nakey* (fiddlehead fern fronds), the latter typically smothered in the ever-present *datse.*

Although there is plenty of white rice, many Bhutanese prefer a locally grown red variety, which has a slightly nutty flavour. At high altitudes wheat and buckwheat are the staples. In Bumthang, *khule* (buckwheat pancakes) and *puta* (buckwheat noodles) replace rice as the foundation of many meals. Dessert is most often a modest presentation of fruit – apple, banana, pineapple or orange, depending on the season.

Foremost among several Tibetan-influenced snacks are *momos,* small steamed dumplings that may be filled with meat, vegetables or cheese – delicious when dipped in a chilli sauce. Fried cheese *momos* are a speciality of several Thimphu restaurants.

Responsible Travel

Climate Change & Travel

It's impossible to ignore the impact we have when travelling, and the importance of making changes where we can. Lonely Planet urges all travellers to engage with their travel carbon footprint. There are many carbon calculators online that allow travellers to estimate the carbon emissions generated by their journey; try resurgence.org/resources/carbon-calculator.html. Many airlines and booking sites offer travellers the option of offsetting the impact of greenhouse gas emissions by contributing to climate-friendly initiatives around the world. We continue to offset the carbon footprint of all Lonely Planet staff travel, while recognising this is a mitigation more than a solution.

Visit the East

By venturing to eastern Bhutan, you can spread your tourist dollar to the far reaches of the country. There are local hotels and homestays that cater to, and depend on, trekkers and birdwatchers. You may even save on the Sustainable Development Fee (p33).

Choose a Homestay

There are government-approved and -audited homestays throughout the country and they offer an unparalleled opportunity for you to immerse yourself in local culture and to contribute money directly to local people.

When dining with a group of people, wait till everyone has been served before you start. If you offer something to a local person – for example, a tip for your guide or driver – it is customary for them to initially decline the offer before they accept.

Avoid pointing directly at a statue when in a lhakhang. Also avoid touching any religious object. If you walk around a Buddhist chorten, goemba or lhakhang, or even an altar inside a lhakhang, remember to do so in a clockwise direction.

CARBON NEGATIVE

Bhutan is recognised as the first carbon negative country. The country's greenhouse gas pollution is offset by its extensive forest reserves, around 60–70% of the country, and its generation and export of renewable (hydro) energy.

REDUCE YOUR CARBON OUTPUT

There is a proliferation of wood-burning furnaces (*bukhari*) in hotels in rural Bhutan, and air pollution in winter can be particularly bad. Help reduce air pollution from wood-burning stoves by wearing warm clothes and asking for extra blankets.

Buy Local

Sometimes it's necessary to go local where a dedicated tourist restaurant simply doesn't exist. And perhaps the only shop in town is selling religious paraphernalia for home altars, perfect for discovering new tastes and experiences and just maybe that ideal memento.

Plastic Bags

Although officially banned in Bhutan since 1999, plastic carry bags are still in wide use and unfortunately still a litter problem. You can keep your own waste to a minimum and reinforce the intent of the ban by bringing a reusable bag and refusing plastic bags when shopping.

Don't shout the name of a Bhutanese at night. It might attract a ghost.

Make a small donation at a temple to keep it running and to receive a blessing.

Temple Etiquette

Shoes, hats and umbrellas should be removed before entering any lhakhang of a dzong, goemba or other religious building. Photography is also banned inside lhakhangs but it is usually permitted in temple courtyards.

RESOURCES

bhutan.travel
Official website of the Department of Tourism has all the background you need for planning a visit, plus hints to help you be a responsibly aware visitor.

wwfbhutan.org.bt
Background on specific conservation initiatives involving protected areas, wildlife corridors, forestry, community initiatives and sustainability.

responsibletravel.com
Reputable travel company website that provides information and promotes responsible travel in all its facets around the globe.

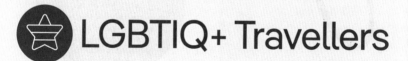

Accessible Travel

Touring Bhutan is a challenge for a traveller with a disability; for a start, there's barely any natural land that is flat and level. However, you'll have a guide, driver and vehicle at your disposal, so it is possible with some planning. The Bhutanese are eager to help, and agencies should be able to arrange a companion to assist with moving about and getting in and out of vehicles.

Airports

Paro International Airport has ramps and accessible toilets. All facilities are accessible, and wheelchairs are available on request. Domestic airports are not as well set up but assistance is usually available.

Accommodation

Homestays and even many standard tourist hotels are unlikely to provide sufficient services to accommodate people with disabilities. Larger hotels, especially five-star hotels, are likely to be the best option when it comes to accessibility.

Sights & Public Spaces

Museums, dzongs and public buildings rarely have wheelchair access or lifts. Public toilets are virtually non-existent, and where they do exist are unlikely to be wheelchair accessible.

Roads & Pavements

Mobility-impaired travellers will find that roads and verges of roads are rough and uneven. Verges sometimes disappear altogether. Sidewalks and pavements, where they exist, often have holes, deep drains with broken tops, and sometimes steps.

LGBTIQ+ Travellers

Although deeply conservative, Bhutanese Buddhism does not condemn homosexuality, and this has been highlighted by high-profile filmmaker and Buddhist Lama Dzongsar Jamyang Khyentse Rinpoche. In a YouTube video posted in 2015 he said that being LGBT in no way impacted one's understanding of or adherence to Buddhism, which is the official religion of Bhutan, and that Bhutanese should not merely tolerate, but should respect LGBTIQ+ people.

Acceptance

Attitudes appear to be changing, as exampled by politicians and prominent Buddhist leaders occasionally speaking out in support of the LGBTIQ+ community and preaching acceptance. Nevertheless, there are still no Pride festivals or similar big marquee events, and there are no recognised queer-friendly bars, bookstores or nightclubs. Nor are there any pink neighbourhoods or queer districts. What there has been is a slow and deliberate coming out of a small number of individuals willing to help present a public face. This has included the creation of dedicated LGBTIQ+ Facebook pages.

LEGALITIES

Bhutan does not provide any form of legal recognition for same-sex couples. On the other hand, same sexes checking into a hotel will not face any issues or discrimination. Since 2021 same-sex sexual activity has been legal, and there are growing calls in government, traditional media and social media for gender recognition for transgender people.

Nuts & Bolts

OPENING HOURS

Banks 9am–5pm (4pm winter) Monday–Friday, 9am–11am or 1pm Saturday

Bars Close at 11pm on weekdays and midnight on Friday and Saturday. Closed Tuesday – the national 'dry' day.

Clubs Generally close at midnight most weekdays, and at around 2am or 3am on Wednesday, Friday and Saturday

Government offices 9am–1pm and 2pm–5pm summer, until 4pm winter, Monday to Friday

Shops 8am–8pm or 9pm

Internet Access

Free wi-fi is offered in most tourist hotels and many cafes and restaurants in larger cities. Bhutan Telecom and Tashi Cell offer 3G and 4G networks that are constantly expanding, and buying a local SIM is an inexpensive way to use data on your mobile phone.

GOOD TO KNOW

Time zone
GMT/UTC+6

Country code
975

Emergency number
112 (ambulance)
113 (police)

Population
800,000

PUBLIC HOLIDAYS

Public holidays follow both the Gregorian and lunar calendars. Several major festivals are considered local public holidays.

Nyilo (Winter Solstice) 2 January

Birthday of the Gyaltse (crown prince) 5 February

Birthday of Fifth King 21–23 February

Birthday of Third King 2 May

Coronation of Fourth King 2 June; also marked as 'Social Forestry Day'

Coronation of Druk Gyalpo 1 November

Constitution Day/Fourth King's Birthday 11 November

National Day 17 December; the date of the establishment of the monarchy in 1907

The following holidays are set by the traditional lunar calendar and Gregorian dates vary:

Losar January/February, New Year

Zhabdrung Kuchoe April/May; death of the Zhabdrung

Buddha Parinirvana/Saga Dawa May/June; enlightenment and death of Buddha

Birthday of Guru Rinpoche June/July

First sermon of Buddha July/August

Dashain September/October; Hindu celebration

Smoking
Smoking in public places is prohibited, except in the dedicated smoking rooms in some bars and restaurants.

Electricity 220V/50Hz

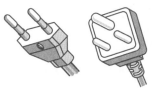

Type C
220V/50Hz

Type D
220V/50Hz

Language

The official language of Bhutan is Dzongkha. While Dzongkha uses the same script as Tibetan – and the two languages are closely related – Dzongkha is sufficiently different that Tibetans can't understand it.

TOOLKIT

Basics

Hello. kuzuzangbo la
Goodbye.
(by person leaving) läzhimbe jön
(by person staying) läzhimbe zhû
Yes. ing/yö
No. mê
Thank you. kadinchey la
Good luck. trashi dele
What's your name? chö meng gaci mo?
My name is ... ngê meng ... ing
Can I take a photo? pâ tabney chokar la?

Directions & Transport

Where is a...? ... gâti mo?
What time does the bus leave? drülkhor chutshö gademci kha jou inna?
How far is the ...?
... gadeci tha ringsa mo?
left/right öm/yäp
Go straight ahead. thrangdi song

Time

What time is it? chutshö gademci mo?
(Five) o'clock. chutshö (nga)
morning drôba
afternoon pchiru
night numu
yesterday khatsha
today dari
tomorrow nâba

Emergencies

I'm ill. nga nau mä
I feel nauseous. nga cûni zum beu mä
I keep vomiting. nga cûp cûsara döp mä
I feel dizzy. nga guyu khôu mä
I'm having trouble breathing. nga bung tang mit shubä
doctor drungtsho

Eating & Drinking

Do you have food now? chö dato to za-wigang in-na?
I don't eat meat. nga sha miza
I don't like food with chillies. nga zhêgo êma dacikha miga
This is too spicy. di khatshi dû
This is delicious. di zhim-mä
Please give me a cup of tea. ngalu ja phôp gang nang
It's enough. digi lâm-mä

Trekking

Which trail goes to...? ... josi lam gâti mo?
Is the trail steep? lam zâdra yö-ga?
Where is my tent? ngê gû di gâti in-na?
What's the name of this village? ani ügi meng gaci zeu mo?
Let's go. jogey-la

NUMBERS	
1	ci
2	nyî
3	sum
4	zhi
5	nga
6	drû
7	dün
8	gä
9	gu
10	cuthâm
11	cûci
12	cunyî

Pronunciation

The simplified pronunciation system used in this chapter is based on the official Romanisation system (used for writing Dzongkha in Roman script), so if you read our pronunciation guides as if they were English, you'll be understood. There are three accent marks: the apostrophe represents a high tone (eg 'ne) or a 'soft' consonant (eg g'), the circumflex accent (eg ê) represents long vowels, and the diaeresis (eg ö) alters the pronunci ation of some vowels, namely ä (as the 'a' in 'hat'), ö as the 'ir' in 'dirt' (without the 'r' sound), and ü (like saying 'i' with the lips stretched back).

An h after the consonants c, d, g, l, p and t indicates that they are 'aspirated' (released with a slight puff of air) – listen to the 'p' sounds in 'pip'; the first is aspirated, the second is not.

Practise pronouncing the ng sound (as in 'sing') at the beginning of a word, eg ngawang (a name). The 'dental' consonants, t and th, are pronounced with the tongue tip against the teeth. Note also that c is pronounced as the 'ch' in 'church', and zh as the 's' in 'measure'.

Regional Languages

Due to the isolation of much of Bhutan, a number of other languages survive, and it's common for regional minorities to have their own language. Some are so different that people from various parts of the country can't understand each other. In eastern Bhutan most people speak Sharchop (meaning 'language of the east'), which is totally different from Dzongkha. In the south, most people speak Nepali. Bumthangkha is a language of the Bumthang region. Also spoken are Khengkha from Zhemgang, Kurtoep from Lhuentse, Mangdep from Trongsa and Dzala from Trashi Yangtse.

DZONGKHA & ENGLISH

English is the medium of instruction in schools, so most educated people can speak it fluently. There are English signboards, books and menus throughout the country. Road signs and government documents are all written in both English and Dzongkha.

THE BHUTAN

STORYBOOK

Our writers delve deep into different aspects
of life in Bhutan.

A History of Bhutan in 15 Places

Bhutan's history is a tale of a small nation trying to define and maintain its distinct identity.

Bradley Mayhew

p232

Meet the Bhutanese

The Bhutanese are known for their humbleness, kindness and simplicity, and they treat every person on the street with respect.

Galey Tenzin

p236

Gross National Happiness

Bhutan has chosen its own unique identity, centred on a different kind of measure.

Galey Tenzin

p238

Bhutan: Beyond Shangri-La

Articles will tell you that Bhutan is an undiscovered Shangri-La. There's a lot more to it than that.

Bradley Mayhew

p240

Decoding Bhutan's Temples

Understanding these conduits between the sacred and profane.

Bradley Mayhew

p242

Monks studying, Chimi Lhakhang (p125)
PETER ADAMS/GETTY IMAGES ©

A HISTORY OF BHUTAN IN
15 PLACES

Bhutan's history is a tale of shifting religious, royal and secular power – of saints, kings and noblemen – and of a small nation trying to define and maintain its distinct identity. To truly get to grips with Bhutan's past, you have to move beyond simple facts and figures into myth, magic and reincarnation. By Bradley Mayhew

A FEW KEY events have shaped Bhutan's history over the centuries. The introduction of Buddhism in the 8th century, and the later dominance of the Drukpa school of Buddhism in the 12th century, has defined religious life in Bhutan. Modern Bhutan also owes much to its founding father Ngawang Namgyal (1594–1651), otherwise known as the Zhabdrung, who defined many aspects of what makes Bhutan unique, from its dress codes and social interactions to its system of government. For centuries a series of religious leaders, abbots, reincarnated lineages and noblemen further shaped the nation, alongside a secular ruler known as the *desi*. Only in 1907 did the Wangchuck family establish itself as Bhutan's royal family.

Bhutan has deep trade and religious ties with its neighbour Tibet to the north, and many of Bhutan's most important religious leaders arrived as exiles from Tibet. Yet until the 1970s Bhutan was largely cut off from the rest of the world. Its recent history has been a determined effort to keep its national identity and sovereignty intact.

Compare Bhutan's recent political history with that of its neighbours Sikkim (absorbed by India), Tibet (controlled by China) and Nepal (its royal family overthrown) and its cultural and national strength appear all the more remarkable.

1. Kyichu Lhakhang
THE FIRST TEMPLE IN BHUTAN

The exquisite Kyichu Lhakhang outside Paro is generally considered to be the oldest temple in Bhutan, along with the Jampey Lhakhang in Bumthang. Both temples were ordered built by the Tibetan King Songtsen Gampo in 659 CE, as part of a project of 108 geomantic temples designed to pin down a gigantic demoness that was preventing Buddhism from taking hold in Tibet. The king's Chinese wife Wencheng (known as Ashe Jaza, or the 'Chinese Princess', in Bhutan) helped divine the location of the demoness; Kyichu Lhakhang was built to pin down the demoness' troublesome left leg.

For more on Kyichu Lhakhang, see p94

2. Kurjey Lhakhang
THE ARRIVAL OF BUDDHISM

In 746 CE the ruler of Bumthang, Sindhu Raja, begged the magician-saint Guru Rinpoche to rescue him from the clutches of the local demon Shelging Kharpo. The guru eventually subdued the white demon, converted the raja to Buddhism, and persuaded the local spirits to act as protectors of the Buddhist faith (thus ensuring a continuity of belief with Bhutan's pre-Buddhist beliefs). Today visitors can see the guru's body *(kur)* imprint *(jey)* in the rock wall of Kurjey Lhakhang, as well as the location of Sindhu Raja's original Iron Fort at Chakhar Lhakhang; both sites pinpoint the moment that Buddhism took root in Bhutan.

For more on Kurjey Lhakhang, see p152

3. Phajoding Goemba
THE RISE OF THE DRUKPA KAGYUD

The Phajoding Goemba meditation retreat, high in the forested hillside above Thimphu, owes its name to Phajo Drukdom Shigpo, a 13th-century Tibetan yogi from Ralung in southern Tibet, who is credited with bringing the Drukpa Kagyu school of Buddhism to Bhutan in 1222. Thanks to Phajo, it was the Drukpa lineage that came to dominate Bhutan, eventually beating out the rival Lhapa school. Phajo, who based himself in Thimphu's first dzong, also established Thimphu's Changangkha Lhakhang and formalised the Zorig Chusum, the 13 types of arts and crafts that still defines Bhutanese arts.

For more on Phajoding Goemba, see p71

Kurjey Lhakhang (p152)

4. Tamshing Goemba
THE TREASURE FINDER PEMA LINGPA

Bhutan has a long tradition of *terton* (treasure finders), tantric lamas who are able to unveil and interpret *terma* (sacred texts) hidden by earlier masters. Pema Lingpa (1450–1521) was the most important of Bhutan's *terton* and his many discoveries and teachings significantly shaped Bhutan's heritage. While based at Kunzundrak in the Tang valley he discovered texts in nearby Membartsho and established Bhutan's most important Nyingma goemba at Tamshing Goemba, where you can still get a blessing from the chain mail forged by the blacksmith Lingpa himself. Descendants of the saint's three lineages include the important Gangte *trulku* (reincarnated lama) and the royal family of Bhutan.

For more on Tamshing Goemba, see p155

5. Tamchog Lhakhang
TIBET'S IRON BRIDGE BUILDER

Just below Tamchog Lhakhang on the road between Paro and Thimphu is a photogenic iron chain-link bridge that was originally built by Tangthong Gyelpo. Tangthong was a 15th-century Tibetan yogi, engineer, blacksmith, philosopher, musician, dramatist and inventor of Tibetan opera, often called the 'Leonardo of the Himalaya'. He first came to Bhutan in 1433 in search of iron ore and eventually built eight iron chain-link bridges across the country. As well as building bridges and passing on his expert blacksmithing skills, he also built the ingenious conch shell-shaped temple of Dumtse Lhakhang, which you can still visit in Paro.

For more on Tamchog Lhakhang, see p104

6. Laya
THE ARRIVAL OF THE ZHABDRUNG

The remote mountain region of Laya is one of several high valleys long used as a trans-Himalayan trading route by merchants and pilgrims headed to and from Tibet. At the time Bhutan was known as Lho-Mon (Southern Darkness) or Menjong (Land of Medicinal Herbs). It was Laya that first welcomed Tibetan exile Ngawang Namgyal as he fled from Tibet in 1616. Namgyal would later become known as the

Zhabdrung, and play the role of founding father of Bhutan, unifying its rival kingdoms, codifying the first system of laws, and building dzongs across the country.

For more on Laya, see p206

7. Simtokha Dzong
BHUTAN'S FIRST DZONG

Simtokha Dzong, at the southern end of the Thimphu valley, is not Bhutan's most impressive dzong, but it is considered to be the oldest still standing. Built in 1629 by the Zhabdrung to house both the monastic and administrative bodies, it was crucial to establishing the dual system of governance that continues in Bhutan to this day. For the next few centuries the monastic body was headed by the Je Khenpo and the government by the Druk *desi*, a secular ruler that was eventually replaced by the kings of Bhutan. Simtokha Dzong was also instrumental in battling against invading Tibetans in 1624.

For more on Simtokha Dzong, see p79

8. Drukgyel Dzong
KEEPING THE TIBETANS AT BAY

For centuries Bhutan has had an uneasy relationship with Tibet to the north. Bhutan shares many cultural, religious and linguistic connections with its larger neighbour, and Tibetan lamas often fled power struggles in Tibet to set up religious centres in Bhutan. Tibet also had a nasty habit of sending its armies over the passes to plunder Bhutan. Drukgyel Dzong was built in 1649 as a reaction to three Tibetan invasions within a decade; the dzong burned down in 1951 but finally reopened in 2023. The dramatic Punakha Dromchoe festival reenacts one of these Tibetan invasions.

For more on Drukgyel Dzong, see p100

9. Trongsa Dzong
THE RISE OF THE WANGCHUCK DYNASTY

The 16th-century Trongsa Dzong is Bhutan's largest fort, and has long served as Bhutan's political lynchpin, binding the country together from its strategically central location. The main road connecting east and west even led right through the dzong until the arrival of modern roads in the 1960s. Bhutan's first king rose to power here as the *penlop* (governor) of Trongsa

and tradition has since dictated that Bhutan's crown prince serve as Trongsa governor before ascending to the throne. Today the dzong's watchtower fittingly houses a museum devoted to the royal Wangchuck dynasty.

For more on Trongsa Dzong, see p144

10. Punakha Dzong
THE ESTABLISHMENT OF THE MONARCHY

In December 1907 the country's de facto leader Ugyen Wangchuk was crowned in Punakha Dzong as Bhutan's first Druk Gyalpo, or 'Dragon King', thus establishing the Wangchuck family dynasty that rules Bhutan to this day. The second and third kings were subsequently also crowned here (in 1927 and 1952), at a time when Punakha was Bhutan's capital and seat of gov-

Simtokha Dzong (p79)

IPEK MOREL/SHUTTERSTOCK ©

ernment. In 2011 the current, fifth, King Jigme Khesar Namgyel Wangchuck, was married here, as his father had been. It was also in the dzong that Bhutan and Britain signed a 1910 treaty guaranteeing Bhutan's sovereignty; unlike India, Bhutan was never colonised.

For more on Punakha Dzong, see p118

11. Royal Manas National Park

PRESERVING THE LAND

Bhutan's first protected area was established in 1963 on the border with India to protect wild elephants, Bengal tigers, rhinos, gaurs and river dolphins. Over the years another nine more protected areas (including five national parks) would follow, totalling an impressive 43% of the country. Today almost the entire northern third of the country is either a national park or wildlife sanctuary, and, vitally, most protected areas are now linked by biological corridors. Bhutan's constitution mandates that the country must maintain at least 60% forest cover; it is currently estimated at over 70%.

For more on Royal Manas National Park, see p165

12. Dochu La

ATONEMENT FOR MILITARY ACTION

The deeply symbolic 108 chortens (stone Buddhist monuments) atop the Dochu La pass were built in 2005 in atonement for the lives lost during the country's 2003 military campaign against insurgents. Rebels had been launching raids on India from the jungles of southern Bhutan for over a decade in their quest for Assamese and Bodo independence. The Bhutanese army led by the fourth king eventually flushed out the rebels; head to the nearby Druk Wangyal (Bhutan Victory) Lhakhang to see modern temple murals depicting the fourth king battling militants.

For more on the Dochu La, see p113

13. Bhutan Gate, Phuentsholing

BHUTAN'S RELATIONSHIP WITH INDIA

Bhutan's main border crossing with India is a symbol of its relations with its massive neighbour. India supplies Bhutan with all of its fuel, 90% of its consumer goods, the bulk of its development aid, and most of its roads. It also operates joint military bases inside Bhutan, which is why it was Indian troops that faced off against China in 2017 after Beijing built roads on Bhutan's remote Doksam plateau. China not only claims Doksam but also Sakteng in eastern Bhutan, as well as most of the Indian state of Arunachal Pradesh. Tiny Bhutan walks a tricky tightrope, squeezed between its tense giant neighbours.

For more on Phuentsholing, see p113

14. Trans-Bhutan Trail

REVITALISING ANCIENT TRACKS

The network of ancient footpaths known today as the Trans-Bhutan Trail existed for centuries as the nation's main thoroughfare for messengers, traders and pilgrims heading east–west, against the region's more natural north–south geographic grain. The trail was rebuilt during the Covid-19 pandemic as a way to employ some of the 40,000 tourism workers left unemployed after the closure of international borders. A royal-funded *kidu* (relief fund) offered financial support to others. Bhutan suffered only 21 deaths due to Covid-19, thanks to one of the world's fastest vaccination programmes and the mobilisaton of the royal-established De-suung (Guardians of the Peace) volunteer programme.

For more on the Trans-Bhutan Trail, see p208

15. Thimphu

BHUTAN'S WINDOW ON THE WORLD

Since becoming Bhutan's capital in 1961, the tiny city of Thimphu has been at the forefront of Bhutan's tentative embrace of the globalised world. It was only in 1999 that television arrived in Thimphu (Bhutan was the last country in the world to allow television), followed four years later by mobile phones. In 2010 Bhutan banned tobacco, only to reluctantly re-legalise it in 2021. Today Thimphu's residents drive electric vehicles, use mobile banking apps and are just as mesmerised by reality-shows like *Druk Idol* as their global counterparts. Slow paced as it may be, Thimphu is the future of Bhutan.

For more on Thimphu, see p46

MEET THE BHUTANESE

The Bhutanese are known for their humbleness, kindness and simplicity, and they treat every person on the street with respect and smiles. Galey Tenzin introduces his people.

A PEA-SIZED COUNTRY, spread over 38,304 sq km, the Kingdom of Bhutan is a constitutional monarchy, whose fifth king, Jigme Khesar Namgyel Wangchuck, is a compassionate leader loved by the country's 800,000 people.

In Bhutan you will meet three ethnic groups: the Tsangla (Sharchop), considered the indigenous inhabitants of eastern Bhutan; the Ngalop, people of Tibetan origin who migrated to Bhutan; and the Lhotshampa, a group of Nepali migrants. All have their own unique dialect – due to the geographical location of the country, as well as its mountainous terrain and valleys, which long separated groups of people.

Bhutanese prefer to spend their holidays visiting temples and circumambulating stupas, while very few choose vacationing hotels and parties. It is not uncommon to find altar rooms in every house, where we do prayers in the early hours, light butter lamps and offer holy water.

Men wear a *gho* (a cloth that falls to the knee and is wrapped around like a robe) and women wear a *kira* (which looks like an apron that goes from the torso to the ankle) – this is our unique national dress.

In Bhutan, it is OK to refuse once when offered food or drinks because we will ask you again. For Bhutanese, a first 'No, thank you' is not exactly a 'No'. Sometimes – or even most of the time – it might mean, 'Of-fer me once again'. We have the habit of refusing first (just as a polite gesture) before we accept or take something from others.

If you visit a Bhutanese house, get prepared to handle some spiciness. Bhutanese love chillies, especially dried red chillies, and it is a love that goes beyond any health advice. You should not be surprised to see a five-year-old enjoying chilli cheese with red rice.

It is also a part of our tradition to eat food with our hands. You might see a lot of our parents and grandparents cleaning their hands before eating with a small dough of rice, which is rolled between two hands, and you might hear them say that the stickiness of the rice removes the germs from your hands. When dining in a group, both the host and guest wait for everyone to be served.

The sense of community vitality among Bhutanese is admirable. If we have someone ill at home, we must expect every neighbour to come for moral support. If we have a special occasion or ritual at home, we invite enough guests to finish off our monthly ration.

Call out my name, 'Galey', and you will see many faces turn towards you. Bhutanese names are not limited but also not that many. There will be at least two or three Galeys in the neighbourhood, although it need not be Galey Tenzin – you might come across Galey Rinchen or Galey Tshering as well.

The Language

Dzongkha (National Language) is spoken by about 95% of Bhutanese, while a minority speak their own dialects, of which there are at least 19. You needn't worry about getting lost without a guide due to the language barrier – the majority of Bhutanese can speak English fluently.

BHUTAN'S MOST BEAUTIFUL VALLEY

I was born and raised in Bumthang, the most beautiful valley in Bhutan and which is often called the mini Switzerland. Bumthaps usually have a typical look, of which I am a good example: tall, average build and medium skin tone. We have our local dialect, the preferred means of communication for most Bumthaps, which is unique and might sound alien to even people of our own country.

For more than a decade now, I've lived in Thimphu, the capital city and the most populated place in the country. Like other Bhutanese, I came here for opportunities and employment. You can mostly find middle-aged people like me and more than half of the country's youth population.

GROSS NATIONAL HAPPINESS

Bhutan has chosen its own unique identity, centred on the concept of Gross National Happiness. Galey Tenzin gives a local's insight into what it's like living under the system.

WHEN YOU TALK about Gross National Happiness (GNH) with non-Bhutanese, it is clear that people often misunderstand its meaning and make certain generalisations about the Bhutanese people. Outsiders might assume, for example, that every Bhutanese remains happy all the time simply because we embrace the principles of GNH. The truth is much more complex; individual happiness still differs from one person to another.

The concept of GNH is based on the developmental philosophy put forth by the fourth king of Bhutan, Jigme Singye Wangchuck, in the early 1970s during a phase of major development of education, agriculture, health and road construction as well as the country's foreign relations. The GNH concept aims to balance the economic development of the nation with the wellbeing of human society and nature – without ever vying for military or economic power.

In terms of economy and wealth, Bhutan stands nowhere near major world players, but it is undergoing steady growth – and doing so without sacrificing the growth

Bhutanese in *gho* and *kira* (traditional robes)

and development of individuals. The Bhutan government judiciously uses what it earns to fund free education, free health and subsidised living standards – with the idea that people are happy when they have opportunities for the future and are also fit and healthy.

There are many small yet impactful initiatives that His Majesty implemented to ensure that his people remain in harmony. Bhutanese receive direct and prompt government services that ensure a comfortable life while maintaining environmental conservation for future generations and keeping cultural and traditional practices intact while also adapting to modern times. Under these circumstances, every Bhutanese is able to enjoy the gift of the country's natural landscape and there are many reasons to be happy.

His Majesty believed that if his people were unhappy, there was no point in having governance. For this reason he set up

IN TERMS OF ECONOMY AND WEALTH, BHUTAN STANDS NOWHERE NEAR MAJOR WORLD PLAYERS, BUT IT IS UNDERGOING STEADY GROWTH – AND DOING SO WITHOUT SACRIFICING THE GROWTH AND DEVELOPMENT OF INDIVIDUALS.

Kidu offices in every *dzongkhag* (administrative district) to make sure that people's problems were heard and resolved. You can see that every Bhutanese student going to school wears a uniform so that there is no discrimination and distinction between poor and rich by the clothes they wear. The government also provides 100 units of electricity free to citizens who live in rural areas.

Furthermore, Bhutanese believe that you assume positive energy by interacting with people and sharing interests. Participating in our cultural life, and preserving our own local traditions and cultural heritage, creates a strong community vitality. Our healthy family relationships, community activities and religious practices are factors for achieving happiness. It gives us a strong sense of values and identity.

The fourth king reigned for 34 years, during which time he made all his decisions based on the people's happiness and led by example. He believed so strongly in the concept of GNH that he gave ruling power to the people. In 2006 he abdicated at the age of 51 to make way for his eldest son, Jigme Khesar Namgyel Wangchuck, the fifth and present king, and in 2008 Bhutan became a democratic constitutional monarchy – a gift from the monarch.

GNH is not just a concept or philosophy; it lives in the heart and soul of every Bhutanese. We strive for the sustainable development of the country while making sure each one of us lives each day in harmony. You might find it complicated to understand GNH, but, really, it's quite simple: when people are self-sufficient, have strong connections to their government, live in solidarity with nature and enjoy every aspect of their culture and tradition, we believe there is nothing more you can ask for to be happy.

Novice monk lighting candles

BHUTAN: BEYOND SHANGRI-LA

Travel articles on Bhutan will tell you that the country is an undiscovered Shangri-La. Luckily there's a lot more to Bhutan than that. By Bradley Mayhew.

BHUTAN'S MARKETING PEOPLE are geniuses. Ever since the unveiling of Gross National Happiness (p238) a quarter of a century ago, the country has become synonymous with benevolent governance and the world's happiest people. Bhutan's environmental achievements are equally famous; the forests that cover 70% of the country absorb almost double the carbon dioxide that it produces, making it one of only two countries on earth to be carbon negative. Its people still enjoy a deep connection to both their Himalayan landscape and their rich cultural heritage.

And yet there's more to this idyllic image than meets the eye. Gross National Happiness is a widely misunderstood concept, focusing as much on good governance and cultural preservation as it does on Western notions of individual happiness. Bhutan actually ranks surprisingly poorly on international metrics of happiness (95th on the UN World Happiness Report), and the suicide rate in Bhutan is higher than in Iraq or Syria, and it is rising.

Bhutan is also at the sharp end of climate change. As its Himalayan glaciers shrink by a million tonnes of ice a year, downstream communities are becoming increasingly vulnerable to outbursts from rising glacial lakes. Fast-growing Thimphu is already starting to have problems with its water

Thimphu

supply. One unexpected byproduct of democracy has been massive road construction, with every hopeful politician promising roads to even the remotest village in return for votes, and roads now scar hillsides in even the remotest valleys.

In 2008 Bhutan got its first taste of democratic elections, thanks to the fourth king's far-sighted decision to abdicate (at the age of 51) and devolve power to a parliamentary democracy. So far Bhutan's three elections have each been won by a different party. Levels of corruption are the lowest in south Asia. But Bhutan is also a deeply stratified society, with a handful of historically important families wielding a huge amount of influence. Criticism of the (admittedly much-respected) monarchy remains unspoken. The expulsion of around 100,000 Lotshampas (mostly Nepali-speaking Hindus) from Bhutan into refugee camps in the name of safeguarding national identity took some of the shine off Bhutan's benevolent image during the 1990s.

LEVELS OF CORRUPTION ARE THE LOWEST IN SOUTH ASIA, BUT BHUTAN IS ALSO A DEEPLY STRATIFIED SOCIETY, WITH A HANDFUL OF HISTORICALLY IMPORTANT FAMILIES WIELDING A HUGE AMOUNT OF INFLUENCE.

Even Bhutan's unique tourism policy is somewhat contradictory. Bhutan's paywall style model of high-value, low-volume tourism is commendable for its sustainable goals (even if it puts the country out of the range of most of us!). Yet the reality is that over 80% of foreign visitors to Bhutan are Indian citizens, who pay a daily sustainable development fee that is less than 10% that of other nationalities. The biggest group of tourists to Bhutan therefore provides the least economic value and the highest cultural impact.

A trip to Bhutan will leave you in no doubt that there is much to admire in Bhutanese society, from its pristine environment and strong community ties, to free healthcare and education. Bhutanese citizens even get free timber to build their first house. And yet not everyone is content with paradise. In the last few years high youth unemployment has spurred an estimated 80,000 Bhutanese to leave the country, mostly for Australia, where around 17,000 Bhutanese live in Perth alone.

While many aspects of Bhutanese life remain deeply rooted in traditional Buddhist beliefs, society is changing fast. Most Bhutanese still consult traditional astrologers before making an important decision, but fewer and fewer wear traditional dress outside of government meetings and festivals, when it is legally required. You may well have heard that Bhutan has no traffic lights; but you probably don't know that it has recently been a major investor in (and miner of) cryptocurrencies. Bhutan has changed more in the last 30 years than the preceding three centuries.

Ever since James Hilton popularised the concept of Shangri-La in his 1937 prewar novel *Lost Horizon,* the remote Himalaya has glimmered in the West's imagination as a last repository of all that has been lost in the modern world. The reality is that the Bhutanese are as varied and contradictory as the rest of us. Seeing Bhutan through the prism of Shangri-La reduces Bhutan; it's a far more interesting place than that.

Road near Mongar

ANDREW GEIGER/GETTY IMAGES ©, FAR LEFT: GNOHZ/SHUTTERSTOCK ©

DECODING BHUTAN'S TEMPLES

Bhutan's temples are conduits between the sacred and profane – understanding them is the key to understanding the Bhutanese. By Bradley Mayhew

BHUTAN'S COLOURFUL TEMPLES, or lhakhangs (literally 'place of the god', or chapel), can be confusing places. Multi-limbed protectors jostle next to a dozen types of Buddha, as demonic figures loom out of the shadows and wall murals depict everything from snow lions to fiery hellscapes. At one temple we even saw a mummified human hand dangling nonchalantly from a piece of string. Making sense of this serene riot is a challenge, but understanding a few key concepts and recognising a few common personalities can quickly open up a whole new level of understanding.

Entering a Lhakhang

Before you even enter a temple or monastery chapel, pause at the entry porch (*gorikha*) to view murals of the Four Guardian Kings, each representing a cardinal direction. Look for yellow Namtose, the god of wealth, who holds a mongoose that spits jewels, and white Yulkhorsung who plays a lute. You might also see a mural of the four friends, a visual reminder of how cooperation leads to success (in this case the fruit in the upper branches of a tree). You'll also likely see a mural of an old man with a long beard, alongside a pair of cranes and other symbols of longevity known as the Tshering Namdruk.

One of the most profound images is the Wheel of Life. Held in the mouth of Yama, the Lord of the Dead, the wheel represents of the laws of karma and the endless cycle of rebirths known as samsara (literally 'wandering'). Depending upon one's accumulated merit one ascends or descends the realms of the image's middle circle, from the tortures of hell to the heavenly realms of gods and titans. The outer ring shows the 12 links of dependent origination, from sex and birth to grasping, suffering and death. It's a complex and subtle teaching tool, perfectly suited to a historically illiterate congregation.

Head into the inner courtyard and you'll likely see images of mythological animals, such as the snow lion and dragon, as well as a shrine to the *tshomen* – a half-woman, half-snake lake deity, whose roots lie deep in the pre-Buddhist animism of the Himalaya.

Inside a Lhakhang

The central statue in a lhakhang is normally of Sakyamuni, the historical Buddha, sometimes flanked by 'Past' and 'Future' Buddhas in a trinity known as the *dusum sangay*. Especially popular in Bhutan is Guru Rinpoche ('Precious Teacher'), known in Sanskrit as Padmasambhava (the Lotus Born) and sometimes called the 'Second Buddha', an 8th-century teacher, demon-subduer and miracle worker from Swat in Pakistan who was fundamental to the spread of Buddhism across the Himalaya. Almost all of Bhutan's religious sites claim some kind of connection with Guru Rinpoche. You'll recognise him from his staff (known as a *katvanga*) and his jaunty moustache, but he also has seven other manifestations, known collectively as the Guru Tshengye, including one (Dorji Drolo) riding a tiger.

You'll almost certainly also see bearded statues of the Zhabdrung Ngawang Namgyal (1594–1651), the founder of the Bhutanese state, as well as one or more of Bhutan's historical Je Khenpos, or chief abbots.

The Altar

The main way a Bhutanese altar differs from a Tibetan altar is the elephant tusks that flank the altar. These days plastic tusks are used in new goembas.

Look for seven bowls of water, which some say refers to the Buddha' s first seven steps (or Tibet's first seven ordained monks). Also here is a ewer of holy water *(drub chuu)*, a mandala of seeds and some incredibly ornate coloured sculptures (*tom* or *torma*) made from flour and butter. Make an offering of a few ngultrum and you will receive a handful of holy water and sometimes a protective, coloured thread called a *sungke*.

Most altars also hide a relic or two somewhere, often a stone marked with the miraculously 'self-arisen' *(rangjung)* hand- or footprints of past masters, or even sacred scraps of cloth or walking sticks that once belonged to them.

Tantric Influences

All temples have a *goenkhang,* or protector chapel, a spooky side room painted in black and home to a collection of ancient weapons and bloodthirsty, wrathful demons, some of whom are so terrible that they have to be concealed behind screens. Very few *goenkhangs* are open to foreign visitors, but you might find puppet-like statues or masks of local protectors *(tsen)* hanging from pillars in the main chapel. Each valley and region of Bhutan boasts its own local protector, in addition to national protectors such as Yeshe Goempo (Mahakala) and Palden Lhamo.

The richly decorated interiors and fearsome statues can be overwhelming, which is partly their purpose; to instill a sense of reverential awe. But there is also a deeper metaphysical plane at work here. Multiarmed protectors, for example, represent aspects of the ego (one's 'inner demons') to those with religious training, and demons symbolise the political forces that historically prevented Buddhism from taking root.

Bhutanese visit a temple for many reasons – to show devotion or gain merit, protection, a blessing or good luck. Over the centuries a visit here has offered the chance to control the uncontrollable, and explain the unexplainable, and Bhutanese still come whenever there is an important decision to make; rolling altar dice and consulting monk astrologers to determine the most auspicious date or course of action for any major event. Whatever the motivation, temples and monasteries remain the centre of a Bhutanese community, essential to every aspect of life, from birth through to death. The more you learn to decode them, the more interesting they become. **243**

INDEX

accessible travel 226
accommodation 26, 219
activities, see rafting, trekking & hiking
air travel 217
airports 216
Aja Ney 180
altitude sickness 221
animals 15
archery 53
art galleries, see museums & galleries
arts & crafts 16-17, 58-9, 75
  carpet-weaving 134-5
  incense 66, 105
  paper-making 66, 92
  textiles 16, 149, 177, 185
astrology 55
Autsho 177

Balakha 198
Barshong 203
Bhonte La 203
Bhutan Gate 235
Bhutanese people 236-7
birdwatching
  Mongar 173-5
  Nabji Trek 213
  Phobjikha 129-30
black-necked cranes 129-30
blue poppies 112
Bondey 102
books 29
border crossings 216
  Gelephu 164
  Phuentsholing 134
  Samdrup Jongkhar 187

Map Pages 000

breweries 35
  Bumthang Brewery 153
  Namgyal Artisanal Brewery 92
  Ser Bhum Brewery 114
bridges 106
  Bazam bridge 119
  Geynizampa 208
  Kizum 158-9
  Nyamai Zam 87
  Tamchhog Lhakhang 104, 233
Brokpa people 186
Buddha Dordenma 78
Bumdrak Trek 196-8, **197**
Bumthang 24, 147-61, 237, **148**
  accommodation 157
  food 154
Bumthang Cultural Trek 211
business hours 227

camping 219
car travel 217
cell phones 216
central Bhutan 136-65, **138-9**
  itineraries 22-3, 140-1, **22-3**
  navigation 138-9
  travel seasons 140-1
changing money 218
Changlimithang Archery Ground 53
Chasilakha 135
Chazam 181, 185
Chebisa 205
cheese 153, 223
Cheli La 108
Chendebji 144
Chha Shi Thang 201-2
Chhokam Tsho 202
Chhokortse 71
Chhume valley 149
Chhuzom 105-6
children, travel with 220
chillies 153, 222
Chodeyphu 198
Chokhor valley 23, 151-5
Chompa 180

chortens
  Chendebji Chorten 144
  Chhuzom 105-6
  Chorten Dangrim 110
  Chorten Drimed Namnyi 105
  Chorten Kora 186
  Khamsum Yuelley Namgyal Chorten 122
  Khuruthang 121
  National Memorial Chorten 54
  Pumola 71
Chozo 208
Chumphu Ney 100-1
Chutigang 211
cinema 29
climate 26-7, see also individual regions
climate change 224
clothes 28
  traditional clothing 61-2
  trekking 43
costs 218
crafts, see arts & crafts
credit cards 218
crocodiles 134
culture 14, 236-7
currency 218

Dagala Thousand Lakes Trek 208-9, **209**
Damche Gom 195
Damnongchu 213
dances 37-8
Dangochang 201
Danji 208
disabilities, travellers with 226
Do Zam 155
Dochu La 113-16, 235
Dolam Kencho 203
Dom Shisa 203
Dongney Tsho 198
Drak Kharpo 105
drinks 222-3
drivers 217
Druk Path Trek 195-6, **195**
Duer 208
Dungkhar 178

Dzongkha language 29, 69, 228-9, 236
dzongs 8-9
  Dho-Ngen Dzong 67
  Dobji Dzong 135
  Drukgyel Dzong 100, 234
  Dzong Chung 119
  Jakar Dzong 151
  Jili Dzong 196
  Lhuentse Dzong 178
  Lhuentse Rinchentse Phodrang Dzong 178
  Paro Dzong 87-8
  Punakha Dzong 118-19, 234-5
  Sey Dzong 203
  Shongar Dzong 174
  Simtokha Dzong 79, 234
  Trashi Chho Dzong 67-8
  Trashi Thongmoen Dzong 126
  Trashi Yangtse Dzong 186
  Trashigang Dzong 182
  Trongsa Dzong 144-5, 234
  Wangchuck Lo Dzong 108
  Wangdue Phodrang 126-7
  Yugyel Dzong 205
  Zuri Dzong 90

eastern Bhutan 167-87, **168-9**
  itineraries 24-5, 170-1, **25**
  navigation 168-9
  travel seasons 170-1
electricity 227
emergencies 227
environmental issues 240-1
etiquette 28, 37
  at religious sites 103, 225
events, see festivals & events, tsechus

family travel 220
farmstays 219
festivals & events 27, 36-9, see also tsechus
  Jampey Lhakhang Drup 151

Ngang Bi Rabney 155
Punakha Dromchoe 119-20
Royal Highlander Festival 126, 205
Trongsa monk migration 146
films 29
fishing 165
food 34-5, 41, 222-3

galleries, see museums & galleries
Gangla Karchung La 207
gardens, see parks & gardens
Gasa Dzongkhag 126
gay travellers 226
Gaytsa 149
Gedu 135
Gelephu 164
gho 28, 61-2
goembas, see also nunneries
  Cheri Goemba 75
  Chhokhortse Goemba 71, 196
  Choedu Goemba 100
  Dechen Chholing Goemba 161
  Dechen Phodrang 65
  Demon-Subdued Monastery 75
  Deothang Goemba (Dawathang Goemba) 156
  Dodeydrak Buddhist Institute 72
  Drak Kharpo 103
  Drametse Goemba 181
  Dranje Goemba 95
  Drolay (Dalay) Goemba 124-5
  Dzongdrakha 101-2
  Gangte Goemba 130-1
  Jamtey Goemba 110
  Katsho Goemba 111
  Kharbandi Goemba 135
  Khuruthang Goemba 121
  Kuenzang Chholing Shedra 131
  Kunzangdrak Goemba 157
  Kunzendrak Goemba 159
  Lungchutse Goemba 115
  Neyphu Goemba 103
  Nimalung Goemba 150
  Pangri Zampa 74
  Pelri Goemba 102
  Pelseling Goemba 157

Phajoding Goemba 71, 196, 233
Phongchu La 175
Rangjung Yoesel Chholing Goemba 184
Sangchen Choekor Shedra 197
Senlung Goemba 175
Taktsang Goemba 96-9, 198
Talo Goemba 124
Tamshing Goemba 155-6, 233
Tango Goemba 76
Taphey Goemba 144
Tengchen (Tenchhen) Chholing Ani Goemba 95
Tengchu Goemba 110
Thadrak (Thadranang) Goemba 72
Thangbi Goemba 154, 211
Tharpaling Goemba 149, 158
Thujidrak Goemba 71, 196
Tiger's Nest 96-9
Trashigang Goemba 115
Wangditse Goemba 65
Yangthang Goemba 111
Gogu La 206
golden langurs 163
golf 68
Gom Kora 185
Gross National Happiness 238-9
Gung Kharpo sky burial site 112
Gunitsawa 203
Gur 208
Guru Rinpoche 74, 97, 151-5
Gyalpozhing 175

Haa 108-9
Haa valley 20, 107-12, 107
health 221
  traditional medicine 61
  trekking 43
hermitages
  Choedrak 149
  Juneydrak 110
highlights 8-17
hiking, see trekking & hiking
history 232-5
  Dochu La 235
  Drukgyel Dzong 234
  Kurjey Lhakhang 232-3
  Kyichu Lhakhang 232
  Laya 233-4
  Paro Dzong 88
  Phajoding Goemba 233

Phuentsholing 235
Punakha Dzong 118, 234-5
Royal Manas National Park 235
Simtokha 79, 234
Tamchog Lhakhang 233
Tamshing Goemba 233
Thimphu 235
Trans-Bhutan Trail 235
Trongsa Dzong 234
holidays 227
homestays 14, 219, 224
hot springs
  Duer tsachhu 208
  Gasa 126
hotels 219
hot-stone baths 101, 219

illness 221
incense 66, 105
Indian travellers 32
insurance 221
internet access 227
itineraries 20-5, 21, 22-3, 25, see also individual locations

Jakar 151, 211
Jangchhu Lakha 196
Jangothang 201
Janye Tsho 196
Jhari La 206
Jhomolhari 194-203, 207
  beyond Jhomolhari 204-9
  Jhomolhari Trek 199-203, 200
Jili La 195
Jomo 209

Kaley La 112
Keche La 208
Khadey Gom 198
Khaling 187
Khardung 184
Kharung La 187
Khedo Tsho 202
Khoma 177, 178
Khuruthang 121
kira 61-2, 185
Kitephu 211
Koina 206
Kori La 180-1
Kuri Chhu 177-8
Kuri Zampa 175
kushutara 177

Labana La 196
lakes
  Jimilang Tsho 196
  Membartsho 159
  Tshophu 203
  Utsho 208
language 29, 69, 228-9, 236
langurs 163
Langye Ja La 196
Laya 126, 206, 233-4
Laya Trek 205-6, 205
LGBTIQ+ travellers 226
lhakhangs 242-3
  Benri Lhakhang 103
  Bondey Lhakhang 102
  Buli Lhakhang 149
  Bumdrak Lhakhang 198
  Chakhar Lhakhang 110
  Chandana Lhakhang 116
  Changangkha Lhakhang 55
  Chasilakha Lhakhang 135
  Chimi Lhakhang 125
  Choechotse Lhakhang 197-8
  Choejam Lhakhang 160
  Chorten Nyingpo Lhakhang 150
  Chhundu Lhakhang 110
  Damcho Lhakhang 130
  Dho Jhaga Lama Lhakhang 121-2
  Doley Lhakhang 102
  Dongkala Lhakhang 104
  Druk Wangyal Lhakhang 114
  Dumtse Lhakhang 91
  Dzongdrakha 101-2
  Gönsaka Lhakhang 90
  Guru Lhakhang 94-5, 102
  Jaiphu Lhakhang 175
  Jampa Lhakhang 71
  Jampey Lhakhang 151-2
  Jongsarbu Lhakhang 101-2
  Khangza Lhakhang 71
  Khewang Lhakhang 130
  Konchogsum Lhakhang 156-7
  Kumbhu Lhakhang 130
  Kurjey Lhakhang 152-3, 232-3
  Kyichu Lhakhang 94-5, 232
  Larjung (Larjab Drakar Choeling) Lhakhang 180
  Lhakhang Kharpo 108
  Lhakhang Nagpo 108-9
  Luege Rowe 156
  Mani Dungkhor Lhakhang 57

lhakhangs *continued*
 Narut (Pelphug)
  Lhakhang 160
 Ngang Lhakhang 154-5,
  211
 Ogyen Chholing Manor
  159-60
 Pema Sambhava
  Lhakhang 156
 Pena Lhakhang 91
 Prakhar Lhakhang 150
 Radak Neykhang 127
 Rinchen Jugney
  Lhakhang 161
 Sey Lhakhang 155
 Singye Drak 92
 Ta Rimochen Lhakhang
  158, 159
 Tago Lhakhang 102, 104-5
 Tamchhog Lhakhang
  104, 233
 Tashichholing Lhakhang
  144
 Thinleygang Lhakhang
  116
 Tseringma Lhakhang 102
 Ugyen Tshemo Lhakhang
  99, 198
 Ura Lhakhang 161
 Wengkhar Lhakhang 180
 Yakgang Lhakhang 175
 Zangto Pelri Lhakhang
  56-7, 99, 134, 155, 198
 Zhambhala Lhakhang 149
 Zungney Lhakhang 150
Lhedi 208
Lhuentse 24, 176-8, **177**
libraries 68
Limithang 206
Lingzhi 202
literature 29
Longte 143
Lungtenzampa 184

M
malaria 221
markets
 Centenary (Weekend)
  Market 56
 Handicrafts Market 56
 Norzin Lam 58
 Paro weekend market
  91-2

meditation retreats, *see*
 goembas
Membartsho 159
Menlong Brak 187
Merak 184, 213
Merak–Sakteng Trek
  184, 213
Mesithang 158
migoi 15, 184
Mila Seykhar Guthog 135
miracles 155
Mo Chhu 121
mobile phones 216
Mon La 184
monasteries, *see* goembas
money 218
Mongar 24, 172-5, **172**
Motithang 71, 72, 196
movies 29
museums & galleries
 Art Gallery Jatra 57
 Craft Gallery 58-9
 Dilgo Khyentse house
  museum 95
 Faculty of Traditional
  Medicine 61
 Folk Heritage Museum 69
 National Museum 88-9
 National Textile Museum
  55-6, 58
 Ogyen (Ugyen) Chholing
  160
 Postal Museum 62
 Simply Bhutan 62
 Sisichhum Heritage
  Home 106
 Tower of Trongsa Royal
  Heritage Museum 146
 VAST Bhutan 57
music 29

N
Nabji Trek 213
Naktshang 181
Namchena 213
names 55
Namgo La 198
Narethang 207
National Assembly 68
National Institute for Zorig
  Chusum 66
National Library 68
National Museum 88-9
national parks & reserves
  15
 Jigme Dorji National
  Park 126
 Royal Manas National
  Park 165, 235
nature 15
Ngang-yul 154-5
nightlife 222-3

Nobgang 125
nunneries
 Kila Dechen Yangshi
  Nunnery 108
 Pema Tekchok Choeling
  Shedra 158
 Sangchen Dorji Lhendrub
  Choling Nunnery 124-5
 Zilukha Nunnery 69
Nyile La 201

O
Ogyen Chholing Manor
  159-60
Om Tsho 208
opening hours 227
Owl Trek 211

P
palaces
 Kuenga Rabten 163
 Wangdichholing Palace
  150
 Yundrung (Eundu)
  Chholing 163-4
Pangalabtsa 208
Panka 209
paper 66, 92
parks & gardens, *see
  also* national parks &
  reserves
 In Situ Rhododendron
  Garden 173
 Ludrong Memorial
  Garden 68
Paro 20, 21, 86-92, 200, **87**
 beyond Paro 93-106
Paro Valley 93-106, 194-203
 beyond the Paro Valley
  204-9
Pele La 122, 132
Pema Lingpa 155-7, 208
people 236-7
phalluses 125
Phephe La 211
Pho Chhu 121
Phobjikha 22, 128-32, **128**
Phongchu La 175
Phuentsholing 133-5,
  235, **134**
Phurji Laptsa 175
pilgrimage sites 12-13,
  see also goembas,
  lhakhangs
Pinchinang 187
planning
 Bhutan basics 28-9
 booking 30-3
 clothes 28
 festival dates 37
 Indian travellers 32

Sustainable
  Development Fee 33
 tour agencies 32-3
 trekking 40-3, 192-3
 visas 31, 216
politics 240-1
poppies 112
population 227
prayer flags 59, 115
Preng-La 213
public holidays 227
Punakha 21, 117-22, **118**
 beyond Punakha 123-7

R
Rabana 196
Radi 184
rafting
 Punakha 121
 Royal Manas National
  Park 165
Rang La 211
Rangjung 184
red pandas 15
regional languages 229
religious sites 12-13,
  see also goembas,
  lhakhangs, nunneries
responsible travel 224-5
rhinos 15
rhododendrons 27, 173
road trips
 Mongar 173-5
 Paro to Thimphu 104-6
 Phuentsholing to
  Thimphu 135
Robluthang 206
Rodang La 212
Rodang La Trek 212-13
Rodophu 207
Rukubji 143

S
safe travel 221
Saga La 198
Saga La Trek 198, **199**
Sambitang 211
Samdrup Jongkhar 25, 187
Sangaygang 71
Sarpang 162-5, **163**
Sephu 144
Shaba 104
Shakshepasa 206
Shelkar Drak 109-10
Sherichhu 181
Shershong 180
Shertang La 161
Shing Karap 200
Shingkhar 160, 161
Shodu 202
Shomuthang 206

Map Pages **000**

SIM cards 216
Simkotra Tsho 196
Sinche La 206
Singye Dongma 92
smoking 227
Snowman Trek 206-8, **207**
Soi Yaksa 203
Soi Yaksa (Jhomolhari
  Loop) Trek 203, **200**
spas, see also hot springs
  Paro 91
  Shaba 104
stamps 62
statues
  Buddha Dordenma 78
  Guru Rinpoche statue 178
Sustainable Development
  Fee 33
Swiss Farm 153

Takethang 201
Takhung La 203
Taki La 178
takins 72
Taktshang Goemba 96-9,
  198
Talakha 209
Tale La 209
Tandingang 211
Tang Valley 23, 158-60
Tangling-Tsho 213
Tangmachu 178
Tangthong Gyelpo 233
Tarina 207
Tasheri Jathang 206
taxis 217
temples, see lhakhangs
Thampe La 208
Thampe Tsho 208
Thangthangka 200
Thangtong Gyalpo 106
Thanza 208
Thimphu 21, 22, 46-79, **48-9**
  accommodation 61-2,
    67-8
  central Thimphu 52-62,
    53
  food 55-7, 60-1

greater Thimphu 63-9, **64**
history 235
itineraries 50-1
navigation 48-9
nightlife 57
north of Thimphu 73-6, **74**
shopping 58-9, 62
south of Thimphu 77-9, **78**
Valley Rim 70-2, **71**
walking tours 58-9, **59**
Thombu La 203
Thombu Shong 203
Thrumshing La 173
Tiger's Nest Monastery
  96-9
time 227
tipping 218
tour agencies 32-3
traditional medicine 61
traffic police 54
Trans-Bhutan Trail 10, 122,
  208, 235
  Dochu La 115-16
  Haa valley 111-12
  Paro valley 100
  Phobjikha 132
Trashigang 25, 179-82, **180**
  beyond Trashigang 183-7
Trashi Yangtse 25, 186
travel seasons 26-7, see
  also individual regions
travel to Bhutan 216
travel within Bhutan 217
trekking & hiking 10, 40-3,
  189-213, **190-1**
  Bumdrak Trek 196-8, **197**
  Bumthang 157-8, 160
  Bumthang Cultural
    Trek 211
  Chokhor Valley 152
  Dagala Thousand Lakes
    Trek 208-9, **209**
  Druk Path Trek 195-6, **195**
  equipment 43
  Gangkhar Puensum Base
    Camp Trek 201
  Haa 110
  Haa valley 111
  health 43
  Jhomolhari Trek 199-203,
    200

Laya Trek 205-6, **205**
Merak–Sakteng Trek
  184, 213
Mongar 175
Nabji Trek 213
Naro Six Passes Trek 201
Nub Tshona Pata Trek 201
Owl Trek 211
Paro 90
Paro Valley 95, 100
Phobjikha 132
  planning 40-3
Punakha 121
Rodang La Trek 212
routes 42-3, 190-1
Royal Manas National
  Park 165
  rules 41
Saga La Trek 198, **199**
  seasons 192-3
Snowman Trek 206-8,
  207
Soi Yaksa (Jhomolhari
  Loop) Trek 203, **200**
Thimphu 65, 71, 72, 78
Trans-Bhutan Trail 10,
  100, 111-12, 115-16, 122,
  132, 208, 235
Trongsa 143-4
Trongsa 22, 142-6, **143**
tsechus 8, 27, 36-9
  Gasa 126
  Gom Kora 185
  Haa 109
  Jakar 151
  Kurjey 151
  Lhuentse 178
  Paro 88
  Phobjikha 129
  Punakha 120
  Talo Goemba 124
  Thimphu 68
  Trongsa 146
Tsendho 100
Tshokam 196
Tsomo La 207

Ura 160

vaccinations 221
vegetarian & vegan
  travellers 35
visas 31, 216

walking, see trekking &
  hiking
walking tours 58-9, **59**
Wamrong 187
Wangdue Phodrang 23,
  126-7
Wangkha 135
water 221
waterfalls
  Lehleygang 165
  Namling 174
weather 26-7
western Bhutan 81-135,
  82-3
  itineraries 20-1, 84-5, **21**
  navigation 82-3
  travel seasons 84-5
wi-fi 216, 227
wildlife sanctuaries
  Bomdeling Wildlife
    Sanctuary Visitor
    Centre 187
  Sakteng Wildlife
    Sanctuary 184, 213
Woche 208

Yadi 181
yathra 149
Yeli La 202
Yong Khola 173, 175
Yongphu La 187
Yoselgang 198
Yotong La 149

Zhemgang 162-5, **163**
Zorig Chusum 16, 66

'Favourite memory from this trip? Staring open-mouthed at snow-capped peaks of Jhomolhari and Jichu Drake framed by the twin mountain lakes of Tsophu, Soi Yaksa trek (p203).'

BRADLEY MAYHEW

'I lost count of the times on this trip when I found myself in a remote temple transfixed by tales of magical flying stupas, demon-battling saints and troublesome snake spirits.'

BRADLEY MAYHEW

Mapping data sources:
© Lonely Planet
© OpenStreetMap http://openstreetmap.org/copyright

THIS BOOK

Commissioning Editor
Darren O'Connell

Production Editor
James Appleton

Book Designer
Fabrice Robin

Cartographer
Corey Hutchison

Assisting Editors
Gabby Innes, Anne Mulvaney, Gabbi Stefanos

Cover Researcher
Mazzy Prinsep

Thanks Ronan Abayawickrema, Jessica Boland, Hannah Cartmel, Fergal Condon, Karen Henderson, Alison Killilea

MIX
Paper from responsible sources
FSC™ C021741
www.fsc.org

Paper in this book is certified against the Forest Stewardship Council™ standards. FSC™ promotes environmentally responsible, socially beneficial and economically viable management of the world's forests.

Published by Lonely Planet Global Limited
CRN 554153
8th edition – Dec 2023
ISBN 978 1 78868 785 0
© Lonely Planet 2023 Photographs © as indicated 2023
10 9 8 7 6 5 4 3 2 1
Printed in Singapore